SPEEDBOAT

D.W. FOSTLE

Mystic Seaport Museum Stores
Mystic, Connecticut 06355

Distributed by
International Marine, Camden, Maine 04843

For Betty Sue and Melissa

Man's precarious adventures in terrific speed are nearing the point where the laws of nature will say finally: "Thus far and no farther."

Sir Henry Segrave
1929

Published jointly by United States Historical Society and Mystic Seaport Museum Stores

Trade Edition distributed by:
International Marine
Camden, ME

Designed by: Marie-Louise Scull

Cataloging in Publication Data

Fostle, Donald W., 1942–
    Speedboat / D.W. Fostle. — Mystic, Conn.:
Mystic Seaport Museum Stores, c1988.

    Bibliography: p.
    Includes index.
    1. Motorboats—History. 2. Motorboat racing—History. I. Title.
GV835.18F6
ISBN 0-939510-07-3

Printed in Japan

CONTENTS

PREFACE

*T*his book began one day in the summer of 1987 with a remarkable opportunity. Through Joe Gribbins, editor of *Nautical Quarterly*, an invitation was extended to visit The Rosenfeld Collection at Mystic Seaport to see what might be done in the way of a book on powerboats. The Rosenfelds had published several collections of their sailing photos over the years but had never turned their attention to the hundreds of thousands of powerboat photos they had taken over more than half a century. At first it seemed that a general history of powerboating would be best. But the tree of powerboat development is thick with branches, altogether too many to be treated in a single volume. There were cruisers, houseboats, workboats, skiffs, outboards, yachts, and many others, each type with its own appeal and story. It appeared reasonable to focus on a single distinguishing characteristic and that, clearly, was speed.

Speed and the desire for it separated powerboats from their wind and muscle-driven ancestors. So this book came to be titled *Speedboat*. A further demarcation, though not entirely satisfactory, was made in the time period covered. This volume concludes with events of the early 1960s. The activities of the last 25 years may very well be judged by the future as a time of consolidation and refinement. The production powerboats of today are not very different in materials or technology from those of the 1960s. Accordingly, this volume ends with the ascendancy of the fiberglass deep-V hull and the inboard-outboard drive.

It is remarkable, but nonetheless true, that a book tracing the development of high-speed American boats has not been written before. Save for a brief period early in this century, there is also an almost total absence of the types of technical papers in which the fields of aeronautical and automotive development abound. The main records chronicling powerboating are magazines and, in periods of great popularity, newspapers. The pleasure-boating journals — *Rudder, Motor Boat, Yachting, Powerboating* and *Motor Boating* — are the prime repositories, supplemented by newspapers such as *The New York Times*. It would not have been possible to work with this vast record were it not for the recent development of computerized textbase systems that work as electronic file cards. More than 1,500 articles and items were selected and "textbased" for this book, and the sheer number prevents their appearance in the bibliography, which is principally devoted to books that proved useful.

Many people contributed their time, knowledge and effort in the course of the creation of this book. Among them were Tom Aageson, Mystic Seaport Museum Stores; Roger Alan, Philadelphia Maritime Museum; Lee Barnett, State of Michigan Archives; Helen Bisby, Grand Rapids Public Library; John Canby, Society of Naval Architects and Marine Engineers; Lorna Condon, Society for the Preservation of New England Antiquities; Tom Crew, The Mariners' Museum; Harriet Culver, Culver Pictures; Jeff Flannery, Library of Congress; Ben Fuller, the curatorial staff at Mystic Seaport Museum and particularly the Rosenfeld Collection personnel; Kurt Hasselbalch, Thousand Islands Shipyard Museum; Richard Heckman, General Dynamics; Scott Peters, Michigan Historical Museum; Jerry Morris and staff at the G.W. Blunt White Library, Mystic Seaport Museum; Margaret Rice, Amesbury Public Library; Daniel Savitsky, Stevens Institute of Technology; Richard Scharchburg, General Motors Institute; Neil Van Allen, GM Research Library; Bill Wilkinson, The Mariners' Museum; and David Zarringer, Webb Institute Library.

For their insights, recollections and manifold contributions, the following people deserve special thanks: John Atkin, Martin Beebe, Richard Bryan, Bill Cantrell, Henry Austin Clark, John Deknatel, Tom Flood, Mickey Hacker, Dyer Jones, Ron Jones, Ted Jones, Fritz Kahlenberg, Beverly Rae Kimes, Norman Lauterbach, Elinor Hacker Lowther, David P. Martin, Mark Mason, Pearce McLouth, Mary Horn Printz, Stanley Rosenfeld, Bill Schroeder, Duncan Scott, Everett Smith, Harsen Smith, John Staudacher, Les Staudacher, Henry Steinway, Olin Stephens, Brooks Stevens, Ion Sutton, Gar Wood, Jr., Jim Wynne and Nelson Zimmer. A special mention must be made of the contribution of Joe Gribbins, who served not only as a catalyst but as the consummate editor, invariably displaying a combination of tact, perspective and insight.

The chronicles of high-speed boat development contain the stories of remarkable men and extraordinary achievements. In the main, these were the accomplishments of small groups and of individuals. Some possessed genuine genius and vision, a few were never recognized by their contemporaries, and many more have been forgotten. This book attempts to plot the bearings of their lights through the fog of time.

D.W.F.

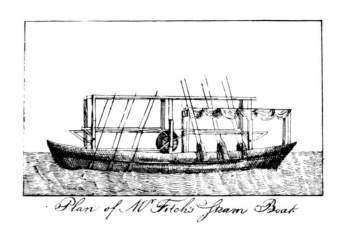

Plan of M.r Fitch's Steam Boat.

I have given my Country a most Valuable Discovery on the 30 of August 1785, for which I have received no Compensation, and I doubt not but common justice will induce them to do something for me, especially when they can do it for the benefit of our Empire ————

Another inducement which urges me to pursue this Scheme is, to put it out of the power of future Generations to make excuses for the present one — And if I should die in penury, want, wretchedness and rags, that my country may have no excuse; and that I may have the severest pleasure, in the Contemplation of receiving real pitty from future Generations

all which is humbly submitted to the Company

By

25.t Dec.r 1790

John Fitch

BEFORE THE BEGINNING

(opposite)

John Fitch's sketch of his first steam vessel and his letter to the future. The sketch does not show the engine, as Fitch was not yet sure of its appearance.

President George Washington politely demurred when asked for an introduction to the Virginia legislature, but offered his guest the hospitality of Mount Vernon. Ben Franklin would not provide a public endorsement, but offered a few dollars in support. Mr. Franklin had his own ideas for a jet-propelled vessel. Of the 3,900,000 residents of America in the years just after the Revolution, few had a grander vision than John Fitch: vessels moving on the waters of the new nation, not by the force of wind or muscle, but by machinery.

Born near Hartford, Connecticut, in 1743, Mr. Fitch had apprenticed as a clockmaker, the ultimate in eighteenth-century high technology. He briefly operated a bronze foundry before abandoning his family in 1769. During the Revolution Fitch gunsmithed at Valley Forge. Later he speculated in real estate, was captured by Indians in Ohio and, after being freed by the Army, took up residence near Philadelphia. It was there that he formed his vision of mechanical propulsion for a vessel, probably about 1785. The exact inspiration is unclear; perhaps he saw the only steam engine operating in America at the time. His was not an entirely original vision. For centuries men had dreamed of a such a thing: "It roweth, it draweth, it driveth, to pass London Bridge, against the stream at low water," wrote the Marquis of Worcester as he described his experiments with mechanical propulsion before his death in 1667. And there were others, many others, lost in the folds of history.

It is unlikely that Fitch knew of prior efforts. Not dissuaded by the response of the Founding Fathers, the Continental Congress and several state legislatures, Fitch took his proposal to the citizens of Philadelphia. He raised $300 from twenty men and commenced construction. The boat was built at the yard of Brooks & Wilson in Philadelphia and the engine constructed by Henry Voight, who had worked on Newcomen engines in England. With a length of 45' and a beam of 12', twelve steam-driven paddles pushed the boat along at 3 miles per hour at a trial on August 22, 1787. The speed was judged insufficient, and *Columbian* was broken up.

(below)

Benjamin Franklin proposed this water-jet-propelled boat in the Proceedings of the American Philosophical Society *in December 1785. Note the pump-like handle and the four 90-degree turns in the water path.*

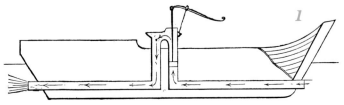

1

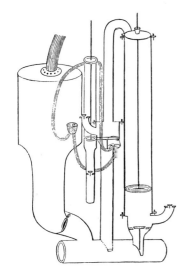

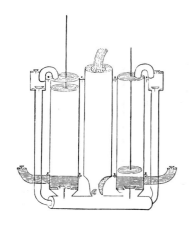

Undeterred and with a fresh infusion of capital, John Fitch commenced *Perseverence*. At 60' by 8' beam, *Perseverance* proved a success and was witnessed "navigating against the wind and tide, with a very considerable degree of velocity by the force of steam only." By 1790 Fitch had built a third boat that made 8 miles per hour on a carefully measured course. He had also obtained the exclusive rights to steam navigation for the waters of New York, New Jersey, Pennsylvania, Virginia and Delaware. In the summer of 1790 one of John Fitch's boats was making trips from Philadelphia to Trenton. Though passengers and freight were carried, profits were not forthcoming. When a new boat was destroyed by storm, the shareholders lost patience. Later Fitch would write, "I know of nothing so perplexing and vexatious to a man of feelings, as a turbulent Wife and Steam Boat building . . ."

Fitch lived his life in the cold shadows of misfortune, and they darkened further, this time through an invitation to go to France and build a boat there. The French Revolution flared, and Fitch could not build his boat. One of his investors — and the source of the invitation — gave his plans and specifications to Robert Fulton. A destitute John Fitch retrieved his designs but was stranded in France. Working his way back to America, Fitch was now an impoverished alcoholic experimenting with propellers and paddle wheels on Collect Pond in Manhattan.

Unable to raise capital, John Fitch fled to what he thought was the Kentucky wilderness. There he owned 2,200 acres of land, the product of an earlier speculation. Arriving at Bardstown, Kentucky, in the winter of 1795-1796, he found that squatters had cleared his land and had begun farming. The destitute John Fitch struck a bargain with a local saloon keeper. In

Early nineteenth-century diagrams of the cylinders and condenser of a Fitch engine. Fitch faced the formidable task of having to invent and construct every component of the hull, engine and propulsion systems.

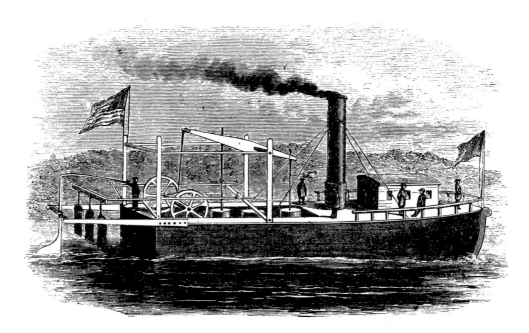

A Fitch packet in operation on the Delaware in 1790.

return for board and one pint of whiskey a day, he would deed to the saloon man 150 acres of his holdings. After Fitch forecast that he did not expect to live long, the barkeep accepted the offer. Within a few months another 150 acres changed hands, and the allotment was increased to two pints per day. Claiming pain, John Fitch obtained opium from a local doctor. On July 2, 1798, he died by his own hand, consuming the opium and whiskey together. Revolutionary, visionary, and the inventor of mechanical propulsion in America, John Fitch was buried in an unmarked grave.

For seventeen years after Fitch's effort of 1790, powered navigation in America was torpent, punctuated by the occasional experiment. But the fires of John Fitch's innovations, though deeply banked, were not extinguished. After a decade of experimenting with torpedoes, submarines, canals, bridges and weaving machines, Robert Fulton decided — along with Robert Livingston — to build a steam vessel in America. The wealthy Livingston was the brother-in-law of John Stevens, a New York inventor from whom Fitch failed to raise funds many years before. Fulton had been experimenting in France; Livingston and Stevens had built engines and boats in America. When Robert Livingston went abroad as Minister to France, it was natural that the men

Fitch's Collect Pond experimental boat fitted with both paddle wheels and a screw propeller. On the site of this pond in Manhattan now stands The Tombs.

should strike an alliance. Lubricated by capital and connections, the project moved to completion with relative smoothness. Much progress had been made with engine development in the years since the Fitch efforts. Fulton wisely did not build his own engine, but instead went to the firm of Watt & Boulton with his requirements. The machinery was shipped to America, where it was installed in a hull built by Charles Brown on the East River. Livingston was meanwhile occupied with obtaining or restoring the rights needed to operate the vessel on state waters.

This replica of North River Steam- boat of Clermont was built to celebrate the centennial of Fulton's Hudson River operations. The reproduction Clermont operated for years, and this photo of her was taken at West Point in 1915.

The *North River Steamboat of Clermont* was 140' overall, 16' in beam with a draft of 28 inches. Propulsion was by two 15'-diameter paddle wheels. Not new, paddle wheels driven by oxen had been used on Roman boats to invade Sicily during the Punic Wars. They had also been used by John Fitch. In fact, little about this boat was new, as detractors were quick to point out. *Clermont's* lack of innovation was probably the prime factor in her success. The objective was not invention; it was profitable commercial operation.

At her first trial one observer reported in the convoluted prose of the time: "The jeers of the ignorant, who had neither the sense nor feeling enough to suppress their contemptuous ridicule and rude jokes, were silenced for a moment by a vulgar astonishment which deprived them of their powers

of utterance, till the triumph of genius extorted from the incredulous multitude which crowded the shores, shouts and acclamations of congratulations and applause.'' On August 17, 1807, *North River Steamboat of Clermont* left on her first trip to Albany, a journey which took 36 hours for a rate of about 4 miles per hour. As the few who remembered John Fitch noted, this was not very fast. The fare was fourteen dollars round-trip, equivalent to about eight days wages for a skilled artisan and thirty days for a laborer.

While Fulton's enterprise was successful, the general adoption of mechanical propulsion moved no faster than the boats. A decade after *Clermont*, only 10 of the 1,087 new vessels constructed in America were mechanically powered. By 1825 41 of 1,000 vessels built were powered, according to the Bureau of Navigation. In 1850 this had risen to 197 out of 1,412 or 14 percent. It was not until 1880 — almost a century after Fitch's earliest experiments — that the tonnage of new steam construction matched that of sail.

The development of yachting in the early years of the nineteenth century was equally slow. Among the earliest yachts recorded was *The Jefferson* owned by George Crowninshield of Salem in 1801. The 22-ton sloop also operated as a privateer and a fishing vessel, suggesting some ambivalence of purpose on the part of her owner. By the time the New York Yacht Club was formed in 1844 there were a few dozen pleasure vessels at both New York and Boston. There also existed a bias by yachtsmen against mechanical pro-

Cornelius Vanderbilt's awesome North Star, *a pioneer American steam yacht. She was 270' of ante-bellum conspicuous consumption with 34' diameter paddlewheels.*

pulsion. England's Royal Yacht Squadron forbade steam with sternly worded resolve: "The object of this club is to promote seamanship to which the application of steam is inimical, and any member applying steam to his yacht shall be disqualified hereby, and shall cease to be a member."

So exotic and demanding was the technology, so expensive was its use, that mechanical propulsion did not appear in American pleasure boats until the 1850s, almost seven decades after John Fitch's first experiments. Given the complexity and cost, there is little surprise in finding that among the pioneers was Cornelius Vanderbilt, who in 1853 built the steam-powered *North Star*. At 270' she was a side-wheeler of full commercial proportions. A more modest 98' steamer was commissioned by William Aspinwall, President of the Pacific Mail Steamship Company, in 1854. Yachtsmen of lesser means moved on the water

at the whim of the wind, by such physical exertion as they or their servants might provide, or not at all. And so it would remain until well after the Civil War. In the wider view, boats and ships were not a very large factor in the development of what was sometimes known as "inanimate power." Of the 8,271,000 mechanical horsepower in use in the United States in 1870, only 7.6% was found in steam vessels. It was the railroads which led the way with 54% while factories accounted for 30%. The balance was used for mining and farming machinery.

Steam engines grew to be the pride of America, a symbol of prosperity, productivity and progress. Their builders finished the frames with the finest enamels, polished the brass parts, applied gold striping, and sometimes decorated them with painted flowers. This was called "industrial beautification." At the great expositions of the mechanical arts, thousands stared in wonder at the iron icons of power. These were the machines that drove the

machines that gave unfailing light, warmth, and cool fresh water, that moved men across the earth with unprecedented speed and opulent comfort.

Steam engines were ministered to by "engineers" who risked scaldings, maimings and death. These were not minor risks. Each year on late-nineteenth century railroads about 1 in 25 employees was injured, and 2,000 to 3,000 died. Nor were passengers at smaller peril: deaths averaged about 8,500 per year with injuries to about 64,000 men, women and children. Water travel was slightly safer. The Bureau of Navigation carefully tabulated an average of 1,550 "Disasters · to Vessels," covering rammings, sinkings, fires, explosions and groundings each year. Involved, on average, were about 28,000 people. Murder, mutiny and other mayhem were catalogued separately. But progress was not measured by risk. The criterion was speed, the reflexive relationship be-

An immense Corliss engine at the Centennial Exposition in Philadelphia. President Ulysses S. Grant started the engine to signal the opening of the exhibition, and legend has it that Nat Herreshoff helped build and run the machine.

tween velocity and time. In the first half of the nineteenth century speed on the water improved by about 3% per year. On the New York-Albany route, times fell by a factor of five from the 36 hours of *North River Steamboat of Clermont* in 1807 to the 7 hours, 20 minutes of *Daniel Drew* in 1860.

By the 1880s transatlantic racing was in vogue, and the steamship companies vied for the fastest crossing by building vessels of ever-escalating speed. Crossing times fell each year and travelers lined up for passage on the fastest ships, hopeful of obtaining a berth in history and a topic of conversation for years to come. Steaming into a fog bank at 20 knots was thought to be safer — at least by some captains — since the time spent in the fog would be half that proceeding at 10 knots. Higher speeds were also claimed to improve maneuverability in avoiding icebergs, derelicts and other ships. These vessels consumed coal and water in immense quantities. The *City of New York*, for example, needed 800,000 pounds of coal and 3,840 tons of water per day to develop her rated 18,000 to 20,000 horsepower. By the fall of 1890 owners of the "ocean greyhounds" jointly announced an end to ocean racing, citing their concern with passenger safety. Whether the operating economies of lower speeds, reduced maintenance and less pressure to build new ships entered into the decision is unrecorded by history, but in the summer of 1891 records were falling again. The demand for speed was insatiable.

Yet the transatlantic ships and the crack trains represented institutional speed. No matter how exhilarating, no matter how fashionable or glamorous, this was public speed; the experience was available to anyone with the price of a ticket. The machines and their systems were so complicated, so vast, that they were necessarily controlled by trusts, combinations and governments. The "prime movers" were not yet sufficiently small, inexpensive or reliable for the use of individuals. To accomplish that would require different technologies.

The seers of mechanism were already at work on the problem in machine shops, foundries and barns across the land. They called them "explosive motors" at first, an appellation that did not originate in any advertising department. Later these one-man powerplants were known as "internal combustion" engines, a phrase more accurate and less threatening. Had the new "explosive motors" been developed in the late twentieth century, they would have undoubtedly been called "micro-motors" or, perhaps, "personal engines." A fine way to use the new prime mover was in a boat, and since the engines were of low power, a small boat was best. Another revolution was about to begin. John Fitch would undoubtedly have been pleased.

2

A FEW
FORGOTTEN MEN

His was one of the finest minds of the time and perhaps of all time. He was the first to use the pendulum in a clock; he improved the telescope, found the planet Saturn, invented the micrometer, made important contributions to the theory of probability, and discovered the polarization of light. He was Christian Huygens (1629-1695), Dutch physicist, mathematician and astronomer. In 1680, at the age of 51, Huygens proposed a "gunpowder engine," then built one, and demonstrated it to the French Minister of Finance. The Huygens engine exploded a small quantity of powder in a cylinder. Leather check valves let the gases out, and as the remaining gas cooled, a partial vacuum was formed. Atmospheric pressure then pushed a piston down to the bottom of the cylinder to lift a weight or do other work. In collaboration with French physician, physicist and visionary Denis Papin, another Huygens engine was constructed. By some accounts it was used about 1690 to propel a boat by pumping water onto a paddle wheel. The result was not entirely successful, and the sound of an "explosive engine" was not heard for a century.

In 1794 an Englishman, Robert Street, patented an engine that burned turpentine in its cylinders to pump water, but marine application of "explosive engines" was not tried again until the work of Samuel Brown in the 1820s. Brown was greatly interested in locomotion and experimented with both carriages and boats. He realistically but optimistically took into account the economics of operation. Fueling his engines with coal gas, Brown claimed in 1832 that the power generated was free since the coke and coal tar by-products could be sold at prices that produced a profit for the entire enterprise. Brown's work was sufficiently credible to bring the Lords of the Admiralty to a demonstration on the Thames in January of 1827. According to a witness, the 36' vessel moved at a rate of 7 to 8 miles per hour, "with all the regularity of a steamer, and the paddles worked quite smoothly, and seemed capable of continuing to go as long as gas was supplied." A company was formed to build boats, but Admiralty interest waned, and the firm was dissolved.

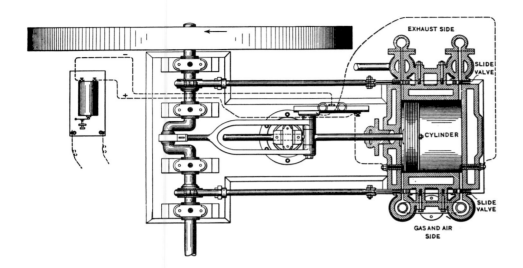

EXHAUST SIDE

SLIDE VALVE

CYLINDER

SLIDE VALVE

GAS AND AIR SIDE

Lenoir's engine owed much to steam practice. Like many steam engines it was double acting; an explosion occurred alternately on each side of the piston.

Until the 1860s explosive engines remained the domain of mechanical prophets. The earliest commercial success followed a pattern similar to Fulton's steamboat: invent as little as possible and draw heavily on previous practice. "The Lenoir engine uses the piston according to the patent of Street, it is direct and double acting as Lebon's engine, it is electrically ignited as that of von Rivaz, it can be operated by hydrogen as proposed by Herskine-Harzard and one probably would recognize Talbot's splendid ideas in the slide valve as used by Lenoir," wrote an M. Lefeyvre in 1864. Whether this was candor or slander cannot now be determined.

Pierre Lenoir's successful synthesis was first constructed in 1860 by Hippolyte Marinoni in Paris. Lenoir's brilliance lay in taking what was essentially an ordinary steam engine and converting it to internal combustion. The fuel was again coal gas. Within five years 400 engines were sold in powers from a half-horsepower to three-horsepower. They drove printing presses, lathes, and stone cutters; they polished marble and cut chaff. It was not long before a Lenoir engine found its way into a boat. Coal gas was not available on the water, so a system was devised to vaporize "light hydrocarbons." Lenoir's boat was said to have made several trips per week on the Seine for two years. The route was from Paris to Charenton le Pont southeast of the city and back. This was, the evidence suggests, the pioneering practical motorboat. Yet Lenoir's major contribution lay elsewhere, largely in demonstrating the existence of a market. He was rewarded with an avalanche of competitors, all seeking to improve on fuel economy, an outstanding weakness of the Lenoir machine.

In 1862, the second year of Lenoir's transient triumph, a pamphlet by a French engineer, M. Alphonse Beau de Rochas, appeared. In the slim booklet were the keys to the future of engine development not simply for the nineteenth century but for the twentieth as well. Monsieur Beau de Rochas set forth the architecture of the high-speed, high-compression, four-cycle engine with a large bore and a short stroke. He also explained with what now seems stunning clarity exactly why engines should be built along the lines he described. Almost predictably, Beau de Rochas's work became prophecy with but little influence on practice.

It is likely that many nineteenth-century explosive engine builders did not correctly understand how the mechanisms they constructed worked. This seems to have been the case with one of the most famous, Nikolaus August Otto. Described in 1909 as "the greatest and most successful gas engine inventor who has yet appeared," Otto's seminal patent specification of 1876 explained the workings of his four-cycle engine. It was based on a "slow" explosion controlled by the arrangement of gases in the cylinder. The gases were said to be "stratified." Dr. Otto's patent gave his firm effective control of four-cycle engine technology for many years. In the first decade about 30,000 engines were sold, and the four-stroke cycle patented by Beau de Rochas became indelibly known as the "Otto cycle." The first of the Otto engines could produce one horsepower for one hour using about 40 cubic feet of gas. This was about twice the fuel economy achieved by Lenoir.

Technical journals recorded more than a few learned struggles between the believers in Otto's stratification and those who maintained that Beau de Rochas's concept of compression was the secret of the engine's success. Experiments escalated from simple demonstrations using a cigarette and a water tumbler to the construction of full-scale working engines made of glass. At stake was more than theory; the Otto patent was in conflict with that of Beau de Rochas if compression was accepted as the key to operation. Dr. Otto died in 1891, apparently never accepting that his immensely successful engine owed its efficiency to the use of compression, not the stratification in which he believed.

With the path of development blocked by controversy and controlling patents, the flow of innovation turned in a new direction, that of the two-cycle engine. In the four-cycle, the engine made two revolutions in which the explosive mixture was first inducted, then compressed, burned and expelled. In the two-cycle there was an explosion every revolution of the crankshaft. This had the intuitively appealing advantage of developing more power and the practical benefit of being less assiduously protected by patents.

Dugald Clerk was among those who pioneered the two-cycle form in England, obtaining his first patent in 1877. By 1881

Intended to operate on coal gas, this early Otto four-cycle had separate entry ports for air and gas. The horizontal section shows the very long stroke of the motor. This was thought important in creating the "stratification" of the gases which Otto believed was the secret of his engine's relatively high fuel efficiency.

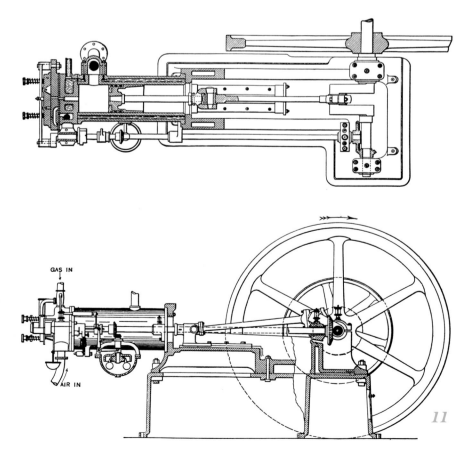

GAS IN

AIR IN

he had developed a type which pressurized a mixture of fuel and air in one cylinder (called the "displacer") and transferred it to another cylinder for combustion. In some quarters the two-cycle principle was known as the Clerk cycle. Clerk and the other developers of two-cycle engines in Europe were less aggressive in the pursuit and prosecution of patents than the Otto interests, and so it came to be that the Clerk cycle formed the basis for much American development in the 1880s. Clerk, for example, never received a patent on his engine of 1881 in the United States. Meanwhile, American developments were accelerating. Only seven gas and oil engine patents were granted in 1880. By 1883 this had grown to 40, and in 1890 62 patents were granted while an estimated 20,000 engines were in use. It was during the 1880s that the explosive motor was transformed from a tentative and experimental alternative to steam to a potentially practical prime mover.

New technology attracts the young and others who have no vested interest in the established order. So it was with the explosive motor. At the Detroit Dry Dock & Marine Company a young man fresh from the family farm in Dearborn encountered the new explosive motor. His name was Henry Ford.

Across the state in Niles, Michigan, two young men watched their father's encounters with the new machines. John and Horace Dodge would reshape America, first with Ford and later in competition with him. Midway between Ford and the Dodges was Ransom Eli Olds, first watching his father and then laboring alongside him building engines and boats in Lansing, Michigan.

All this was less coincidence than a natural outgrowth of the state of the technology.

A Pliny F. Olds & Son stationary engine. The Olds family also built marine engines and launches in their shop on the Grand River at Lansing, Michigan.

12

The early engines were large and heavy, although less so than the steam engines they would ultimately replace. They operated slowly, changing speed only reluctantly and then over a narrow band. While adequate for use in pumping water, threshing grain, sawing wood or doing similar work, they were not yet sufficiently efficient to propel themselves on land. The technical problems were staggering. They involved basic issues of fuel availability, method of fuel vaporization (the French term carburetion had not yet been coined), ignition systems, metallurgy, engine mounting, transmissions, steering, starting, stopping and a thicket of related obstacles. Not the least of these was the condition of roads, where these existed at all. The real challenge confronting the builder of a self-propelled land machine would today be recognized as the design of an off-road vehicle.

By contrast, the marine environment appeared commodious. Hull forms could be borrowed from existing practice; space was ample; and compared to the steam engine, even a primitive explosive engine was relatively small. In the mid-1880s the light power vessel was a rarity. A scant 781 had been built in America since the Civil War. When a wealthy family commissioned a 30' steam launch for transport to their island summer home, they received a launch with the ability to cruise at seven knots, burning a half-ton of coal to run 100 miles. A government-licensed captain was required to operate the engine, and government inspections of the machinery were mandatory. Boiler explosions and fires were regularly reported in the newspapers, so regular examination of the machinery that filled the middle third of the hull was not merely required; it was prudent.

An entirely ordinary steam launch of the late 1880s. This was the benchmark for the work of Clark Sintz and many others.

Waste heat from the boiler and engine could be stifling in summer, clothing was frequently fouled by smoke and fumes, and half an hour was needed at each end of the voyage to prepare and secure the machinery. Hot ashes and clinkers had to be removed and safely disposed. "One who has never been off for a day's pleasure in a small steam launch cannot imagine the amount of misery that one of these small craft is capable of creating," wrote mechanical engineer Edward Birdsall in the 1890s. In light of the operational realities, it is not very surprising that launches were a relative rarity among America's more than 5,000 steam vessels. Yet the steam launch did have its partisans. Jacob Lorillard, the tobacco magnate, designed and built more than thirty of them in his search for perfection.

Industrial history does not record who first took aim at the plodding, puffing target of the late-Victorian steam launch, but in 1885 Clark Sintz was said to have demonstrated his explosive-motored launch on the waters of Michigan. A largely unheralded but pivotal figure in the history of locomotion, Sintz was born near Springfield, Ohio, in 1850 and grew up, like the vast majority of Americans of his time, on a farm. At the age of 23 he began the manufacture of a steam engine, and while visiting the Centennial Exposition in 1876, became interested in internal combustion. Perhaps he saw the Otto & Langen engines on exhibit in the Hall of Machinery. By 1885 he had formed the Sintz Gas Engine Company to manufacture a Clerk-cycle engine with separate compression and combustion cylinders. A true pioneer of explosive engines, it was Sintz who patented what became a fundamental feature of all engines: ignition advance. He supplied engines to Elwood Haynes, among the earliest to build a car in America, to the brilliant artist-engineer Charles Brady King, who built both boats and engines as well as the first automobile in Detroit, and to a blacksmith and decoy carver turned boatbuilder from Algonac, Michigan, named Christopher Columbus Smith.

At New York about 1889 a steam launch moves through the harbor, probably with a sightseeing party. In the background is the crack steamer Monmouth, *which plied the Sandy Hook route.*

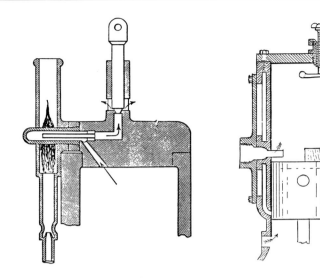

The Sintz engine used a "make and break" ignition with an electrode inside the cylinder. Contact with the piston triggered a low-voltage spark. Also common was the hot-tube ignition where a metal tube inserted in the cylinder was heated at one end by a Bunsen burner. The hot tube ignited the compressed charge. Once the engine reached operating temperature the flame was turned off.

Not long after moving to Grand Rapids, Michigan, Clark Sintz obtained the basic patent for a three-port, two-cycle engine. From this fundamental advance would flow untold millions of outboard motors, lawn mowers, motorcycles and chainsaws in a line which continues to the present day. As an almost incidental feature, the engine also had direct-port fuel injection. Engineer A.E. Potter wrote at the turn of the century: "The early developments of 2-stroke-cycle motors were made in the vicinity of Grand Rapids, Michigan, gradually extending toward the Atlantic Seaboard." The method of extension was simple: other builders copied the engines and built them under their own names. Potter went on to give an eyewitness account of how the then-better-known Palmer engine was copied from the Sintz motor and how the Lathrop was copied from the Palmer. Each would in turn spawn further generations of quasi-legitimate offspring until by the early years of this century more than a hundred shops were turning out two-cycle marine engines. An occasional effort was made to enforce the Sintz patent. In 1906 it was reported that the patent was owned by a Detroit man, ". . . said to represent the Olds Motor Works, who is demanding pay from those who have made and are making," Sintz-type two-cycle motors. The patent had four years remaining, and Clark Sintz had another sixteen. After leaving Grand Rapids he journeyed to Panama, then farmed in Alabama. In 1922 Clark Sintz was working in a machine shop. He died that year at age 72 from injuries received in an automobile crash. Neither his ironic death nor his accomplishments in life received much notice.

A Patent drawing for the seminal Sintz three-port two-cycle engine. A. exhaust port; B. intake port; C. bypass port; D. fuel pump; E. fuel injection; F. ignition. From this design grew nearly all small two-cycle engines in use today.

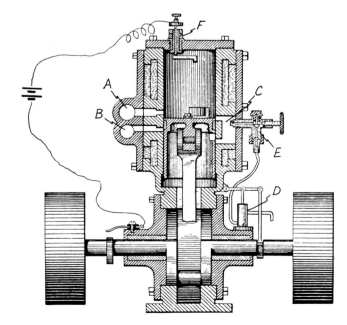

William Steinway

3

GAS, ELECTRIC
& PIANOS

Clark Sintz's two-cycle engines were not the only ones with promise. Among the four-cycle forces, leadership and control rested with the Germans. Wilhelm Maybach, an engineer with the Otto works, was on a reconnaissance mission in 1876 when he toured America. Stopping to visit his brother in New York, he met his brother's employer, William Steinway. Mr. Steinway took an interest in the engines; and Maybach, a very astute engineer, promised to keep Steinway abreast of activity in the field. It is indicative of the pace of development that the matter sat for a dozen years. In the interim Maybach and Gottlieb Daimler had set up their own firm and were licensing patents for their new "high-speed" four-cycle engine.

Accounts vary as to the circumstances that rekindled William Steinway's interest, but by 1888 he had negotiated successfully with Daimler for the American and Canadian rights to the engine. Negotiations may have been assisted by the fact that both men enjoyed choral singing as a recreation. The Steinway name was best-known, of course, for its pianos; but there were other interests: street railways, ferry lines, a gas works, real estate and banking.

Undoubtedly William Steinway saw what today would be called "strategic linkages" between his businesses. Daimler's engine could be used to power streetcars or propel ferry boats; stationary engine buyers would consume gas produced by his works; and the piano company's woodworking knowledge might be readily transferred to building boats. The Steinway plant on Long Island was conveniently located on the East River, and the company's name provided the boats with an indelible imprimatur of quality.

Nor was Mr. Steinway unfamiliar with salesmanship: the advertising programs of the piano company were mainly responsible for the idea that no home was suitably furnished without a piano and that no young lady's education was complete until she could play one. According to family sources, William Steinway took promotion very seriously, personally writing

Best known as a piano-maker, William Steinway was also a powerboat pioneer. Obtaining the North American franchise for Daimler engines, Steinway opened a Manhattan showroom for boats and motors next door to Steinway Hall and invested heavily in the business until his death in 1896.

catalogs and advertisements. With $20,000,000 in assets under his control at a time when the average working American made $438 a year, Mr. William Steinway must have been as well-qualified as any man of his time to secure the success of the explosive motor as a prime mover.

The first meeting of the new Daimler Motor Company was held on February 2, 1889. Things did not move quickly. It was April of the next year before three motors were operating at the works. At Daimler's recommendation, actual construction of the engines had been subcontracted to a Hartford, Connecticut, machine shop. Thanksgiving Day 1890 found William Steinway correcting the Daimler Motor Company catalog, its first, for the year 1891.

One-, two- and four-horsepower engines were offered that year. Prices were high: $690 for a complete one-horsepower marine unit with reverse gear, shaft, propeller, tank and fittings. A comparably equipped two-horsepower unit was $910, and the four-horsepower cost $1,225. This

A Steinway raceboat circa 1892. "Her length is 42 feet overall, is equipped with a 10 H.P. motor, and we are now ready to demonstrate to persons interested in this kind of sport, what we can do in speed, inviting anything of her size afloat to a friendly contest," read the catalogue.

$1,225 engine represented nearly three years' labor for the average American and a labor-equivalent cost in the mid-1980s of about $60,000. Despite the price, the engines began to sell, and in February of 1892 Steinway wrote in his diary, "At last a demand seems to arise for the Daimler Motors." A few months later Steinway decided to expand the Daimler plant. The success was apparently transitory, and by fall Steinway was in the new plant, personally examining boats and motors after receiving an "ably drawn" report on the "unfortunate Daimler Motor Company." Management changes followed.

In 1893 prices were cut; the one-horsepower engine was reduced 47%, the two-horsepower 37%, and the four-horsepower engine by a third to $825 installed in a boat. A seven-horsepower vertical twin and a twelve-horse vertical four were added to the line. That these engines were technically superior seems beyond doubt in retrospect. Comparing the four-horsepower Daimler with its weight of 678 pounds and operating speed of 580 rpm to the competitive Globe engine which weighed 1,200 pounds and operated at 225 rpm clearly indicates the Daimler's superiority. But the company's fortunes continued to oscillate while the volatile Gottlieb Daimler himself moved in and out by transatlantic steamer, volubly and vehemently pushing a move into motor carriages, delivering new engine designs, skirmishing with stockholders, leaving the parent company, then rejoining it, and generally vexing William Steinway. At the Columbian Exposition in 1893 the company received much notice when the launch it had on display was used to save the lives of six souls whose sailboat had capsized in Lake Michigan. Reports claimed the Daimler boat was capable of achieving 16 miles per hour.

Later there were small triumphs and large tragedies. The Panic of 1893 resulted in the failure of 15,000 businesses including 155 railroads and 550 banks. Called the "rich men's panic," it undoubtedly dampened demand for Daimler boats and engines. William Steinway persisted. A Steinway-built race boat was refused entry in a naphtha launch race at Larchmont Yacht Club on Independence

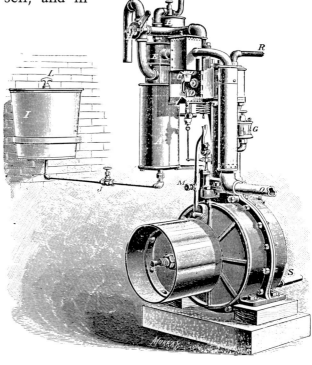

The basic two-horsepower Daimler engine set up for industrial use. A. carburetor; B. fuel supply for hot tube burner regulated by valve F; C. platinum hot tube; D. burner; H. mixture regulator; I. fuel supply; O. exhaust pipe; S. starting crank.

Day, 1894. It ran the course anyway and finished eight minutes ahead of the naphtha boats. In August the Steinway racer won a cup at another race. William Steinway found a buyer — at $5,000 — for his personal cabin launch, only to have it destroyed by a hurricane in September of 1894.

The year 1895 brought an improved climate, largely due to external events. The economic situation was improving, and in Europe Daimler automobiles had swept a pioneer race in France, the Paris-Bordeaux. In America *The Chicago Times-Herald* was promoting a horseless carriage race from Chicago to Evanston, Illinois, and public interest was approaching frenzy. Orders for boats and motors grew sharply. Showing unusual endurance, William Steinway funded yet another expansion of the plant, this time to include a dredged harbor for customer boats. Good fortune was not to last. "I have serious apprehensions as to monetary outlook and curse the Daimler Motor Company for its draining me of money and resolve to stop it," wrote Steinway in March of 1896. The firm was still spending heavily, advertising, and exhibiting at sportsmen's shows.

A large Steinway-built cruiser underway about 1894. A 40' cabin boat of this type cost $4,000 to $5,500 with two 12-horsepower engines; a 50' cost up to $7,000. Bilge pump, cleats, chocks, fenders, anchor, lights, name board, flag poles and brass rails were extra-cost options.

William Steinway did not live to solve the company's problems. Shortly after his death on November 30, 1896, his $181,100 investment in the stock of the Daimler Company was declared worthless by an appraiser. Through reorganization, the firm itself staggered along, building boats, motors and finally only cars in America for a few more years. In Europe Daimler's company agreed to change the name on their cars in return for an order of 36 vehicles from Emil Jellinek. A banker and diplomat for the Austro-Hungarian Empire, Jellinek named boats, yachts, estates and other possessions after his beloved daughter. The motives in this nomination may have involved more than paternal affection, as they allowed Mr. Jellinek and *Daimler Motoren Gesellschaft* to circumvent the company's existing distribution contracts. The young lady's name was *Mercedes.*

What was needed, it seemed, was a transitional technology, a bridge between the old steam and the new explosive engines. An engine that operated on the familiar principle of expansion, like a steam engine, but without its obvious liabilities would have been ideal. Whether or not Frank W. Ofeldt thought of his engine this way is unknown, but this is most certainly what he designed. Working in his Newark, New Jersey, shop, the Swedish immigrant devised a conceptually brilliant engine. Light, reliable, cheap to build, simple to repair, familiar in its operation, burning a petroleum by-product that was often thrown away, the naphtha engine was developed by Frank Ofeldt beginning about 1883.

Naphtha was the trade name for a medium-weight hydrocarbon that appeared in the petroleum refining process just before kerosene and just after benzene. Not much use had been found for the compound; some oil companies promoted its use in stoves. Unless deodorized, it had a vile organic smell. According to reports, naphtha was often burned off as a marketless by-product. In a few years it would become known as "gasolene," with shortages and high prices a common occurrence. It was probably not a coincidence that Standard Oil executive Jabez A. Bostwick was an early investor in Ofeldt's naphtha engine.

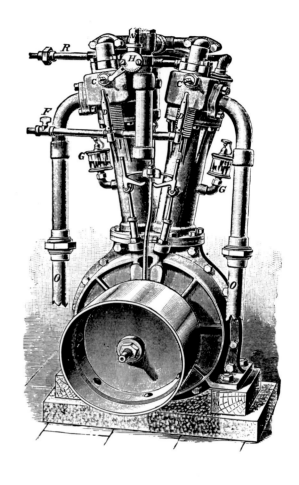

Using the same principle as the steam engine, Mr. Ofeldt heated the naphtha until it turned into a gas. The expansive power of the gas operated on the pistons in the engine in the same manner as steam. After the gas had expended most of its energy on the pistons, it entered a pipe that ran along the bottom of the boat. Here it was condensed into a liquid and returned to the tank. A relatively small amount of the naphtha was used in a burner to heat the hydrocarbon, which was the working fluid. Today we would say that the Ofeldt engine boiled gasolene instead of water.

In one ingenious stroke, Ofeldt had simultaneously solved a number of problems. The volatility of the naphtha meant that the engine's boiler could be miniaturized to a remarkable degree, thereby reducing the size and weight of the engine. A two-horsepower engine weighed only 200 pounds, and the company claimed that this was one-fifth the weight of a steam engine of comparable power. The engine could be set in the stern, liberating the amidships area for enlarged passenger capacity. The use of a liquid fuel removed the problems of shoveling coal and the disposal of ashes. The naphtha was vastly easier to handle although much more hazardous. The oily quality of

Daimler offered V-type engines as early as 1891 in both two- and four-horsepower models. A four-horsepower motor was claimed able to drive a 25' hull at 12 to 15 miles per hour.

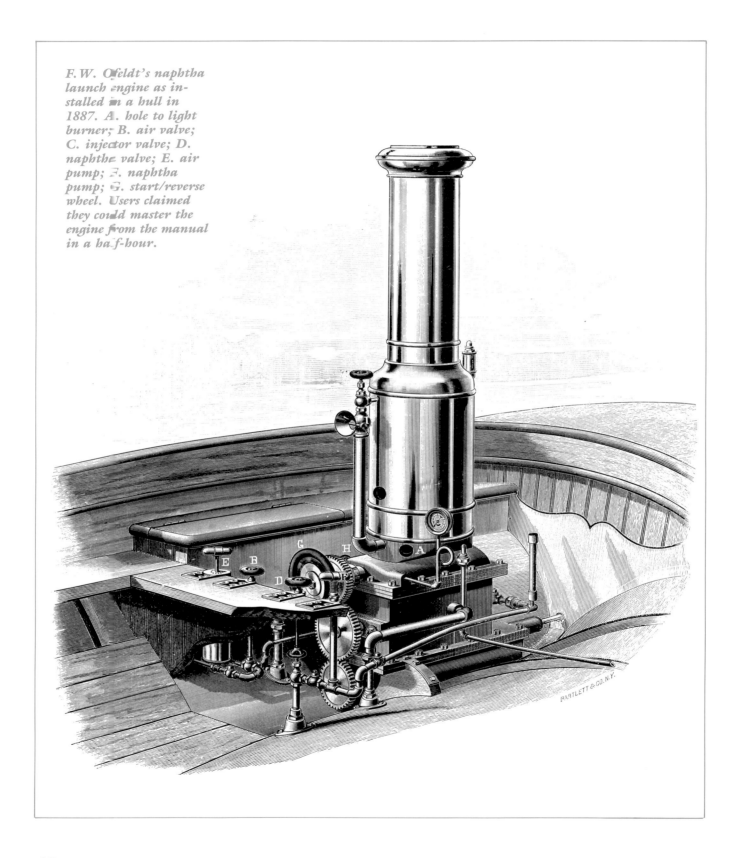

F.W. Ofeldt's naphtha launch engine as installed in a hull in 1887. A. hole to light burner; B. air valve; C. injector valve; D. naphtha valve; E. air pump; F. naphtha pump; G. start/reverse wheel. Users claimed they could master the engine from the manual in a half-hour.

the naphtha made the engine self-lubricating, ending yet another unpleasant task and improving its reliability. Since the engine operated at relatively low pressures — about half that of steam — it could be more lightly built. Perhaps its most miraculous feature was its ability to be underway in less than five minutes, no matter how cold the weather.

Of significance at least equal to the design achievement was the engine's exemption from the laws governing the inspection, licensing and operation of steam engines. Several years later (after an accident involving a naphtha launch) a member of the United States Steamboat Inspectors Board commented: ''It is necessary when naphtha is used as a fuel only, and steam is the expansive power, to get an inspection and a pilot's license, but when naphtha becomes the power as well as the fuel, we have no discretion over them whatsoever.'' If it was a regulatory absurdity that boiling water required a license but boiling gasolene did not, it was equally ridiculous that the regulations did not distinguish between a transatlantic steamer and a 20' steam pleasure launch. Each required a licensed master and pilot. Attempts to require the same of naphtha engines failed, despite the efforts of steam engine builders, captain's associations and pilot's guilds to bring the naphtha engines under regulatory purview.

A naphtha launch man might ''entertain his friends without the espionage of inquisitive employees'' and enjoy waterborne pleasures ''without hired assistance.'' One owner testified that operation was simple enough that he was able to turn the task over to his wife and that she was entirely successful in managing the engine. Apparently these were compelling sales points.

A 30', 6-horsepower naphtha launch with standing roof as it appeared about 1896. The roof was a $150 option to be added to the $1,550 price of the boat. Cushions for the seats cost up to $5 per foot, and 32' were needed for this boat. As with Steinway boats, all basic equipment was ''extra.''

BARTLETT & CO N Y

A small and typically equipped Gas Engine and Power Company launch underway. This 21' model was popular on inland waters, and the company would build hundreds of them over the winter for sale in the spring.

The first naphtha launch was sold in 1886 to the owner of the schooner yacht *Dauntless* for use as a tender. Other yacht owners followed. In 1886, the first year of commercial sales, a naphtha launch race was held at the American Yacht Club. Three boats participated in the three-mile contest, and the winner made the course at a rate of about seven knots in a two-horsepower, 21' launch that had cost its owner about $900. Such races became a fixture at many regattas.

At the 1890 race — 150 boats and an additional 50 engines had been sold that season — 19 boats were entered. They were described as "dainty little craft, frail as canoes, pretty as pictures, and capable of running at nine knots without crowding." Steam launches, running alongside, were "rapidly outdistanced by their smokeless and noiseless competitors." It was not just on the race course that the naphtha boats exceeded their competitors. In 1890 The Gas Engine and Power Company built 200 launches in advance of the season and sold them all. In five years of business their production was about equal to the small steam launch construction of the previous quarter century. The years of greatest popularity still lay ahead. By 1900 roughly 3,000 naphtha boats would be built. Mute testimony to the market power of the naphtha engine was provided by the Monitor Vapor Engine and Power Company of Grand Rapids, Michigan. For a few years in the 1890s their line of seven two-cycle internal combustion engines was fitted with brass stacks which emulated the funnels of the naphtha engines.

The engines and the boats grew in size. By the mid-1890s naphtha yachts of up to 76' were offered for $12,500. These twin-screw yachts were equipped with a pair of 16-horsepower engines, and because of the small size of the naphtha powerplant, were probably equal in accommodation to steam yachts 15' to 20' longer. Two of these flagships were sold for the season of 1896.

The naphtha engine was not without its weaknesses. "It is surprising, in view of the fact that there are in use many thousands of gas machines — all using Naphtha — that so few people are familiar with its peculiarities," said the owner's manual in 1891. There followed a lengthy explanation of the explosive qualities of the liquid, its care and handling. The company took fire safety seriously and lined the interior of the boats with copper sheet in way of the engine. A potentially serious problem could occur if the propeller was fouled by weeds or otherwise overloaded; engine pressure could rise to a point where the packing in fittings would give way, spraying hot naphtha and naphtha gas into the boat.

"Don't give this book away," admonished the manual. Among its two-dozen commandments was "Don't shoot through your tank" and "Don't go out without tools in the boat." The biggest public fear, conditioned by years of grisly steam accidents, was apparently explosion. To counter this, Gas Engine and Power offered a reward of $500 to anyone who could make an engine explode at their works. For the privilege of conducting the experiment, a fee of $100 was levied. History does not record if there were any takers or explosions.

Perhaps the ultimate weakness of the naphtha engine was its fuel economy. It consumed about three quarts of naphtha per horsepower per hour. By contrast, Daimler's engine burned only a pint of fuel per horsepower per hour, achieving six times the fuel efficiency. To the wealthy, the nine cents-per-gallon price of naphtha was undoubtedly a trivial expense, particularly for those who hung the launches on the davits of $50,000 steam

Naphtha cabin launches of this type (known as "street-car" cabins) were popular for coastal cruising. Boats were sold world-wide, and naphtha launches could be found in Hawaii, India, Turkey, Japan and South America. There were two dozen in England by 1896.

The flagship of the Gas Engine and Power Company's naphtha fleet. Carrying two 16-horsepower engines, this 76' yacht provided a less expensive alternative to steam yachts 15'–20' longer and, like its smaller sisters, completely circumvented steam licensing and inspection requirements.

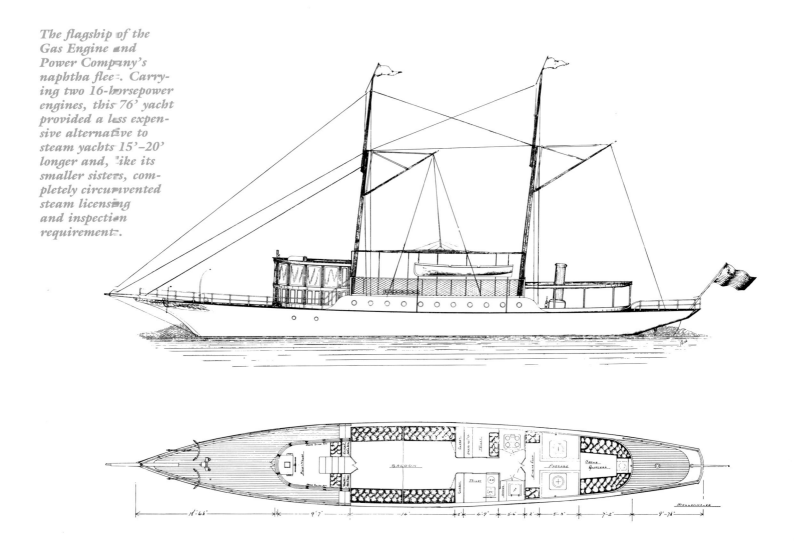

yachts. But the large market lay with the middle class, and they were less likely to ignore the fact that the price of a gallon of naphtha and a pound of pork chops were about the same.

Gas Engine and Power did not focus on the naphtha engine to the exclusion of other prime movers. William Steinway met with Clement Gould, Gas Engine's president, in one of the Daimler Motor Company's more difficult phases. Given that Steinway was entertaining another offer to sell the company, it seems possible that Gould's "long talk" with Steinway involved the possibility of acquisition. Less than a year later Clement Gould died; but he had already involved Gas Engine in another advancing propulsion technology, the electric launch.

In 1892 the trial on the Hudson of an electric launch was page-one, center-column, news. "Those on board were unanimous in their opinion that this system of electrical propulsion was all that could be desired, and far ahead of other motive power for launches.'' The weight of the batteries was said to act like ballast in the keel, giving ''great seaworthy qualities'' while ''the whole operation of the boat is under the control of one person, and simple in the extreme.'' A speed of eight to ten miles per hour was claimed for the 30-footer, while the batteries were said to contain sufficient energy for a run of ten hours, according to *The New York Times*. The builder of the boat was Charles L. Seabury, a founder of Gas Engine and Power Company, and the designer was the incandescently brilliant C.D. Mosher. In the manner of the times, greater note was made of the fact that William K. Vanderbilt had bought an identical model the year before and named it *Alva*.

Gas Engine's aggressive management shortly arranged with the General Electric Launch Company of New York to build the hulls for their launches and rented the firm a building on their property in which to build electric motors. The electric launches were operated at the World's Columbian Exposition (the same event where the Daimler boat performed its rescue) and were claimed to have carried a million passengers at the fair. The Gas Engine and Power Company continued its relationship with the electric

Photographed at Consolidated in the early 1920s, the boat was claimed to be the first commercially sold naptha launch. The condition is remarkable considering that the boat had apparently spent decades outdoors.

A small Alco-Vapor launch by F. W. Ofeldt. The rectangular metal motor cover distinguishes these from the naphtha engine.

This 36' electric launch cost $2,400 at the turn of the century. A 5 1/2-horsepower motor had five forward speeds between 4 and 9 miles per hour. Depending on the size of the battery, this Elco had a radius of action between 45 and 75 miles at "medium speed." The padded after deck was a $70 option and the brass rails were another $54.

launch builders for a half-dozen years. Motivated by a high-stakes patent-control game, a series of corporate metamorphoses took place, and the electric launch operation moved to Bayonne, New Jersey. There it ultimately became known as Elco.

In 1896 a 21' mahogany electric launch of 1-1/4 horsepower cost $1,225 when bought through Gas Engine and Power while a naphtha boat was $850 with a two-horsepower engine. For about the same price as the 21' electric, it was possible to buy a 25' naphtha boat. A two-horsepower naphtha engine sold for $500, suggesting that the value of the hull was about $350 in either

case. On this basis, electricity as a motive power was significantly more expensive at about $875 for the batteries and machinery. The naphtha and the competitive Daimler boats were roughly the same in price with the Daimler enjoying a slight price advantage of $50 in the 21' size. William Steinway was apparently mystified as to why his motorboats were not a paying proposition. He had superior technology, better fuel economy and very competitive prices. It is no less a mystery today, but one factor may have been that Gas Engine and Power built stock boats for immediate delivery while Steinway apparently built only on a time-consuming custom basis.

The naphtha engine had a surprisingly long life. It was still being manufactured and sold (largely to older yacht owners) in 1910, a quarter-century after its invention. The design and the price were unchanged. Perhaps this was testimony to Frank W. Ofeldt's brilliant conception as well as to the conservative nature of elderly yachtsmen.

The Ofeldt patents were superbly drawn and completely protected the naphtha engine from imitation. They had been assigned to the Gas Engine

An electric launch moves silently through the water at Chicago's World Columbian Exposition in 1893. More than 50 launches were in service, and it was claimed that a million people rode in them before the fair closed.

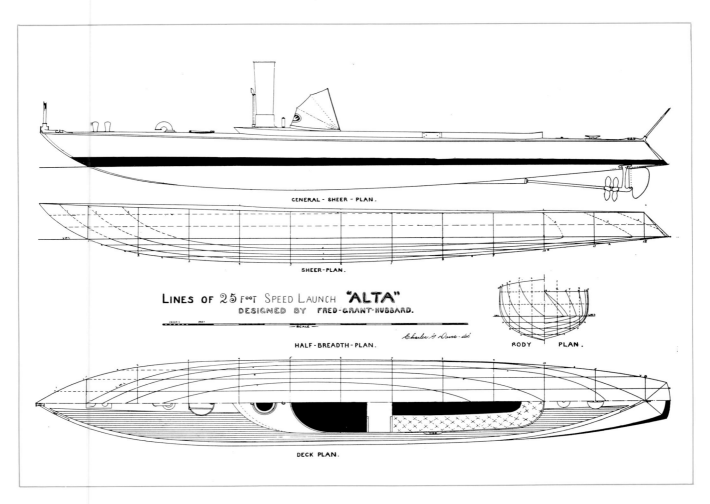

GENERAL - SHEER - PLAN.

SHEER-PLAN.

LINES OF 25 FOOT SPEED LAUNCH "ALTA"
DESIGNED BY FRED-GRANT-HUBBARD.

HALF-BREADTH-PLAN.

BODY PLAN.

DECK PLAN.

An exquisite 1896 design for an Alco-Vapor speed launch. The twin propellers were counter-rotating to neutralize the effect of engine torque. The boat was 24' by 3' 6'' with a hull designed to lift and reduce wetted surface. A compound six-cylinder radial engine was used, but no horsepower rating was given.

and Power Company at the time of their grant in 1886. What compensation Ofeldt received for these ultimately very valuable patents cannot now be determined, but he did not stay with the company. The Gas Engine and Power Company's voluminous catalogs never mentioned him.

Over the remaining eighteen years of his life Ofeldt moved from Newark to Jersey City and finally to Brooklyn. With his sons he continued to build steam engines and his own version of the naphtha engine called the Alco-Vapor. This machine was also exempt from the steam regulations. It used alcohol mixed with water as the working fluid and kerosene as the fuel. By comparison to the heavily promoted, well-capitalized naphtha launch, sales were modest. Ofeldt developed many innovative engines, patenting clever designs for V-2 and V-4 steam engines, as well as triple-expansion radial configurations. By the late 1890s the Ofeldt family was building prototype steam carriages, but these were not produced in any quantity. Frank W. Ofeldt died on September 29, 1904. There was a three-line obituary in the Newark newspaper. Had there been a fourth line, it might have said ''inventor of the first power pleasureboat engine.''

4

THE PROPHET
OF PLANING

*T*he power was not yet there to make them fast. It was challenge enough to make them run. When the early explosive engines putted and popped across the nation's waters, 10 miles an hour was an excellent performance. A light 30' launch might make this speed on 15 horsepower, about the limits of practical technology in the later years of Victoria's reign. High speed demanded high power, and high power still required steam. In an interlocking series of corollaries, steam implied great weight, high complexity, and large expense. It also meant well-developed engineering disciplines, the science of steam and the ships it powered. Published tables could tell a designer the difference in resistance to motion that would result from the use of a copper bottom or a painted one. Nomographs charted the horsepower developed versus coal consumed at various boiler pressures. These and hundreds of other variables could be controlled, arranged and manipulated to suit the purpose at hand. Often that purpose was speed — speed for war, speed for commerce and speed for sport.

The three purposes were more alike than different. An Eastern millionaire might challenge the United States Navy to a race. Passenger steamers raced yachts. A yacht could be built, then sold to a foreign government as a gunboat. Arms traders followed the availability of yachts as closely as they watched the fortunes of antagonists in minor wars. This was not a one-way relationship; representatives of governments, both United States and foreign, were often seen on club verandas or on board when a fast vessel was at trial. It began, for these purposes, with the advent of the spar torpedo during the Civil War. A spar torpedo was simply an explosive charge on the end of a long pole. The attacker moved alongside the target vessel by stealth and cover of night, placed the charge under the hull and detonated it. Pulling boats or small steam launches crewed by very brave men deployed spar torpedoes. Their operational effectiveness was reduced by the advent of searchlights and deck-mounted automatic weapons.

This amidships section of Cushing *from the official Navy drawings shows not only the shape of the hull but the extent to which the machinery was packed into it. The engine and coal bunkers occupy the entire width of the hull.*

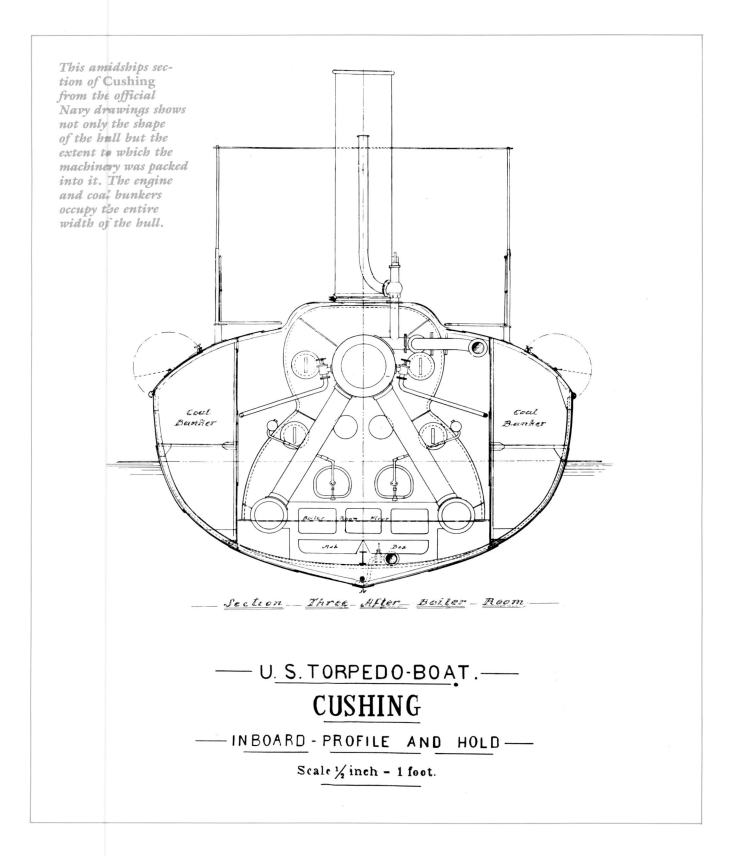

Coal Bunker

Coal Bunker

Section Three After Boiler Room

— U.S. TORPEDO-BOAT. —

CUSHING

— INBOARD-PROFILE AND HOLD —

Scale ½ inch - 1 foot.

In a classical technological see-saw of threat and counter-threat, the self-propelled torpedo made its appearance. Basically a buoyant bomb with a propeller, the Whitehead or "automobile" torpedo was developed in England in the 1870s. Much larger and heavier than the earlier American spar type, automobile torpedoes required special boats to deliver them. It also appeared that speed was an advantage both to pursue the target and to hasten departure after firing the torpedo. The torpedo was a revolutionary weapon, one that allowed a small boat with a few men to engage and destroy capital ships. There were the customary disagreements on strategy, tactics, boat design and doctrine, but the world's navies embraced the concept, building more than 1,280 torpedo boats by the mid-1890s.

The United States, something of a laggard in naval matters, had 22 torpedo boats built or budgeted. By coincidence, the size and desirable characteristics of the deadly torpedo boat and the benign, if profligate, steam yacht were very similar. Both were most useful at 100' to 125' in length; both required high maneuverability and speed. America did not lag in steam yacht development; there were more than 400 on the lists by 1890.

The Herreshoff Manufacturing Company was among the first to exploit the potential in the United States, building *Lightning* to deliver spar torpedoes in 1876. Described as a "large wooden launch," she made the respectable speed of 17.5 knots on trial but was rapidly eclipsed by vessels of the European powers. In the United States more than a decade passed before the Navy purchased *Stiletto*, a Herreshoff private venture, and refitted her as a torpedo boat. The 86' 6" by 11' beam "torpedo yacht," with 31-ton displacement, made 18 knots in 1888. The U.S. pace accelerated, and the Navy commissioned the torpedo boat *Cushing* from the Herreshoffs. With 1,750 indicated horsepower pushing her 105 tons on a length of 137' 6", *Cushing* made 22.53 knots. About two thirds of her interior volume was given over to engines, boilers, bunkers and related machinery. She carried three torpedoes, one in a bow tube, two more in racks. The speed, as commentators were quick to point out, was below the benchmark for European performance.

The Navy, with long-awaited Congressional consent, had put in place a plan to build 20 more torpedo boats; this struck a public resonance, and naval and marine topics filled the newspapers of the day. Technical descriptions of vessels, reports of trials, successes, failures, speed records, explosions, wrecks and policy disputes filled the Eastern newspapers, often on page one. Steam speed had become a spectator sport. The Herreshoff Manufacturing Company was awarded contracts for three more torpedo boats. They continued to build for the static steam pleasure fleet which numbered about 450 yachts throughout the 1890s. But if they ever held it, the Herreshoffs lost the mantle of technological supremacy.

Amesbury, Massachusetts, had been eclipsed by neighboring Salisbury by 1880. Many years before, the residents of Amesbury had ordered a group of citizens to settle on the other side of the Merrimac River, thereby founding

Charles Dell Mosher

William Gardner

Nathanael Greene Herreshoff

John Brown Herreshoff

C.D. Mosher's Buzz with its unusual destroyer-type ram bow which ran relatively clear of the water at speed. Buzz was timed at 27 miles per hour, an unprecedented speed for a 50' boat.

Salisbury. It was at Amesbury that Charles Dell Mosher found employment in the power plant of a textile mill and set up housekeeping with his wife in company-provided housing in the mid-1880s. During the 10-hour, six-day work weeks that were customary at the time, C. Dell Mosher, as he was then known, mastered the intricacies of power generation, extending his abilities by designing boilers, engines, condensers, safety valves and other arcana of external combustion engines.

On his own time Mosher worked on the related problems of hydrodynamics and hull shape. His methods were as unique as his accomplishments. Finding an unused mill race, Mosher placed glass in its side and bottom panels. In the race he placed his models. Tied to the model was a cord running over a pulley. To this Mosher attached weights. When the pull of the model matched the weight on the cord, the hull became stationary. Mosher then recorded the resistance of the model and watched its behavior as the water rushed past. Threads attached to the model traced the flow of water around it. By varying the volume of water in the race, Charles Dell Mosher examined hull behavior and resistance over a wide range of speeds.

A series of models was painstakingly modified, mistakes corrected by building up a model with beeswax. Mosher had created a personal test tank, a primitive but elegant system in which the water moved while the model remained stationary. Mosher's ability to observe the model from the top, sides and bottom was also unique. The test tanks of European governments — then the leaders in testing — moved the hulls on carriages, making them much more difficult to observe. The boats which grew from C. Dell Mosher's pragmatic but precise testing astonished the design establishment.

They were the fastest vessels on the face of the earth. Few but Mosher himself comprehended the accomplishment: the boats planed. They lifted themselves out of the water and reduced their own resistance to movement.

Edward P. Hatch was 55 years old and well into creating his second fortune as president of Lord & Taylor, purveyors of dry goods; the first had been made selling sewing machines. Hatch wanted a steam yacht for use at his summer home on Lake Champlain, and he purchased a boat called *Buzz* which Mosher designed and built in 1887. It is no longer clear whether *Buzz* was built on speculation or specifically for Mr. Hatch. She was 50.0' long with a 6.6' beam, drawing 1.4' at rest. C. Dell Mosher had designed and built not only the distinctive hull with its destroyer-like ram bow, but the engine as well. It had two cylinders of 8'' diameter with an 8'' stroke. The firm of Maccabe Brothers provided the boiler of a locomotive. *Buzz*, it was reported, ran a mile in 2:34 for a rate of almost 27 miles per hour. This was as fast as — and perhaps faster — than any other boat in America.

Buzz was the first skirmish in a war of steam speed. She was a stunning 30% faster than the Herreshoffs' *Stiletto*, a fact not lost on an unhappy customer, New York publisher Norman L. Munro. The flamboyant Munro collected yachts in the same way that Victorian ladies collected houseplants: in large numbers. His most recent Herreshoff creation had not only failed to meet her contract speed; her boiler exploded during trials, killing a man. The tragedy cost Nat Herreshoff his steam license forever and sent Munro in search of another apostle of speed.

Charles Dell Mosher was the man, and the machine was *Norwood*, 63.2' of mahogany holding 400 horsepower. A trial on the Merrimac River on July 8, 1890, proved — to the satisfaction of some — that she was the fastest boat in America. A mile was timed at 1:58 for a speed of 30.5 miles per hour. Munro immediately announced in *The New York Times* that he was ready

Norman L. Munro's Say When, one of his flotilla of Herreshoff steam yachts that preceded the Mosher-designed Norwood.

The American Yacht Club grounds at the turn of the century. Founded in 1883, the American was exclusively a steam club. Its lists included many of the fastest boats and the club actively, if not too successfully, promoted racing.

Norwood at speed. With 400 horsepower propelling her 63' of mahogany, she achieved 30.5 miles per hour in July, 1890. Her hull shape was revolutionary, and it became the standard form for fast boats for nearly 20 years.

to race *Cushing*. It was further claimed that *Norwood* had only used 105 of the 400 horsepower developed by her triple-expansion engine to achieve 30 miles and that 35 miles per hour could be accomplished with ease.

All was quiet until the late summer of 1891 when the regatta committee of the American Yacht Club announced a race for steam yachts. The American was located at Rye, New York, and was exclusively a powerboat club. Formed in 1883 by a group from the New York Yacht Club, its backers included the famous Jay Gould. While earlier efforts to promote steam racing had been a failure, this one promised to be "the race of the century."

Steam yachting was "in a boom . . . and many sailing yachts are just now going begging for purchasers," wrote one correspondent. But opinion was split: "There is no real love of yachting displayed by the steamboat men but rather a fondness for an outing occasionally under such circumstances as will enable them to avoid the inconvenience of public travel . . ." As events emerged, the owners of the yachts also wished to avoid the inconvenience of publicly demonstrating the speed claims made for their yachts. The race was to include a large field of "flyers." The prize would be $500, an amount sufficient to pay the wages of two servants for a year. The Navy boats *Cushing* and *Stiletto* were invited; from the private sector offers were made to the owners of the yachts *Now Then*, *Javelin*, and the recently built *Vamoose*, Herreshoff boats all. *Norwood* was also invited. Race day was set for Saturday, October 3, 1891, and a course was plotted from New London, Connecticut, to the American clubhouse at Milton Point, Rye, New York. This was a distance of about 90 statute miles down Long Island Sound.

This unidentified steam yacht shows the classic "stream-line" approach to achieving speed. Extremely narrow for her length, such a hull would list heavily if driven at high speed.

William Randolph Hearst's Herreshoff-designed Vamoose. *Carrying 800 horsepower, the 112' yacht was built at a cost of $62,250 and had a contract speed of 25 knots.* Vamoose *never achieved this speed in public trials.*

In the course of a few days the field narrowed to two. The Navy demurred. *Cushing* was in dry dock, claimed the Navy, while *Stiletto* was omitted from mention. The owner of one Herreshoff boat simply did not care to race at that time. The owner of another was secluded deep in the "North Woods" and could not be contacted. *Yankee Doodle* (formerly E.P. Hatch's *Buzz*) was a late entry; but her owners could not obtain an inspection certificate for her novel oil-burning boiler. It came down to *Norwood* and *Vamoose*.

Vamoose was the latest Herreshoff creation and had been commissioned at a cost of $65,250 by William Randolph Hearst. Her contract had required 25 knots, which presumably had been achieved in private trial. She carried 800

horsepower in her 112.5' length. *Vamoose* had also completed the customary rite of passage by venturing out onto the Hudson and beating the passenger steamer *Mary Powell* in an impromptu competition. Late that afternoon *Vamoose* encountered a "fairly fast local passenger train" and vanquished it too, according to a reporter who was on board. This did not impress the aficionados of steam speed: "Her performance with the *Mary Powell* does not go for very much, for the *Stiletto* did practically the same thing six years ago . . ." A few days later *Vamoose* hit the fireboat *New Yorker* while docking. With only minor damage to her stem, the race was still on.

Publishers Hearst and Munro vied in the press, and the contest began to take on a steel-grey overtone of bitterness tinctured with desperation. Hearst ordered the Herreshoff propeller removed from the yacht and a German propeller substituted. Munro engaged not only Hearst but *Norwood*'s designer, first inviting C.D. Mosher to race the yacht, then refusing when Mosher asked for complete control of the vessel. Mosher, in conversation with a reporter, released his estimate of *Norwood*, saying that she was unsafe since repairs made to her high-pressure condenser were defective. "Mr. Munro does not have enough money to induce me on board the *Norwood*," said Mosher. "Mr. Hearst hasn't enough money to induce me to let Mr. Mosher on board," rejoined Norman Munro. Ego vanquished sportsmanship as race day approached.

It was not long until the platoon of journalists covering the race discovered *Norwood*'s radical hull form. On the ways at Wintringham's yard in South Brooklyn, they encountered "an extremely beautiful craft forward, her lines being the perfection of ease and grace. Aft, however, they are more peculiar than beautiful. About twelve feet from the taffrail the hull of the boat is cut away underneath, so that with the exception of a slight slope upward on both sides of the keel she has the appearance of a flat-bottom skiff." The journalists had seen the future but did not understand how it worked. They were not alone.

It was race-day morning, Saturday October 3, 1891. *Norwood* had left her berth in Bay Ridge at midnight. Proceeding slowly through the darkness and some fog, she ran aground at 8:15 A.M. on a very clear morning. Her propeller was damaged beyond repair. The pilot, described as "scarcely a youth," had left the boat and could not be found. So it came to be that "the race of the century" ended before it began on the Penfield Reef, just a few yards from shore at Bridgeport, Connecticut. In the ensuing ennui, the father of the pilot commented that his son "has a pilot's license, but in light of his management of the *Norwood*, it is difficult to understand how he could have secured it."

Rushing to save face, the American Yacht Club arranged for Hearst's *Vamoose* to exhibit her speed on a course at Milton Point. On a mile measured with the same wire that had been used for the *Norwood* trial on the Merrimac River, *Vamoose* steamed at full pressure, listing heavily to port and vibrating viciously. Each lump of coal had been individually selected, it was said. Two runs were completed at 24 miles per hour. "She is just getting warmed up to it,'' said the Captain. A third run also yielded 24 miles per hour, against the wind and tide. On the fourth run with 250 pounds in the boiler and 410 revolutions, *Vamoose* was exhibiting the ''first symptoms of a blow-off.'' The sounds of rending metal were accompanied by an engineer's mate leaping from the hatchway. *Vamoose* had broken her steam-powered steering gear. Improvised steering by cable took *Vamoose* back to her berth, a trip in which she narrowly missed collision with a ferryboat and a navigation buoy. Charles Dell Mosher watched this exhibition from the clubhouse, his reaction unrecorded.

Now it was *Norwood*'s turn. Twenty-nine days later she reeled off a mile in 2:12 on Brooklyn's Atlantic Yacht Club course for 27.2 miles per hour. A back-up run against the wind took 2:26 when the spring in a blow-off valve broke, dropping boiler pressure to 150 pounds. The boat's behavior was described as ''excellent.'' She did not list, she did not vibrate, and she did not squat. She did set a new record.

For the next decade C.D. Mosher became the man to see for those in search of ultimate steam speed. Even as *Norwood* rushed down the Brooklyn course, Mosher was designing another record-breaker with his recently acquired partner William Gardner. The client was William Brown Cogswell, a Syracuse, New York, ammonia manufacturer. The new boat was informally

W.B. Cogswell's Feiseen, *a 78-footer. After setting a record of 31.76 miles per hour she was sold to Brazil as a torpedo boat in late 1893.*

called "Still Alarm" because of the secrecy surrounding her construction at Wood's yard on City Island. At 78' long with a beam of 9.5' and finished in bright mahogany, she was built with the expressed purpose of beating both *Norwood* and *Vamoose*.

While the hull followed *Norwood*'s successful form, the engine was a major advance. Built in Newark to Mosher's designs, the quadruple-expansion engine emphasized not only power but extremely light weight. The crankshaft began as a one-ton forged steel billet. Six months later the finished crank weighed 414 pounds. Each journal was drilled for lightness. The target output was 600 horsepower from a weight of 3,600 pounds. Combined with the 5,400 pounds of boiler and related equipment, the boat developed one horsepower for every 15 pounds of machinery. So advanced was this engine that a decade later 30 pounds per horsepower was still considered a very light engine.

When "Still Alarm" entered the lists she was registered as *Feiseen*, Japanese for "flying arrow." It was not long before the obligatory record was set: 31.76 miles per hour for a mile course. *Feiseen* did not linger on the yacht list. Built at a cost of $30,000, she was sold in the fall of 1893 to Charles R. Flint for an undisclosed price. Flint, known popularly as the "Rubber King" or "the Father of Trusts," had extensive holdings in South America, was a founder of W.R. Grace & Company, cultivated presidents, and when the need arose dealt in munitions. *Feiseen* was converted into a torpedo boat to fight an insurgency in Brazil. The refit, which included a lengthening of 12 feet, the construction of an armored deckhouse, and installation of weaponry, was accomplished in record time to the designs of Gardner & Mosher at the Wood's Sons Yard. In the spring of 1894 the insurgency in Brazil collapsed with some assistance from the United States Navy and Flint-provided "dynamite guns." Among the vanquished was Admiral da Gama, a "lineal descendent" of the explorer. C.R. Flint pronounced that this was good for Brazil, good for the United States and good for business.

C.D. Mosher's stature continued to grow; and he became, first in partnership with William Gardner at 1 Broadway and later independently, the premier designer of high-velocity vessels, yachts that were not merely fast but were record-breakers. Mosher's interests and competence extended beyond high-speed steam, and he did pioneering work with electric launches, first in conjunction with Seabury's yard and later with Samuel Ayer & Son at Nyack. The most spectacular of these electric boats was one built for John Jacob Astor. At 75 feet overall, she was the largest electrically powered vessel built to that date. Sparse descriptions indicate that she may have been flat-sterned like Mosher's steamers but with "much more curve to her sides." The boat was also equipped with two centerboards and a sailing rig in case of electrical failure. Still building in the spring of 1896, her life was short. In September of 1897 she was hit and sunk by the *Mary Powell*. Mr. Astor's electric boat was never recovered from the waters of the North River.

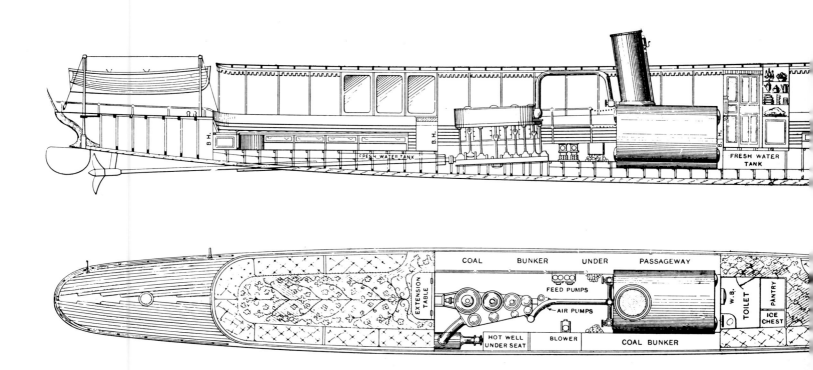

COAL BUNKER UNDER PASSAGEWAY

EXTENSION TABLE

FEED PUMPS

AIR PUMPS

HOT WELL UNDER SEAT

BLOWER

COAL BUNKER

W.B.

TOILET

PANTRY

ICE CHEST

Named for a mythi-
cal Viking ship, the
80' Ellide reached a
record-shattering
40 miles per hour.
C.D. Mosher said
that the hull
lifted 8 to 9" when
traveling at full
speed. A high-speed
run by Ellide was
an annual event on
Lake George for
many years.

At the same time that the electric was being built at Nyack, two Mosher steam yachts were under construction there. Both would achieve amazing speed, yet one was destined to become famous, the other obscure. Very little was recorded about *Viper* other than that she was "of novel design." A tiny 40'-long, 4'-beam launch powered with a quadruple-expansion Mosher-designed engine and boiler, she was built for a young stockbroker, George B. Magoun. Based on the outputs of Mosher's larger engines, *Viper* would have developed between 200 and 250 horsepower. Whatever the power, the boat was reported to have reached the astonishing velocity of 38 miles per hour. The precise speed is not of any great importance. At any speed over 22 miles per hour *Viper* would have been a fully planing boat by modern definition. Just as Frank W. Ofeldt's innovative naphtha engine marked the beginning of a new age of pleasure-boat engine technology, C.D. Mosher's *Viper* was a benchmark for small planing hulls. The line of development that began with *Buzz* reached a zenith with *Viper*, and speeds so high from hulls so small would not be reached again for a decade.

Mosher's other design of 1896 achieved international renown and an impeccably measured speed of 34.73 knots or 40.0 miles per hour. "She rivalled the tempest in speed, and distanced the following eagle" read the line from a Viking poem which inspired the yacht's name, *Ellide*. Her owner

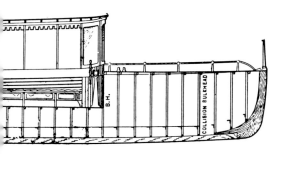

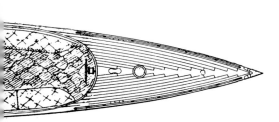

was E. Burgess Warren of Philadelphia, a Harvard-educated "manufacturing chemist" who pioneered in asphalt paving. The "most successful" fisherman on Lake George and an art connoisseur, Mr. Warren expressed surprise at the speed of *Ellide*. The contract had called for a minimum of 30 miles per hour, and C.D. Mosher collected a $6,000 bonus when trials were complete.

Ellide was 80' overall with a beam of 8'4". Her main powerplant was an immense Mosher-patented quadruple-expansion engine which developed 910 indicated horsepower on trial. A half-dozen smaller engines performed such tasks as water pumping and forcing air into the boiler. Construction was of double-planked mahogany which was fastened with Tobin bronze to a steel frame. Five steel bulkheads compartmentalized the boat, and copper flotation tanks were also fitted. *Ellide* did not lack in accommodations; there was a "dining room," galley, china closet, ice chest, head and a commodious cockpit aft. It was reported that Mr. Warren intended to use *Ellide* as a "fishing boat" after the United States Navy completed their "experiments" with her. At one trial seven Navy men were on board, including Navy Constructor Francis T. Bowles. Another observer was Alfred Yarrow, chief of the British warship firm which bore his name. "As a basis upon which to make calculations for torpedo boats, she is indeed a wonder," said A.F. Yarrow.

"Due to the form of the boat the entrance lines become finer and finer as the bow continues to rise out of the water, while due to the breadth and form at the stern, there is no settling or squatting at any speed. It further follows that as the bow rises the run or buttock lines become more nearly horizontal, so that at the highest speeds the after body is in large part simply sliding along nearly parallel to the surface of the water." The words were those of Professor W.F. Durand of Cornell University, describing the planing behavior of the 80' *Ellide* in 1898. In 1899 E.B. Warren moved *Ellide* to Lake George. There she would remain for many years, putting on an "annual demonstration of speed" each Independence Day. History does not record the number of lake trout E. Burgess Warren pulled over the hourglass stern.

Ellide's boiler was patented by Mosher and a similar design was used in several U.S. Navy torpedo boats. Safety valves at the top of the unit would blow off when a pre-determined pressure was reached to prevent a boiler explosion.

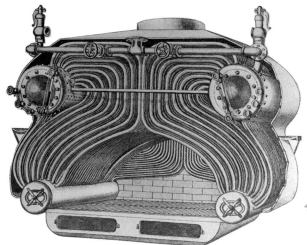

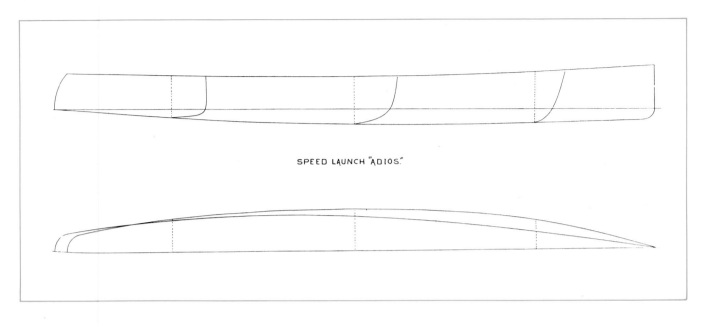

SPEED LAUNCH "ADIOS."

5

FAST, FASTER, FASTEST

*A*dios was the fastest motorboat in the nation. She did not hail from New York City or the technology centers of Jersey City or Bayonne. She was not the fevered vision of a Michigan motor man or a Prussian machinist. She was not commissioned by a robber baron or a builder of banana republics. She would torpedo nothing but egos. In 1902 there were no steamers to mortify on the pond where she was built by Tom Milton, a man whose main product was $25 rowboats. Her hull was based on drawings from magazines. The man who designed *Adios* built her engine as well, his collection of machine tools housed in a third-story walk-up in Syracuse, New York. Herbert J. Leighton, a genius in resonance with the laws of speed on water, would appear and then disappear. He was an enigmatic man who left little behind, only the mute testimony of the record books and fading photographs of white hulls, exhaust pipes jutting into the sky.

Beginning about 1895 when he opened his own engine shop in Syracuse and perhaps when he worked at the strangely named Straight Line Engine Company, H.J. Leighton probed the premier problem of explosive engines: achieving high power with high reliability. This was then, as it is today, the ultimate challenge for designers of prime movers. His engines were Clerk cycle, and he balanced their forces and metallurgy with elegance in an eight-cylinder 120-horsepower motor. This was the engine that moved *Adios* across Onondaga Lake at 24 miles per hour. Leighton, described by a fellow engineer as a "conservative, practical man," was also independent in his thought. Eschewing the fashionable, narrow, hyper-light hulls, Leighton designed boats that were heavily built and beamy. *Adios* carried a beam of 6'6'' on her 55' waterline length, at least 20% more than was considered optimum for speed. The most likely explanation for *Adios*'s performance was that she carried even more power than her designer admitted.

The 23 mile-per-hour-speed of Adios generated great interest in both her hull and engine. D.H. Cox published these "approximate" lines in a technical paper in 1903. Two other hulls were also built from these lines. Equipped with 60-horsepower Leighton engines, they were used on the St. Lawrence for many years.

H.J. Leighton's Adios at full speed. Her 120-horsepower, 8-cylinder engine was the largest marine gasolene engine built by 1902. When not setting speed records, Adios was fitted with a large canopy and used as a cruising launch.

45

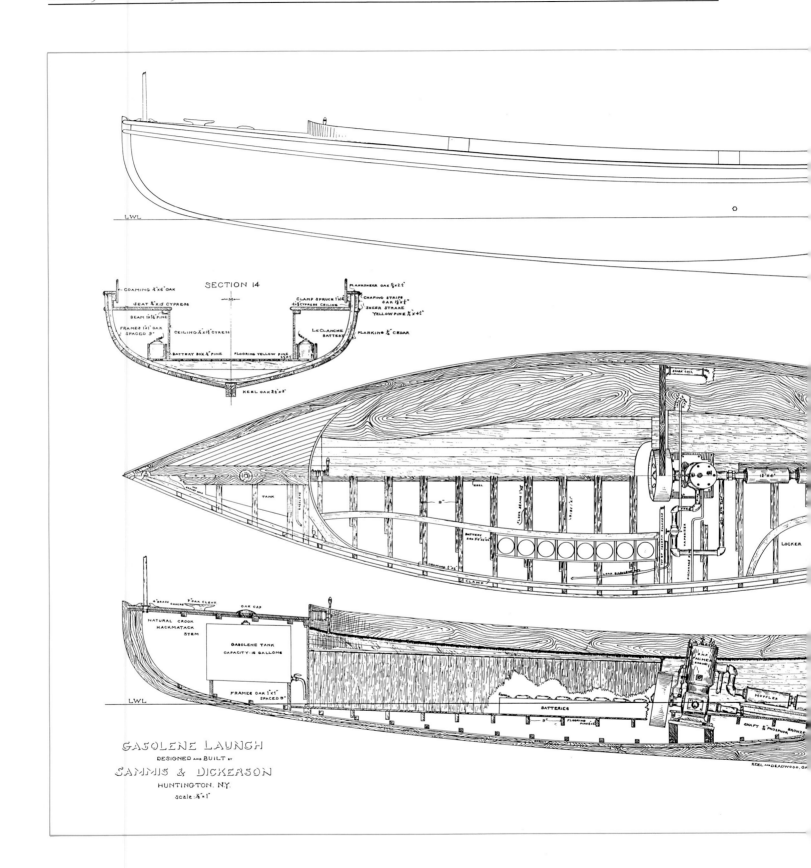

SECTION 14

GASOLENE LAUNCH
DESIGNED AND BUILT BY
SAMMIS & DICKERSON
HUNTINGTON, N.Y.
scale: ⅜"=1'

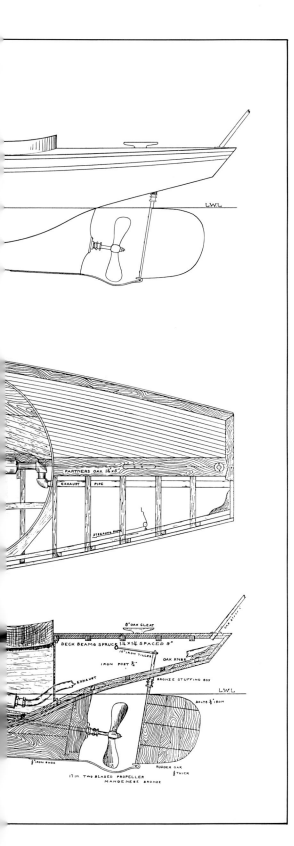

"It honestly makes me smile when I think of how you all will wonder at this bit of news from a little inland town," wrote a *Rudder* correspondent in 1902. Then followed a report of a 23-mile-per-hour run in *Adios.* H.J. Leighton contented himself with selling boats and engines around that "little inland town" and the Thousand Islands. A 60-horse Leighton engine cost $6,000 in 1902, an amount easily equal to the cost of a large new home. Despite the price, there was no shortage of buyers, and dozens of Leighton launches were built in sizes ranging from 20' to 60' in the early years of the century. Many were built to a contract speed, and each Leighton engine came with a one-year guarantee, no small assurance at a time when an engine that started was often regarded as miraculous.

When *Adios* was under construction, the hydrocarbon engine had already assumed supremacy in pleasure boating. Of the 400 yachts reported as under construction by *Rudder* in the 1901 season, powered vessels accounted for 62.25% while sail accounted for 37.75% Of the total 400, almost half (47.5%) were fitted with gasolene engines while about 15% were powered by steam, naphtha vapor, or electricity. A few were auxiliary sailing yachts. Of the "alternative" propulsion systems electricity was the most popular, accounting for 5%, about 20 boats.

So popular was motorboating becoming that H.J. Leighton apparently did not feel any need to campaign *Adios* far from home. There is only one known appearance by the boat outside of northern New York. On October 29, 1903, *Adios* entered a regatta at the Brooklyn Yacht Club. Her sole competitor was the soon-to-be-famous *Standard. Adios* crossed the finish line five minutes ahead of *Standard* on the 12-mile course, averaging 21.2 miles per hour versus *Standard*'s 17.2. This would be *Standard*'s only defeat in several seasons of competition. As *Standard*'s stature grew, it magnified the reputation of *Adios*, the only boat to vanquish her. With remarkable cleverness H.J. Leighton was enhancing his reputation by not racing.

Standard was built as a showcase for a new high-powered engine designed by Carl Riotte and financed by Lewis Nixon, a shipyard owner, steel-ship pioneer and former Tammany Hall politician. By the time of *Standard*, Carl Riotte and his brother Eugene had more than a decade of engine-building experience. Starting in their teens, the brothers had built not only engines but also motorcycles and motor carriages at a series of firms, the most recent being the Empire Engine Company. Like most engine men of their time, the Riottes saw potential in the automobile, and the new Standard engines were built at a firm called The United States Long Distance Automobile Company. Although a few autos were sold, the focus shifted to the Riotte marine engines.

The Standard motor, as it appeared in 1903, bristled with innovation. A six-cylinder machine operating on the four-cycle principle, the open-crankcase design owed much to steam practice. At 3,200 pounds and 110 horsepower, the Standard was considered to be of medium weight and very high power. With a 10'' stroke and an 8'' bore, each cylinder had a swept volume of about 500 cubic inches, and the total displacement was 3,016 cubic inches. A fleet of 33 modern small cars would equal the swept volume of one Standard engine of 1903. Far too large to be turned by a crank, the motor was started by a compressed-air system.

The engine's length was 6' 3'' and its height 4' 2''. While seeming immense today, by the criteria of the time the machine was a marvel of miniaturization. In a technical paper read before the Society of Naval Architects and Marine Engineers, D.H. Cox pointed out that two engines of a similar type could be installed to save five tons of weight while doubling the power of a steam installation.

The awesome 60' Standard. Cruising slowly here, she was built to showcase the engine technology developed by Carl Riotte. Put overboard in 1903, Standard remained competitive for several years and was probably able to exceed 30 miles per hour.

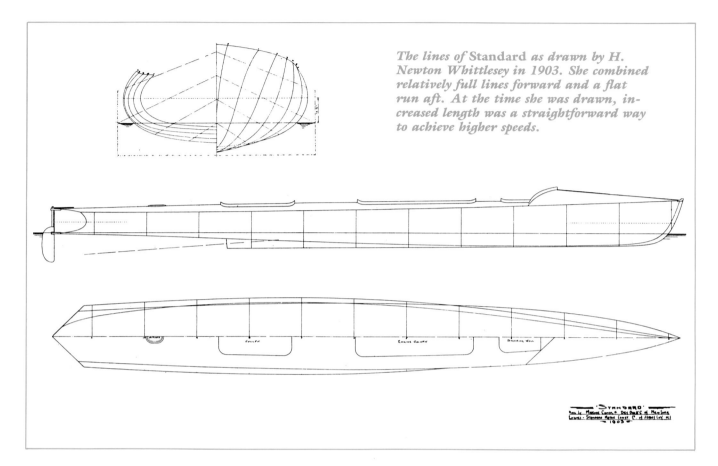

The lines of Standard *as drawn by H. Newton Whittlesey in 1903. She combined relatively full lines forward and a flat run aft. At the time she was drawn, increased length was a straightforward way to achieve higher speeds.*

The 60'-long hull was no less advanced. Drawing on French torpedo-boat practice, 31-year-old H. Newton Whittlesey, a naval architect trained at Webb Institute and the University of Glasgow, designed *Standard*'s astonishingly light hull to weigh less than 1,500 pounds. Planked in 3/16'' mahogany, the hull was given rigidity by two girders running its full length. The tension on the girders was adjustable, allowing subtle changes to be made in the shape of the hull. The 7'6'' beam was wider than usual, and the boat's construction was sufficiently novel to allow Whittlesey to patent it. All this seemed to work well enough, but one passenger commented that ''the extreme thinness of wood between one's self and the water, when driving at high speeds, is an unpleasant subject of thought.'' High speeds in *Standard*'s first season meant 20 miles per hour.

In the fashion of her fast steam ancestors, *Standard* stalked the Hudson, her prey the ever-game *Mary Powell* and the 19-knot passenger steamer *Monmouth*. *Standard* lay dead in the water at an ambush point. Sighting the quarry, she rumbled to life using her air starter and roared alongside the steamer. The steamer's pilot signaled the boiler room, and soon black smoke surged from the funnels as firemen shoveled in frenzy, sweating for a few more turns while the pressure gauge slowly rose. Passengers gathered at the

Standard at full speed as she crossed the finish line to win the first running of the American Power Boat Association's Gold Cup race in June of 1904. The three-race series was run on the Hudson River and the $750 Tiffany-designed cup was actually made of silver which was gold-plated.

rail to watch the low brown hull, her bow wave sparkling in the sunlight, her exhaust rumbling like an earthquake. She pulled ahead, cut across her quarry's bow, dropped astern and pulled ahead again in the ritual demonstration of dominance known as "running circles around her." Then *Standard* was gone. Left behind were the vanquished and a miasmal mix of combustion by-products: coal smoke and petroleum spirits.

If this was sport, it was also sales promotion; and some decried the invasion of commercialism represented by naming a boat after its engine. In 1904, designer and journalist W.P. Stephens inveighed, "The speed bacillus which has done so much within the last dozen years to kill the sport of yacht sailing and to becloud the whole science of naval architecture, has firmly fastened its grip on the pleasure launch." Mr. Stephens reserved his most lacerating invective for a group he called "automoboatists." These were "men who assume that because they know something about automobiles, they also know everything about launches." Limbering up his pen, Stephens went on, ". . . as a class they are utterly ignorant of practical boating and yachting as well as the elemental principles of naval architecture."

But Stephens was also a realist who recognized that "there is no denying that the small power boat, noisy, dirty and ill-smelling as she may be, has attractions of her own for a large number." The intrusion of automotive technology that so disturbed W.P. Stephens was the future of speed on water. It would push prime movers of the *Standard* type out of the yacht clubs into the holds of harbor tugs, and it would banish H.J. Leighton's brilliant conceptions to the nether world of industrial history. But not without a contest.

There were $11.3 million in automobile sales in 1903 and $3.5 million in pleasure boats. While the exact amounts were not then known, it was clear to most in the automobile trade that there was a market for boat engines. Some thought that the potential was at least as large as motorcars. ''We have not GOOD roads, and see what we have done with the automobile? But we have the finest, most accessible and most wonderful system of Rivers, Bays, Sounds, Channels and Lakes and the best Waterways for sport and commerce in the world. We will have every owner of an automobile, own an automobile Launch, for speed, for pleasure, for utility, for power, for economy, for hauling, for touring.'' The words come from an internal memorandum of the Smith & Mabley Company, importers of Mercedes, Panhard, F.I.A.T and Renault automobiles, among others.

A.D. Proctor Smith and Carlton R. Mabley, two aggressive and meteorically successful young entrepreneurs, did more than write memos on the wonders of the ''autoboat.'' They built, raced and promoted their ''fliers,'' correctly seeing that their millionaire motorcar customers were prospects for fast launches. In the first nine months of 1903, Smith & Mabley sold more than a quarter-million dollars of European chassis and custom-built bodies. In 1904 they astonished the New York business world by placing an order for 100 Mercedes automobiles. Smith & Mabley had contracted for a quarter of the Canstatt factory's production in what was literally a ''million-dollar deal.''

While the social elite and their chauffeurs trekked to the lush garage at 38th Street and Seventh Avenue in Manhattan for sales and service of their mobile status symbols, Smith and Mabley were making the most of their

For those desiring speed but unable to afford a boat such as Adios or Standard, this Charles D. Mosher design represented a reasonable alternative. At 26' and fitted with a car-type steering wheel, she would have been called an ''autoboat'' of the latest fashion.

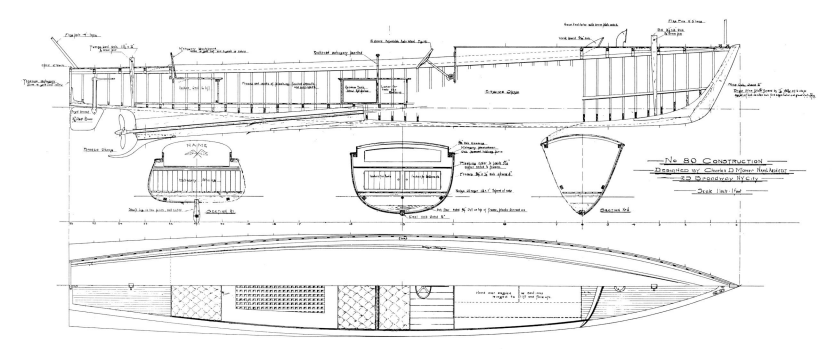

Pioneer automobile manufacturers often participated in racing to promote sales. This is F.I.A.T. No. 2 which was raced with only modest success. The torpedo-like tube is a sight for the helmsman so that he can line up on the buoys.

relationships with prestigious European manufacturers. In the service department mechanics were able to dissect the finest European machines. Did the frame of a $10,000 motor car crack under strain? Was the iron in its pistons resistant to wear? Did its valves burn easily? From the Smith & Mabley service work came the answers: the strengths and weaknesses of the state of the European art. A replacement for a broken part was not necessarily pulled from the shelf. It was often fabricated on the spot. Lack of standardization was one reason; another was the logistical impossibility of ordering a part from Europe in a reasonable time. So Smith & Mabley knew not only how to repair some of the world's finest cars; they learned how to build them. It was not surprising that the company began to make its own motorcars. They grew to be legendary beasts of machines. Chaindrives whining and engines roaring, they bested the best of Europe in road racing and on the the circle tracks. For a brief while Simplex was supreme on both land and sea.

The aquatic edge of the Simplex sword was *Vingt et Un*, French for 21, a designation of the claimed horsepower of the S & M four-cylinder, four-cycle Simplex engine of the "Panhard type." The 30' *Vingt et Un* ran the mile course of the Palisades Boat Club near Yonkers at the unprecedented rate of 26 miles per hour on November 5, 1903. The performance met skepticism outside the popular press. In a thinly veiled reference, E.W. Graef wrote, "Don't expect a 30 foot boat to make over 21 mph for they haven't reduced the weight of engine per hp enough yet . . . . Remember that a newspaper mile varies in length from 1,500 to something like 4,000 feet, but rarely reaches 6,080, which is the actual nautical mile."

Vingt et Un's true velocity was not her ultimate measure of significance. More important was the fact that she was the earliest American manifestation of the *canot-automobile*. The French, with a commanding lead in automotive technology, had done the obvious: place the largest motor in the lightest hull and see how fast it could go. Beginning about 1900 a group known as *Club Helice* was formed to race these nautical mutants. Smith & Mabley, attuned to the ways of the continent, imported the concept.

Vingt et Un was designed by Clinton Hoadley Crane. Harvard-educated, trained in naval architecture at the University of Glasgow, apprenticed at the vaunted Cramp Shipyards, and a sailor of one-raters and half-raters, the tall, handsome designer came from a monied Englewood, New Jersey, family. Thirty-year-old C.H. Crane was the prototypical gentleman naval architect. It is likely that Smith and Mabley were introduced to Clinton Crane by Crane's younger brother Henry, whose name appears in Smith & Mabley sales reports. C.H. Crane drew the lines for a light hull of 30' on the waterline, giving her a beam of 3' 10'' and a draft of 7''. The bow was described as ''perky,'' and there was the requisite torpedo stern. Behind the engine was a cockpit capable of holding eight persons. Three were on board

Panhard II was powered with a 4-cylinder automobile engine by the pioneering French auto manufacturer and raced by the U.S. importer. The small strings which ran over the engine house were used to signal the steersman which way to turn on this Elco-built boat.

Here is the first Vingt et Un, for which the sensational speed of 26 miles per hour was claimed in November of 1903. Owners Smith & Mabley never entered the boat in a race, but widespread publicity of Vingt et Un's *performance touched off an "autoboat" craze that lasted for several years.*

for the trial. Fuel capacity was 25 gallons which, it was claimed, would drive the boat for 300 miles at 20 miles per hour. Reports gave *Vingt et Un*'s dry weight as a phenomenally light 810 pounds, 420 in the engine and 390 in the hull. That the boat was very light is of little doubt, for she was built by Tom Fearon of Yonkers, a builder of very fast rowing shells who had experimented with steam launches for more than 20 years. Fearon planked *Vingt et Un* in 5/16'' mahogany on tiny 1/2'' oak frames. Smith & Mabley announced that they were able to provide similar boats for $2,500 to $3,000. If *Vingt et Un*'s career was short, her advertising value was great; and for the 1904 season Smith & Mabley commissioned *Vingt et Un II*.

This much more substantial 740-pound hull carried a four-cylinder, 75-horsepower engine designed by Edward Franquist, the Simplex chief engineer. *Vingt et Un II* would foal generations of fast boats, each design modified conservatively but not always successfully from its predecessor. She was 38'9'' on the waterline with a 4'7'' beam and a trial displacement of 3,850 pounds. Handled by her designer under the best conditions, *II* ran the mile at 24.2 miles per hour.

If not astonishingly fast, the speed was sufficient as *Vingt et Un II* compiled a respectable racing record in the summer of 1904. Among the defeated was Nat Herreshoff, who had built a large steam-powered racing launch to "teach the younger generation a thing or two," in one correspondent's words. About 60' long, *Swift Sure* was powered by a 4 1/4" by 7" by 11" Herreshoff triple-expansion engine with a 7" stroke. The engine was capable of turning 800 rpm with 275 pounds of boiler pressure and was said to develop 100 horsepower. Whatever her power, she was first beaten by *Standard* at the Atlantic Yacht Club meet. "She will do better later," said the Sphinx of Bristol. *Swift Sure* appeared again at a Newport meet in August of 1904. Her competition this time included *Vingt et Un II*; and while *Swift Sure* was faster than she had been at New York by about 2 miles per hour, she was not fast enough and was beaten by *Vingt et Un II* on the 18.4 mile course. Coming in third was *Mercedes USA*, with her designer W. Starling Burgess pumping furiously to keep his hull afloat in the rough seas. The Herreshoff boat did not compete again.

Bristol steam technology was lagging badly by this time. On the automotive front steam cars were among the fastest in the world; and the demands of road service for light weight, high power and fast starting spawned flash boilers, light engines, liquid-fuel burners and astonishing power-to-weight ratios. The Stanley Brothers, for example, achieved 127 miles per

The interior of the Smith & Mabley boatshop. In the stocks is a hull very similar to Vingt et Un. S & M built and sold high-speed launches which used the same engines as their Simplex automobiles.

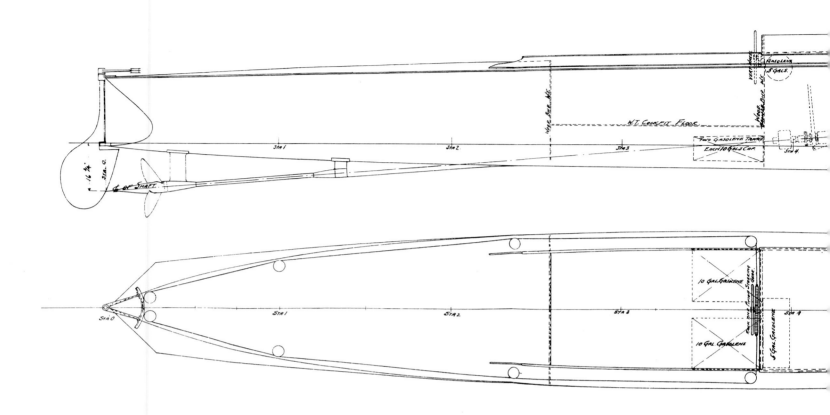

The profile and plan of the very successful Vingt et Un II. *With her 75-horsepower, 4-cylinder Simplex engine, the second* Vingt et Un *reached 24.2 miles per hour. The plumb stem, cowling and V-shaped transom defined the look of speed for years to come.*

hour on the sands of Daytona in 1906, a world land speed record. The engine was steam. The fact that steam was unable to compete with internal combustion engines in boats was not yet limited by the technology; it was limited by the practitioners.

Vingt et Un II was shortly sold to Willis Sharpe Kilmer, a Binghamton, New York, patent medicine maker and newspaper publisher whose passion was fast horses. Mr. Kilmer kept the boat at New York City long enough to win the American Power Boat Association's Gold Cup against a strong field in September of 1904. It was the second running of the race. The first had seen *Standard* walk away with the trophy in a weak field of two other boats — *Water Lily*, a Consolidated product, and *FIAT I*, built by Elco. After ceding the trophy for the second competition, *Standard* was not entered as she too had been sold. Her buyer was Cleveland steel man Price McKinney. Ultimately Mr. McKinney would commit suicide after losing control of his company; but he campaigned *Standard* vigorously for several years with Riotte-built motors of up to 500 horsepower.

Standard and *Vingt et Un II* were scarcely the only combatants. Many of the legendary names of the Edwardian motor world participated. There were Lozier, Chadwick, Winton, Olds, F.I.A.T., Panhard, Mercedes, Mors and

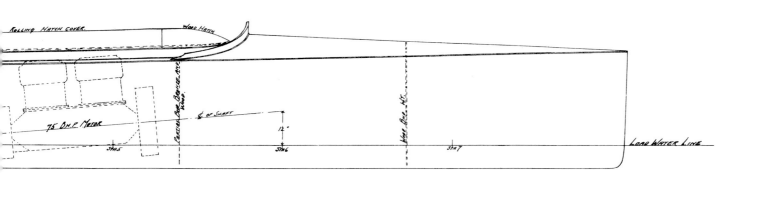

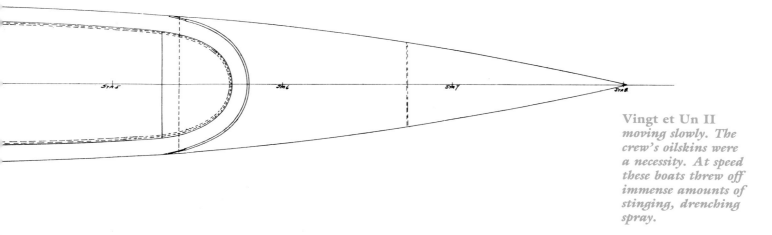

Vingt et Un II moving slowly. The crew's oilskins were a necessity. At speed these boats threw off immense amounts of stinging, drenching spray.

others, each contending for victory and the sales they hoped would follow. They struggled against each other, against cranky hulls that drowned their occupants in spray, against truculent motors, poor-quality fuel, cantankerous ignitions, floating logs, poorly marked and measured courses, and against strange rules concocted by regatta committees. Usually — though not always — there was a winner; but in a $1,500 grudge race between *Vingt et Un II* and *F.I.A.T. III* both boats ran out of gas.

Like some giant dinosaur in the throes of death, the men of steam put on a terminal display of power and speed. To many of the time the names were well-known: Charles Dell Mosher and Charles Randell Flint. It began with a war, this time the Spanish-American, a conflict which flared and died within three months in the spring and summer of 1898. At its conclusion the United States had acquired Cuba, Puerto Rico, the Philippines and a few minor islands from Spain, and C.R. Flint was left with two partially completed steam engines for a torpedo boat project he had been planning with Lewis Nixon. With the war over, demand was very small for such items, a problem compounded by the changing fashions in naval warfare which now favored larger ships.

C.R. Flint was nothing if not resourceful. He decided to put the engines in a fast hull and beat the speed of the renowned British yacht *Turbinia*, built to demonstrate Charles Parson's steam turbines. This was a natural project for C.D. Mosher, whose *Ellide* had already outsped *Turbinia* and who had

designed the engines for Flint. Built at a cost of $160,000 at the Samuel Ayers yard in Nyack, New York, *Arrow* was launched in 1900. She was 132' long by 12'6'' wide with a draft of 3'6'' and a displacement of about 66 tons. This was remarkably light for the size. The lightness was accomplished in part by the usual Mosher strategems of forged and bored engine parts which yielded a powerplant weight of 17.8 pounds per horsepower. Always innovating, Mosher re-heated the steam between each cylinder of the quadruple expansion engines. Each developed 4,000 horsepower at 350 pounds pressure and 540 rpm. The boilers were certified for 440 pounds, and the engines were capable of 600 rpm; so it is likely that *Arrow* might have developed as much as 10,000 horsepower under optimum conditions with a brave crew. The two engines operated twin counter-rotating propellers on a common shaft to nullify the vast torque developed, a force that would otherwise have caused the hull to list badly if her 8,000 horsepower were applied to a single screw.

While Mosher had for many years used metal framing in his designs, this time there was extensive aluminum in place of steel in structure above the waterline. Other items such as *Arrow*'s galley furnishings were also fabricated in aluminum. This stunning example of Victorian high technology was not simply a race boat but a pleasure yacht used by a series of owners for two decades.

Arrow did not have a public trial until 1902. Then she steamed a nautical mile in 1:32 for a rate of 39.13 knots or 45 miles per hour. A *Scientific American* reporter noted that "she made remarkably little fuss, there being no lofty or crested bow wave, such as is seen at the high-speed trials of torpedo boats." On board there was a considerable fuss if not outright terror. A quarter mile into the run at 400 pounds boiler pressure a safety valve blew. The terrified engineer immediately pulled the other three safety valves, and *Arrow* completed the last three-quarters of a mile blowing immense amounts of steam and developing only 250 pounds in the engines. Still she accomplished 45 miles an hour as an average for the mile. Designer Mosher pointed out that *Arrow* had been in the water for several months and that her bottom had not been cleaned in that time. She was also carrying much excess weight as her draft was five inches greater than designed. No further trials were attempted.

C.R. Flint's Arrow *as she appeared when the Mosher-designed 132-footer pushed the water speed record to 45 miles per hour in 1902. Flint later removed one of the two boilers and used her to entertain heads of state and business associates.*

A racer under construction in the Smith & Mabley shop about 1904. The razor-sharp bow was intended to cut the water with minimum disturbance and was very deep so that it remained in the water as the hull lifted.

Charles R. Flint achieved a return on his investment through a $35,000,000 order for ten torpedo boats and eight submarines from the Russian navy. He had sent the Grand Duke Alexander Michaelovitch a model of *Arrow* fitted out as a torpedo boat. Flint later removed one of the two Mosher boilers and used *Arrow* for entertaining, selling her in 1906 to E.F. Whitney.

In July 1904 as *Standard, Vingt et Un II* and the other autoboats were engaged in their first season of real competition, Lewis Nixon wrote in the yacht's log, "In the *Arrow* we see the perfection and maturity of the steam engine. In this we see the need of further advance which will be the gas engine — no boiler — no steam — smokeless — noiseless — always ready." While Lewis Nixon was correct in his assessment, it would be almost a decade before a gas engine moved a boat faster on the water than a steam engine had moved *Arrow* in 1902.

6

AUTOBOATS & SPEED DEVILS

For Edward Russell Thomas it was a life of fast cars, fast horses and beautiful women. He crashed the first, traded the second and married the third. And not just once. He was the youngest bank president in America, using a small slice of the family fortune to seize control of the Seventh National Bank in Manhattan. The next day the bank collapsed. He roared down city streets in his "White Ghost," scattering pedestrians and collecting speeding citations as if they were calling cards. It was not all good clean fun for the twenty-five-year-old "Society Swell." On Lincoln's Birthday in 1902 Thomas's White Ghost "ground to death" seven-year-old Harry Thies on Convent Avenue near 130th Street. The judge ordered E.R. Thomas to pay the family $3,125. For Thomas this was less than a week's income from the family trust, and he did not slow down for long.

Less than three months later Thomas, his wife and chauffeur were attacked on Manhattan's East Side by a gang hurling rocks, cans, pots, and frying pans at their auto. A mob of a hundred boys attacked, a riot started, and the police arrived. Thomas and his party escaped to their home on West 57th Street. Mrs. Thomas, the former Linda Lee of Tennessee and "one of the most beautiful women in America," was treated by a physician for head wounds and shock. Attacks on motorists were common at the time, and public opinion was not unanimously against the practice. As one woman wrote to *The New York Times*, "The auto-mobilist must be encouraged and protected or else he might lose his nerve and not be able to run down pedestrians with the proper amount of sang froid." Open class warfare did not stop E.R., and he skipped bail on his next speeding ticket, only to be caught and hectored by the magistrate. In Cuba the next year Thomas drove his 90-horsepower Mercedes into a ditch, destroying the car and badly injuring his passenger. He had tried to avoid hitting a horse and buggy. Thomas declared that he would never drive at speed again, except at Daytona Beach.

E.R. Thomas then turned his attention to autoboats. The natural place to inquire was the emporium of Smith & Mabley, which had moved uptown to premises only a short walk from the Thomas residence. Mr. Thomas had a specific requirement: his autoboat must reach 30 miles per hour. This would make it the fastest motorboat in the world. Clinton Crane was called, and he apparently pronounced the project feasible. The always conservative Crane modified the lines of his last effort, the vexing and erratic *Challenger*, an extension of *Vingt et Un II*, which was itself derived from the torpedo boat forms of M. Normand of Le Havre. Estimates showed that the 150-horsepower Simplex engine of *Challenger* would propel the new hull at a rate greater than the contract speed.

She was to be called *Dixie* in tribute to Linda Lee's Southern origins. *Dixie* was 40' on the waterline with a beam of 5' 6''; the length was chosen to conform to the rules for British International Cup racing which required a length of not more than 12 metres. She was also a bit portly by the standards of the time, displacing 5,150 pounds ready to race. On the vital measure of power-to-weight, each horse pulled only 34.3 pounds compared to the 51.3 in *Vingt et Un II* of only two years before. If the genes of victory were recessive in *Challenger*, they were dominant in *Dixie*.

Dixie's first public trial proved indecisive if not disastrous. On June 19, 1905, she made her way from the Smith & Mabley shop at Astoria, Long Island, through the Harlem River to the Hudson at 116th Street, where the Navy had established an officially measured nautical mile. During the first timed run *Dixie* hit the wake of a steamer, broke her steering gear and swerved wildly, throwing engine designer Ed Franquist into the river. After Franquist was rescued, *Dixie* and the tender *Simplex* returned to Astoria. The assembled reporters agreed that she was fast. Unanswered was exactly how fast.

With snow on the hillsides, the fast launch Japansky *undergoes a test. Built by Consolidated, she was state-of-the-art in speed circa 1904. Here she is listing to port from the torque of her engine and slightly down at the stern. The streamline theory on which she was designed was soon to become obsolete.*

On July Fourth *Dixie* entered the Indian Harbor Yacht Club races at Greenwich, Connecticut. "It was an ideal day for the sport," according to a reporter, but it was not an ideal day for E.R. Thomas. On the first round of the 32.2-mile race *Dixie* with Thomas at the helm was timed at 27.4 statute miles per hour. Boat speed was probably well in excess of that as *Dixie* was far off course, sailing over the quaintly named Hen and Chickens rocks despite the fact that they were marked with a buoy. The tide was ebbing, and on the second pass over the reef *Dixie*'s running gear was torn away. *Argo*, a 60-footer piloted by Charles L. Seabury, finished the race alone. *Dixie* was towed in. Commenting on Thomas's navigation, an editorial in *The Motor Boat* said that "it is for this reason that owners of motor boats . . . are so lightly held by their half-brothers in other marine sports."

Events turned for Edward Russell Thomas later that month when he swept a 75-mile series of three races at Marblehead, averaging about 25 miles per hour. At the popular Hudson River Motor Boat Carnival in late September *Dixie* turned in the fastest speed of the meet against a strong field that included autoboat entries from Lozier, Winton, Olds and Panhard. The Olds *Six-Shooter* failed to start while *Panhard II* and the 12-cylinder *Winton* did not finish the 30-nautical-mile event. Not the least pressed, *Dixie* averaged 26.7 statute miles per hour.

To spectators it was an impressive performance: "On she came, leaning out of the water like a scared flying fish, the water flying in outcurved, spattering, irridescent walls from her sleek red sides, her motor whizzing like a battery of Gatlings. Owner E.R. Thomas held the wheel, his long frame draped in a yellow oil-skin coat, a big life preserver strapped around his chest

E.R. Thomas's Dixie *at speed in 1905. The 150-horsepower Simplex engine was built from four pairs of two-cylinder units. Her competition lap speeds were in the range of 26–27 miles per hour, fast enough to win most races.*

With Captain Pearce at the helm and engineer Rappuhn at the throttle, the first Dixie leaves the dock to do battle on Long Island. Clinton Crane, Dixie's designer, described her as "very cranky" at high speeds.

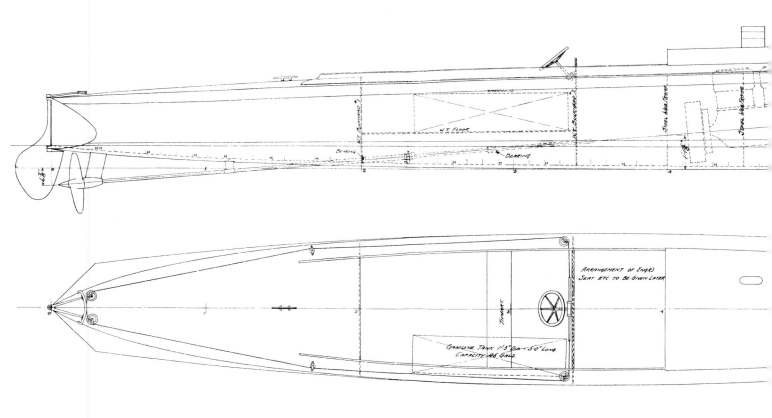

— in case the speed devil should buck jump and hurl him helpless into the water," rhapsodized the *New York World*. And the speed devil almost did hurl Thomas into the water; *Dixie* sheered hard toward a sea wall before her helmsman regained control. The Carnival was the season finale, and apparently E.R. Thomas had fulfilled his desire for speed on water. He sold *Dixie* to Edward J. Schroeder, a Jersey City railway-car lighting manufacturer.

Thomas did not, however, entirely abandon internal combustion exploits. In 1908 his Buffalo-based Thomas Motor Car Company fielded the only American entry in a 21,000-mile race from New York to Paris. The Thomas Flyer left New York on February 12, 1908, and arrived in Paris (by way of Siberia and Tokyo) five and one-half months later, to be declared the winner of the *Grand Prix du Tour Du Monde*. On arriving in Paris the Flyer's crew was arrested for driving without lights. Thomas would go on to corner the cotton market, lose millions in stock trades and flirt with bankruptcy as he had flirted with death on the road. For Edward Russell Thomas, risk was its own reward.

It is unlikely that two men so different could have shared the same interest. E.J. Schroeder was a shy, retiring man. At social gatherings he eschewed the company of his peers and was often found in the garage, conversing quietly with the chauffeurs about matters mechanical. The son of a German welder who had parlayed his metal-working skills into a business supplying gas lights for railway cars, E.J. Schroeder attended Stevens Institute of Technology for a year before joining the business. Shifting the company from gas to electric lighting, he quadrupled its sales volume, managing the growth on a day-to-day basis.

Edward J. Schroeder watches intently as Dixie *wins a race at Palm Beach in 1906.*

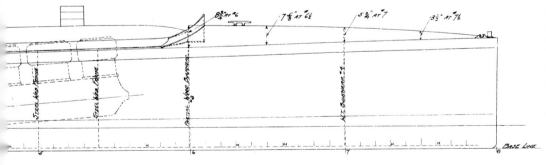

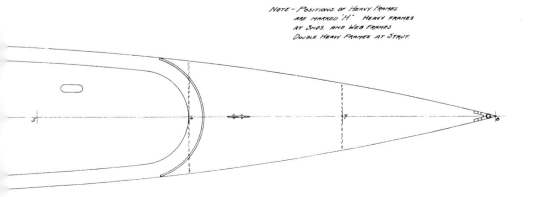

Dixie's profile and plan. Crane believed that a very large rudder helped control the hull's tendency to roll when engine speed was changed. The starboard placement of the fuel tank was intended to counter-balance engine torque. The cowling ahead of the engine kept rogue water from the engine space.

Here is H.J. Leighton's brilliant "rules racer" that won the 1905 Gold Cup on time allowance at an average of 18.4 miles per hour. The 27' 3" Chip was in use 30 years later by a fishing guide.

In the season of 1906 there were not many racing opportunities. After the frenzies and fiascos of 1904 and 1905, public interest in the autoboat had ebbed. The auto manufacturers found that building fast boats was much more difficult than they had thought, and builders such as Olds and Winton withdrew rather than subject themselves to further public humiliation. They raced to gain prestige and sales. Breaking crankshafts at the starting line and crashing into buoys or marker boats did not enhance stature. Despite the forecasts of men such as Smith and Mabley, powerboating, while not stagnant, did not match automotive growth. In just the two years between 1904 and 1906, motor vehicle sales tripled to $62.7 million while boat sales increased only 39% to $4.1 million. In 1904 there had been one dollar in boat sales for every seven in cars. In 1906 the ratio had plummeted to a dollar in boat sales for $14.60 in autos. Struggling to keep up with demand and to fight new competition in their main business, most of the automakers abandoned boating.

The few that remained found themselves in a thicket of changing rules designed to "equalize" the boats through handicap formulae. So complicated that no one was sure who won until well after a race, so subject to interpretation that protests were routine, the rules inhibited the growth of the sport. The American Power Boat Association was responsible for much of this, and while intentions were undoubtedly good, the results were less than salubrious. To arrive at a "rating," the A.P.B.A. used a formula which took into account the length of the boat, its midsection area, its engine horsepower as determined by a formula which changed from time to time, and a few incidental factors such as engine speed and engine type, either two-cycle or four-cycle.

The rating was then used to "correct" the boat's time over the course. It was a noble idea, based on nineteenth-century concepts of naval architecture and yachting tradition filtered through the inevitable organizational politics. Rule changes in 1906, for example, made two-cycle engines noncompetitive, at least according to their manufacturers.

A popular winter sport among autoboat aficionados was calculating the speed required for a fast boat to win a race under the ratings. On more than a few occasions the computations showed speeds higher than had ever been reached, requiring a big boat to average 33 miles per hour to win against the corrected time of smaller boats. That was the speed needed for *Dixie* to win the A.P.B.A. Gold Cup in 1906. At the time she had not exceeded 27 miles per hour in competition, although Clinton Crane said later that she had attained 30 in private trials. Ed Schroeder knew all this quite well but still entered *Dixie* for the Gold Cup.

There was at least one man in America whose command of the rules was strong and who purpose-designed boats and engines to take advantage of them. H.J. Leighton of *Adios* fame was that man. His patron was Jonathan Wainwright, a Philadelphia contractor whose will to win was immense. Even in death Jonathan Wainwright wished to possess the Gold Cup; his last will and testament provided funds for a trophy defense. After *Vingt et Un II* brought the cup to the Chippewa Bay Yacht Club on the St. Lawrence River, it was the work of Leighton, Wainwright and Joseph Leyare, a boatbuilder from Ogdensburg, New York, that kept it there.

In 1905 Wainwright had entered *Chip*, one of his flotilla of Leighton-designed boats. At 27' 3'' inches on the waterline and equipped with a

The Lozier Shooting Star *was unusual in its use of lapstrake construction. Auto manufacturer Lozier was heavily committed to boatbuilding with two large plants, one for hulls and another for engines.*

four-cylinder Leighton engine of only 201 cubic inches, it was the smallest and lowest-powered boat in the race; *Chip* was rated at 10-1/4 horsepower. The big New York autoboats were there: *Panhard, Shooting Star, Flip* with her exotic Darracq engine and *Skeeter*, Ed Schroeder's first boat. At Oak Island on the St. Lawrence, the third running of the Gold Cup began with nine entries. There were three 30-mile races on three days. Ed Schroeder might have won the Gold Cup that year if pure speed had been the criterion. *Skeeter* was turning laps at 26 miles per hour, and so was Henry Lozier's *Shooting Star II*. But after the A.P.B.A. computations were completed, it was *Chip* which won on allowance, her average speed 18.4 miles per hour. Grumbling about the rating system was heard, not all of it polite. The Chippewa club made the politically astute move of providing a special trophy for the fastest boat. H.A. Lozier, Jr., won that, but not the Gold Cup. The ever-affable Mr. Lozier smiled for the photographers, but it would not be long before his firm concentrated exclusively on auto production.

When *Dixie* appeared for the 1906 Gold Cup, there was a field of ten boats, mostly local. The 1904 winner *Vingt et Un II* was back, but flying the colors of the Frontenac Yacht Club. The persistent *Panhard II* was also present. The *piece de resistance* was the Leighton-Wainwright-Leyare creation *Chip II*. ''Leighton has us all stopped,'' remarked one competitor after seeing the boat. Herbert J. Leighton had built one of the most bizarre engines that ever turned a flywheel; its sole purpose was to win a single race.

Studying his rule book, Leighton observed that the new A.P.B.A. rules did not reckon the engine's stroke in calculating its horsepower, but only the bore. The result was a design with a tiny 4'' bore and a 10'' stroke with only two cylinders and a displacement of 251 cubic inches. But Leighton did not stop there. He added a third cylinder with a bore of 6'' and a stroke of 6.5'' which pumped air and fuel into the other two. It was an idea borrowed from that English master of two-cycle engines, Dugald Clerk, who had used the same scheme a quarter-century before but abandoned it. Perhaps Leighton had studied these engines as a Cornell University engineering student. He exhumed the concept and improved it, pumping extra fuel and air into his engine. Today this is called supercharging, and had there been a manifold pressure gauge in *Chip II*, it would have shown about ten pounds boost. With incandescent brilliance H.J. Leighton had defeated the rulebook, turned liabilities into assets and set his competitors raging and rummaging through those rules in search of the critical clause that would banish Leighton and his creativity from competition. A new 30' 2'' hull, beam 4' 8'' and planked in 1/2'' cedar was also built. Ready to win, tethered in her slip in David H. Lyon's boathouse 200 yards from the starting line, *Chip II* displaced 1850 pounds. Her rated horsepower was 15.34; her actual output was at least twice that.

The race was almost an anticlimax. On the first day *Chip II* was beaten by a boat called *Sparrow*, and spirits rose among all but Chippewa Bay Yacht

Club members. The oddly named *Sparrow* was a joint production of a Camden, New Jersey, boatbuilder named E.H. Godshalk and an auto manufacturer called The Packard Motor Car Company. It was 21.95 miles per hour for *Sparrow* and 19.46 for *Chip*. When filtered through the formulae, a *Sparrow* victory was declared. *Dixie*, roaring around the course at almost 28 miles per hour, placed fourth.

The second day saw *Chip II* edge up to 20.68 miles per hour, a scant 1.4 miles off *Sparrow*'s pace, to secure the win. With freight-train-like reliability, *Dixie* tore off 28-mile-per-hour laps; but when the pencils stopped scratching, she was awarded last place. A wind from the northeast brought heavy weather on the third day and slowed the remaining four competitors. E.J. Schroeder did not even start *Dixie* that day. *Chip* ran the 30 miles at 18.8 miles per hour; and *Sparrow*, the contender, was slowed to 16.43, fully 25% off her best performance. When the computations were completed and the points totaled, *Chip II* was declared the winner of the Gold Cup. A firestorm of protest followed, and it raged for months with the principals campaigning in the press, swapping allegations, writing letters and proselytizing the A.P.B.A. Vacillation followed as the local club committee and then the A.P.B.A. seesawed on the critical issue of how to treat *Chip II*'s third cylinder in computing her rating. First *Chip II*, then *Sparrow* and finally *Chip II* was declared the winner.

Dixie appeared at the Hudson River Carnival in September, 1906. There she won the "International Cup," a race for boats fitting the "Twelve Meter Rule." The win was darkened by the deaths of the engine designer and the mechanic of a boat called *Vesuvius*; both drowned wearing oil-skins and heavy rubber boots. The designer, Harry Odiorne, was thrown from the boat when it sheered, and the mechanic, J.S. Ferris, perished when he tried to rescue his partner. *Dixie*'s win was further eclipsed by the mile trials of a refurbished and repowered *Standard*, which now carried an engine developing more than 300 horsepower. *Standard*, with Carl Riotte at the helm, averaged 29.31 miles per hour for six one-mile runs on the Hudson. It was the fastest motorboat mile in the world, but not for long. That winter at Lake Worth *Dixie* ran the mile seconds faster, squeezing out 29.78 miles per hour.

The 4-cylinder Packard engine from Sparrow *was based on the company's Model S automotive engine and was rated at 24 horsepower. A protracted dispute over the rules cost Packard the Gold Cup in 1906, and the company did not return to boat racing until the 1920s.*

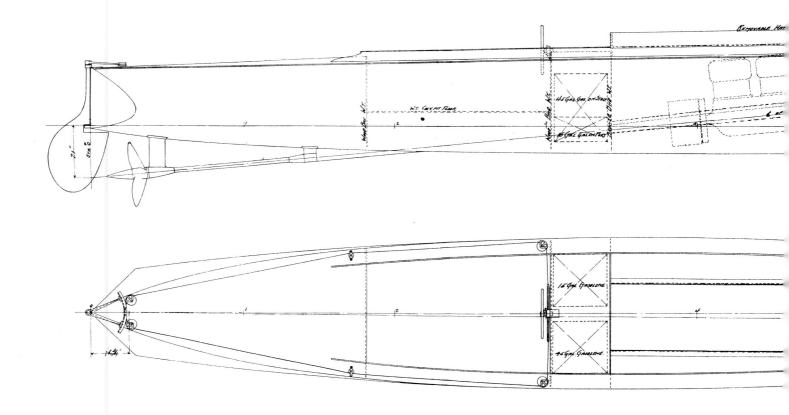

The profile and plan of Challenger. *Designed in 1904, this hull was an intermediate and not very successful step between* Vingt et Un II *and* Dixie.

The next year *Dixie* did not contend for the Gold Cup, leaving *Chip II* to vanquish a small field of local boats with arithmetic ease. Three-time winner Jonathan Wainwright let it be known that "in his opinion the present rules were very poor and that never again would he race any of his boats in a handicap race." *Dixie* meanwhile had been transported to Europe to contend for the British International Cup for Motorboats, usually known as the "Harmsworth Trophy." Not a cup at all, but a sculpture of two autoboats rounding a buoy in heavy seas, the trophy was first presented by Sir Alfred Harmsworth, a publisher, as the marine equivalent of the James Gordon Bennett Cup, an international automotive trophy presented by another publisher. It was the fifth competition for the trophy, but America had only entered once before in 1904. That year Smith & Mabley had sent *Challenger* across and found the experience humbling.

Dixie was given a much better chance of winning by the "boat sharps." Hopes for a *Dixie* victory rose further when French and Italian boats, which had beaten the British earlier in the year, were denied the right to compete. The British said that they were amenable to allowing their continental com-

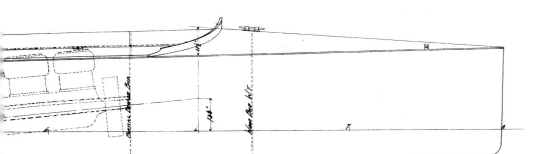

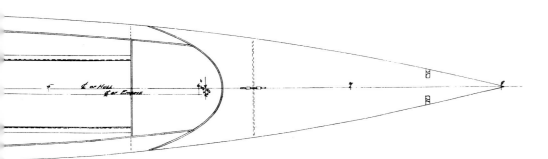

Challenger *was Smith & Mabley's first Harmsworth Trophy contender in 1904. Occasionally fast but always erratic, she was sold to a private party and retired after one season. Clinton Crane used his experience with* Challenger *to develop* Dixie.

petitors to start but also said that the Americans must approve of the decision since the Europeans were late entries. The Motor Boat Club of America, E.J. Schroeder, Commodore, would not accept the late entry of the French boats. The technical exclusion of *Panhard Tellier* and *Rapiere II* resulted in controversy and adverse comment on both sides of the Atlantic. It was also true that the deadline for entry was published months in advance.

At 5:00 P.M., August 2, 1907, at Southampton, England, *Dixie* lay idling about 80 yards from the starting line. At the helm was the unflappable S. Bartley Pearce; at the throttle and in charge of the Simplex engine was Albert Rappuhn. The two Brooklynites would handle *Dixie* throughout her career. The gun went off and 75 minutes and 44 seconds later it was over. *Dixie* had beaten the two English Daimler boats of Lord Howard de Walden. Lord de Walden steered *Daimler I* himself. *Dixie*'s speed for the 35 miles was a rapid 31.8 miles per hour. The consensus was that the course was short since *Dixie* had never made such a speed in America. Clinton Crane shared this view; but Captain Pearce, who was in a position to see the tachometer during the race, claimed it was the actual speed made. In any case, the Harmsworth Trophy was transported in triumph to the rooms of the Motor Boat Club of America at the Waldorf-Astoria.

Political infighting would soon remove Ed Schroeder as Commodore of the M.B.C.A.; but he had already begun planning a new boat with Clinton Crane. Smith & Mabley had gone bankrupt during the Panic of 1907, and the Simplex operation had been taken over by one of its investors, Herman Broesel. Simplex, though it would make superb automobiles for many years, was out of the boat business.

This left Ed Schroeder with a serious problem: how and where to obtain a light, powerful engine. The two major builders of truly high-powered gas engines were Standard and James Craig. Both built engines of the heavy-duty marine type not really suitable for a race boat. The problem was taken to Clinton Crane's brother, Henry M., who had recently begun building custom automobiles in Bayonne. The brilliant engineer proposed a radical configuration at the very edge of Edwardian technology: a V-8 with hemispherical combustion chambers.

By a contract signed that winter, a speed of 35 statute miles per hour was guaranteed or E.J. Schroeder would not have to take the boat. In scarcely six months a new hull and an engine were designed and built. Clinton Crane repaired to the Government Model Basin at Washington, D.C. There he was seen in the company of Naval Constructor David W. Taylor testing two candidate hull forms. A modification of the lines of *Dixie* formed the basis for *Dixie II*. The new hull was flatter aft and had a rounded transom instead of the Normand type of the earlier boats. The tank tests indicated that 207 horsepower would propel the hull to 35 miles per hour if weight could be kept on target. Using the same structural-analysis techniques employed for destroyers, C.H. Crane whittled 600 pounds from the design. The hull was

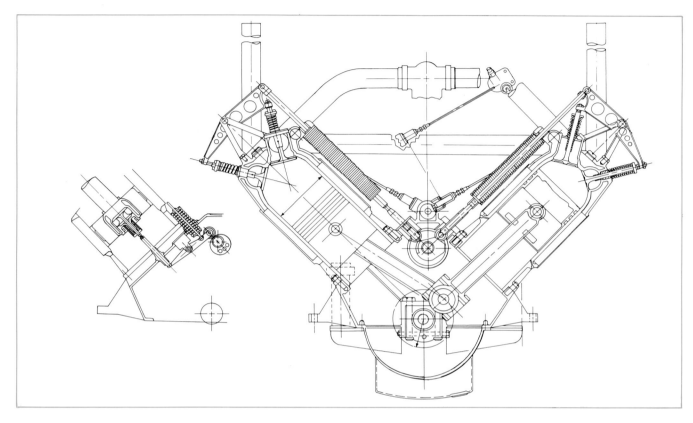

Shown here is Henry M. Crane's V-8 for Dixie II. *A giant leap into the future, Crane's engine was designed, built and tested in only six months. Light and very reliable, it developed 220 horsepower at 900 rpm.*

The 2,477 cubic inch Dixie II V-8 at home in the Crane-Whitman shop. The very light flywheel and drilled rocker arms for the overhead valves show the emphasis on weight reduction. Each of the two exhaust valves in each cylinder had its own pipe.

*Carrying her bow,
Dixie II roars along
the Hudson. Capable
of at least 37 miles
per hour and perhaps
more, the combina-
tion of speed and
reliability made her
nearly invincible.*

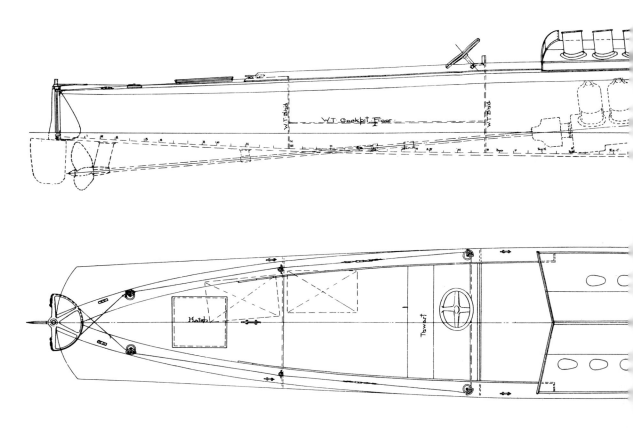

built at the yard of B. Frank Wood, a lawyer turned boatbuilder at City Island. She was planked in mahogany 3/8'' thick below the water and 1/4'' above. The main framing was of rock elm 1-1/2'' by 1/2'' on 24'' centers supplemented by 1/2'' square frames on 6'' centers. Complete and ready for its engine, the hull weighed 1,130 pounds on a length of 39' 3'' with an extreme beam of 5' 4-1/2''. The waterline beam was 6'' broader than the first *Dixie*'s at 4' 8''.

Dixie II's hull was a conservative extension of proven practice; Henry Crane's engine was a giant leap into the future made all the more amazing by the fact that H.M. Crane had never before designed a motor larger than 50 horsepower. *Dixie II*'s engine was designed, constructed and installed in less than six months and met the critical specification of not less than 200 horsepower and not more than 10 pounds for each horsepower developed. An eight-cylinder 90-degree V-8 7-1/4'' square, it had a displacement of 2,477 cubic inches and developed 220 horsepower at 900 rpm. With three valves per cylinder and hemispherical combustion chambers, *Dixie II*'s engine was a preview of the distant future. Taking a leaf from the design notebook of Charles Dell Mosher, exotic steel and aluminum alloys were used with each

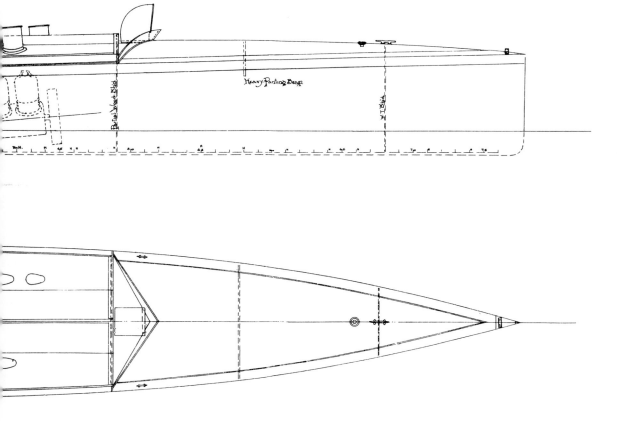

The changes from Crane's earlier designs are clearly seen in Dixie II's plan and profile. The engine is placed further aft; the bearing area at the stern is greatly increased; the transom is revised and the rudder is much smaller. The plumb stem, turtle deck and cowling were retained. Dixie's reverse sheerline was pioneered by Clinton Crane, and is found on high speed hulls to the present day.

Dixie II *at the end of the first round of the Harmsworth Trophy race in 1908. Albert Rappuhn is signaling engine speed to owner Schroeder. Mufflers were required by the rules, and the improvised silencing system that nearly asphyxiated Rappuhn can be seen clearly.*

part machined to a minimum weight consistent with strength. Rather than test and adjust the engine in the boat, a dynamometer was set up in the Avenue A Bayonne shop of Crane and Whitman. The engine was tested for three weeks, culminating in a full-throttle run of one and one-half hours. With her engine installed only one day before the elimination trials for the Harmsworth, *Dixie II* easily bested the field of four other boats.

The challenging British boats had arrived by steamer from England. There was *Daimler II*, different from the boat of the same name which *Dixie* had beaten at Southampton the previous year. This *Daimler* carried triple engines and 420 horsepower. A serious threat was *Wolseley-Siddeley*, owned by the wealthiest man in England, the Duke of Westminster. Fresh from a string of continental victories, the Duke's boat was reported capable of 35 miles per hour, and she carried two straight-eight engines totaling 414 horsepower.

Because of rough water, the race was postponed from Saturday to Monday. Tension heightened. At 3:05 P.M, five boats roared across the line: *Dixie II* followed by *Den II*, *Daimler II*, *Wolseley-Siddeley* and *U.S.A.* *Dixie* never relinquished her lead. Ahead by 47 seconds at the first round, her lead shrank

76

to 16 seconds on the second 10-nautical-mile lap. One hour, four minutes and thirty-seven seconds after the starting gun, it was over, *Dixie II* finishing with a comfortable 33-second advantage. *Daimler II* withdrew after an engine failure, and the two other U.S. boats were 10 and 15 minutes behind. *Dixie II* had averaged 32 statute miles per hour for the course to 31.5 for *Wolseley-Siddeley*.

As she roared across the finish line, Captain Pearce was seen shaking the shoulder of a slumping Albert Rappuhn. Rappuhn had been overcome by exhaust fumes leaking from the hastily installed muffler system. Before passing out he pushed *Dixie*'s throttle wide open, making *Dixie*'s third round her fastest. Steering the boat and simultaneously trying to revive Rappuhn, Captain Pearce crossed the finish wide open. After stopping the boat, he too collapsed from "nervous exhaustion." No serious injury was done to either man, and a few hours later Albert Rappuhn was delivering firsthand reports of the race to those who remained at the clubhouse. "Pearce and Rappuhn! May there never be a time when America is without men such as you," opined *Motorboat*. The next day Albert Rappuhn was back at the throttle while Clinton Crane steered *II* to a new speed record, averaging 31.05 knots or 35.75 statute miles for four runs of a 1.1-nautical-mile course.

E.J. Schroeder and *Dixie II* then migrated to the St. Lawrence, soundly defeating the latest Leighton creation, *Chip III*, for the Gold Cup. With the handicaps removed, Leighton had built an all-out racer carrying two 200-horsepower two-cycle engines. Plagued by overheating, the new *Chip* was unable to stay with *Dixie II*. Pearce and Rappuhn, the consummate professionals, merely stayed comfortably ahead of the competing boats and swept to an easy victory. In October *Dixie II* casually bumped the mile

The Chip III *was the end of H.J. Leighton's dominance in Gold Cup competition. The "organ pipes" were designed to carry exhaust gases above the heads of the crew. Each 6-cylinder, two-cycle engine generated 200 horsepower but cooling problems kept the boat from reaching her potential.*

record to 37.113 miles per hour between the range poles off the Electric Launch Company plant at Bayonne. Clinton Crane had been working on weight placement, and *Dixie* carried her bow high with the forward one-third of the hull out of the water.

And so it went for two years, *Dixie II* winning virtually every race she entered, and she entered many. As things turned out, Clinton Crane had designed *Dixie II* too lightly. She leaked at speed, and a siphon bilge pump became standard equipment. For the 1909 season a new hull was built, and engine output was increased to 250 claimed horsepower by adding a second carburetor. The new boat was soundly defeated at Monaco in the spring of 1909. The new *Dixie II* recovered from the Monaco mortification under the ministrations of Pearce, Rappuhn and Schroeder, going on to dominate the new season in the style of her 1908 namesake. Talk about the "danger of modifications" ceased, but many in the press called the boat *Dixie III*.

Clinton Crane's other new effort, a completely redesigned *Standard*, was capsized by her own torque, throwing four men into the Hudson in March. At Monaco the new *Standard* was a complete failure, listing to her gunwale under the onslaught of torque from her 580-horsepower engine. The crew of *Standard* admitted that they really did not know how much power the engine made. It had broken the dynamometer at 580 horsepower, so that was how it was rated. The new *Standard* was not heard from again, and what Price McKinney did with her is unknown. In retrospect, the failure of *Standard* seemed a signal that the engines had once again exceeded the capabilities of the hulls. Two decades before, the Herreshoffs had battled the power of steam torque and the listing of high-speed hulls. C.D. Mosher demonstrated an alternative and elegant solution in the wide, flat stern. With the new *Standard* Clinton Crane faced the same demon forces. Meanwhile, an American engineer living in France was developing very different hull types. The French called them *hydro-glisseurs* or, sometimes, hydroplanes.

7

DIXIE DYNASTY

In the spring of 1908 a man of average means with the desire to go motor-boating could buy a new 15' launch with a two-horsepower engine for $200, about four months' wages. He paid about 25 cents for the gallon of gas that propelled him along a protected waterway for several hours at four miles per hour. His engine was a one-cylinder, two-cycle, probably built in open disregard for Clark Sintz's patent, which would soon expire. Its manufacturer could have been any of hundreds, for the technology was so well-known and so simple that any foundry or machine shop could build a motor. Many of them did. More complex items such as carburetors were bought from large suppliers for a few dollars. The hull, in all likelihood, was made of pine and painted white. On such a modest boat, varnished trim was used sparingly. It was not built in a factory but by a local boat shop. Rivers and lakes of any size had one, perhaps several such shops.

If a man did not have $200, he could build his own boat. It was the only option; consumer credit was not yet common. Any of several firms would supply a knock-down kit delivered by rail. With the potential skipper supplying the labor, costs were cut by a third to a half. Companies such as Brooks in Michigan claimed that they had sold thousands of kits. Perhaps it was true.

For the industrious but impecunious, the boating magazines — there were at least four by 1908 — published how-to articles and plans for the amateur builder each winter, implying that the boat could be completed by spring. The most important tools were ''elbow grease and gumption,'' said one article. This was considered a fine way to obtain something truly extravagant such as a 25' cruiser, speed 8 knots on 10 horsepower. Such a boat would cost $1,500 if purchased completed, equivalent to about $50,000 today. Young designers on their way to fame or oblivion contributed these designs. So it was that the nation's motorboat fleet grew to 70,000 by the spring of 1908, according to a *New York Times* estimate. It was still necessary to remind many owners that leaking fuel lines should be repaired and that it was not advisable to look for the leak with a match. Each spring the magazines published illustrated articles on how to overhaul the motor.

The idea of self-propulsion, the freedom from dependence on muscle or wind, still seemed miraculous. *Dixie II* might cleave foreign seas at 30 knots, defeat royalty, and bring honors to the nation; but for most the ability to move on water without sweating was wonder enough. As Charles G. Davis, a designer, artist, and journalist, explained in 1909, "A sailboat required a peculiar skill, and even then were only fit for more open stretches of water, and for the benefit mostly of the more fortunate men folks, whereas, motorboats can be used by the masses, and enable people to get around the network of water-ways that spreads over this country, and see sights of beauty that no painting could ever portray. Men, women and children can all be taken along in a motorboat, and when the fair sex can share the pleasure, the success of a pastime is assured."

C.G. Davis wrote with authority. A decade before he had designed for *Rudder* a spectacularly popular small sailboat called *Lark.* The boat was not only popular; its form forecast the functional shape of powerboats to come. Describing his 16' "scow" with its bluff bow, very flat bottom and straight sides, Davis wrote in 1898, "She would run from the top of one wave to the top of the next, actually skipping along the top of the waves." Although the

For many years engine overhauls were an annual ritual. Removing the cylinder head and cleaning out carbon was minimal maintenance. On four-cycle engines, valves needed to be ground. More energetic owners also shimmed bearings and often replaced piston rings.

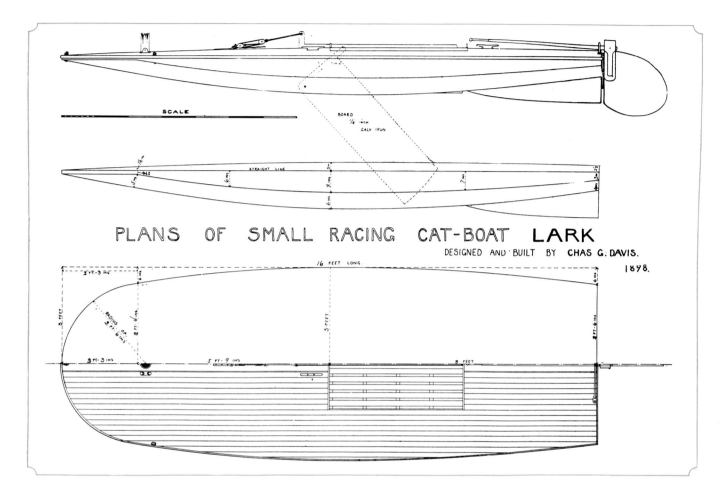

PLANS OF SMALL RACING CAT-BOAT LARK

DESIGNED AND BUILT BY CHAS G. DAVIS.

1898.

term did not exist, Davis's sailing scow was planing, just as C.D. Mosher's steam yachts of the 1890s planed. It may not have been a coincidence. Davis knew Mosher; both worked with William Gardner at the same time. But the connection was not an easy one to make; the notion of a common principle controlling the performance of the 80' steam yacht *Ellide* and the 16' sailing scow *Lark* would have seemed absurd had anyone proposed it. C.G. Davis credited two other craft with the inspiration for *Lark*, both sailboats from earlier in the decade. After a few years of great popularity, Davis's *Lark* was forgotten until in 1907 a report on an early hydroplane built from French patents described the shape of the boat as "like C.G. Davis's *Lark*."

But the roots of the planing boat went much deeper. As an idea it had occurred to many, and there were the obvious parallels of a flat stone skipping across the water, landing ducks and geese and, among Navy men, the ricochet of a cannonball which had missed its target. The earliest recorded attempts to make practical use of the concept were those of Reverend C.M. Ramus of Playden Rectory, Rye, Sussex, England. On April 8, 1872, C.M. Ramus wrote the Commissioners of the Admiralty that he had discovered a

Charles G. Davis's Lark of 1898. The form of this planing sailboat was to be seen again in early hydroplanes.

81

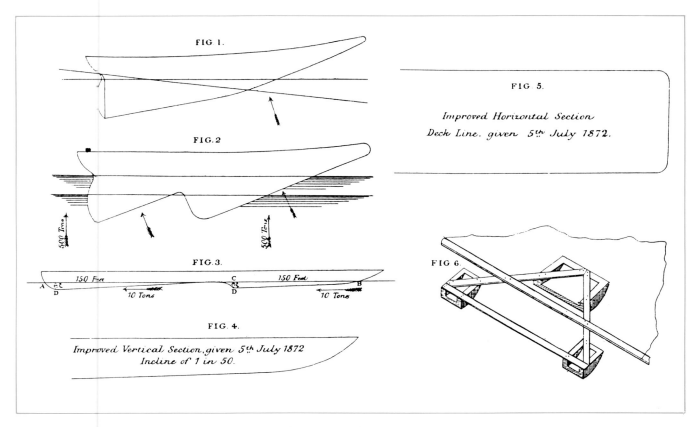

FIG 1.

FIG. 2

FIG. 3.

FIG. 4.

Improved Vertical Section, given 5th July 1872
Incline of 1 in 50.

FIG. 5.

Improved Horizontal Section
Deck Line, given 5th July 1872.

FIG 6.

The drawings for Reverend Ramus's hydroplane as they first appeared in 1872. Figure 1 shows a form which was frequently proposed to increase vessel speeds. Figure 2 shows Ramus's concept for a stepped shape. Figures 3, 4 and 5 give details of this shape as Ramus developed it through model experiments. Figure 6 shows a three-point planing shape with a large plane forward which was also tried.

means by which the speed of ships might be doubled, that he had experimental proof and that "he would place his discovery at once at the service of the public if the Admiralty would assure him that it would be acknowledged as emanating from himself."

Reverend Ramus had already enlisted the enthusiasm of several Members of Parliament, so the Admiralty's response was unusually rapid. Two days later the Admiralty's Chief Naval Architect initialed a memorandum, "Rev. Mr. Ramus has to-day communicated to me the plan of designing steam ships for great speed . . . It consists in forming the ship in two wedge-shaped bodies, one abaft the other. The object is to cause the ship to be lifted out of the water by the resistance of the fluid at high speeds." The Reverend Mr. Ramus's plan was sufficiently credible that William Froude, F.R.S., the premier investigator of ship's forms, was engaged to test the Ramus proposal. Froude tested models built to Ramus's specifications at speeds to 130 knots, and the report he issued was systematically devastating. Describing the Ramus designs as "full of misconception and error" and the idea that rockets might be used to propel a boat as an "irrelevancy," William Froude put the matter to rest. "We shall be very much mistaken," wrote the editor of *Naval Science*, "if these reports do not add to the very high esteem in which Mr. Froude is held by the Admiralty and by the country at large as an investigator of Naval Science."

William Froude was, of course, correct: it was not possible to build a planing ship of 370' as proposed by the Reverend Ramus. The power was simply not available to drive it. Both Froude and Ramus were silent on the practicability of much smaller boats of this type; apparently the idea never occurred to either man. For 30 years the Reverend C.M. Ramus remained a repudiated visionary. Six decades later the first boat in America to achieve 100 miles per hour would use a hull form of the Ramus type. The rockets proposed by Reverend Ramus were instead Packard aircraft engines.

"We can only feel that Mr. Ramus lived too early," wrote Clinton Crane. Yet at the very time when Crane was designing the fastest boats in the country, he was apparently mystified as to how they worked and what hull was best for the purpose. He was not alone. "A glance at the torpedo boats will show the very great differences in the shapes . . . Such differences would seem to show that, with a given displacement and power, the shape of the underwater form was not of the greatest moment," continued Crane in a remarkable display of candor. The trade-off was between seakeeping and speed. Model tests and practical results had shown that the "scow" form was the most easily driven; it went the fastest for a given power and weight. Clinton Crane decided on the side of "seaworthy qualities." It was a decision which led to his eclipse as a designer of fast motorboats.

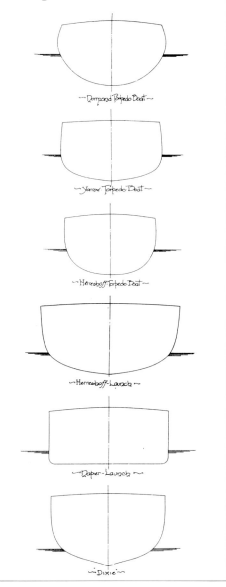

To illustrate the mystifying lack of influence of hull shape on boat speed, Clinton Crane presented this series of drawings before the Society of Naval Architects and Marine Engineers. Crane's key point was that, although the shapes were very different, the speeds of the boats were about the same when adjusted for length and power.

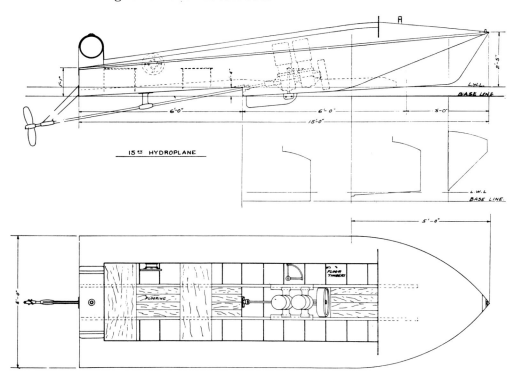

A drawing of William Stern's pioneering American stepped hydroplane of 1906. Controversy over what constituted a hydroplane continued for years. Clinton Crane believed that the hard chines were the critical element.

83

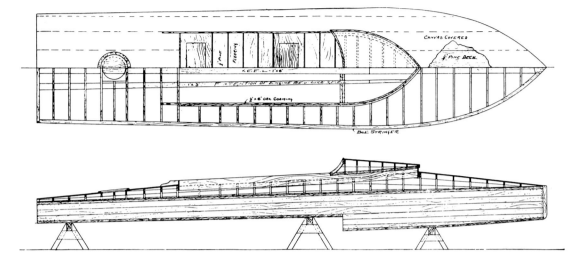

Leon Menzl's plan for a single-step hydroplane as it appeared in Motor Boat. *The publication of his "how-to" article triggered immense popular interest in planing boats.*

This early hydroplane by Sidney Breese presaged the designs of 80 years later with its engine located behind the driver. Four decades after Breese, John L. Hacker also designed raceboats with amidships propellers.

Reports had been filtering in from France of remarkable speeds achieved by the *hydro-glisseurs* of Count de Lambert and Paul Bonnemaison. Matchbox-like little craft, ten feet long and five feet wide, the *hydro-glisseurs* had been rocketing along the Seine at speeds of 15 miles per hour or more. These strange machines seemed to repeal the laws of physics, and it was not long before they appeared in the United States. William Stearns built one of the first at Bridgeport, Connecticut. His *Vida May IV* was 15' long and powered with a Cushman two-cycle twin of 14 horsepower. Weighing about 1000 pounds, the boat clocked 21 miles per hour in the spring of 1907. That same spring there appeared in *Motor Boat* a how-to article for a 20' gliding boat by Leon Menzl. A speed of 15 miles per hour was claimed to be possible from 12 horsepower. An avalanche of inquiries about the crate-like gliding boat ensued, usually asking whether or not more power might be added and what velocity could be expected. A new phenomenon had been

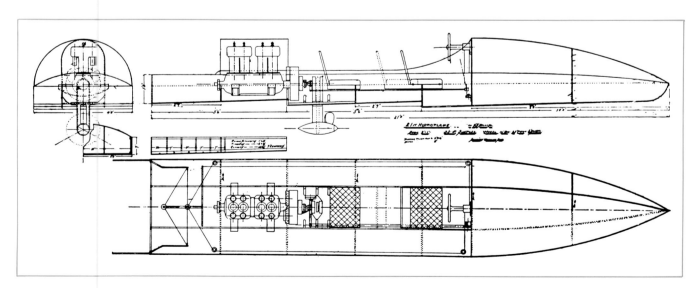

born: cheap speed. No longer was it necessary to spend $6,000 for a Simplex engine, to pay $5,000 for the hull, and to retain the services of a naval architect, driver and engineer. The cost of speed was suddenly cut by more than an order of magnitude: less than $500 for an engine, $75 for lumber, a winter's worth of evenings, and any reasonably handy man could roar across the water at 25 miles an hour. Not too subtly or slowly, a change in attitude took place. If effortless movement across the water was good, then fast, effortless movement was better. Speed was about to be torn from the exclusive domain of the millionaires. Maximum speed, of course, still required maximum expenditures.

As fast as it was primitive, Canadian Albert Hickman's original Viper *was the namesake of a renowned British torpedo boat. Flat-bottomed and hard-chined, the little 20-footer was built in 30 hours by five men. A speed of 27 miles per hour was claimed with 30 horsepower.*

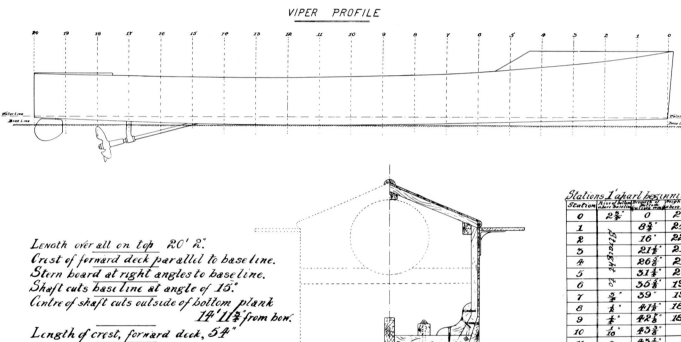

VIPER PROFILE

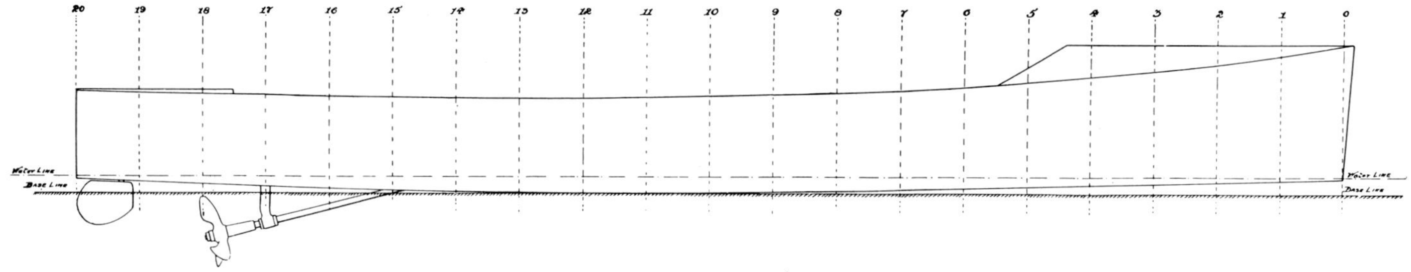

Length over all on top 20' 2".
Crest of forward deck parallel to base line.
Stern board at right angles to base line.
Shaft cuts base line at angle of 15°.
Centre of shaft cuts outside of bottom plank
14' 11¾" from bow.
Length of crest, forward deck, 54"
Length of after deck 30"

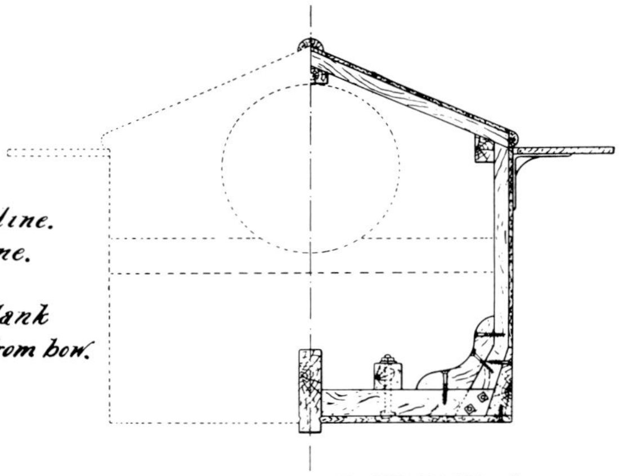

SECTION AT STATION 4

Stations 1' apart beginning at bow.

Station	Rise of bottom above baseline	Breadth of bottom outside meas.	Height of side above bottom
0	2 3/4"	0	26"
1	Straight to	8 3/4"	24 1/16"
2		16"	22 5/4"
3		21 1/2"	21 15/16"
4		26 5/8"	21"
5		31 1/4"	20 1/4"
6		35 5/8"	19 5/8"
7	3/4"	39"	19 1/4"
8	1/2"	41 1/2"	18 15/16"
9	1/4"	42 7/8"	18 3/4"
10	1/16"	43 3/8"	
11	0	43 1/2"	
12	0	43 1/4"	
13	1/8"	42 3/4"	
14	5/16"	42 3/8"	
15	9/16"	42"	
16	15/16"	41 3/8"	
17	Straight	40 5/8"	
18		39 1/2"	
19		38"	
20	2 3/4"	36 1/2"	17"

Dozens of hydroplanes were built by experimenters to test their theories of gliding boats. Some, such as the inventor Peter Cooper Hewitt, were well-funded and carried the imprimatur of establishment technology. Hewitt opted for designs which attached separate planing surfaces to a hull in a manner similar to later hydrofoils. Alexander Graham Bell experimented with similar concepts. This was a seductive approach, as it promised to solve the seakeeping problems of fast small boats. A few tried to make their boats fly by using stubby wings from the nascent technology of flight; W. Starling Burgess was among those who tried flying close to the water. A young man named Sidney Breese pulled a 30-horsepower engine from a sunken launch, built a two-step hull and, after adjusting the engine position, claimed 23 miles per hour in 1908. The boat was unusual in that the engine was placed behind the driver, and it operated a tractor propeller through a chain drive. Education, money or experience did not seem to be a factor in the success or failure of these boats. They swamped, capsized, broke their backs or failed to steer. Some would not plane at all; most did not meet the speed forecasts of their owners. A few worked.

Innovation was suddenly everywhere. The only rule seemed to be that there were no rules. From Nova Scotia came Albert Hickman, promoting flat-bottomed, scow-like forms. A young designer named William Hand built on the pioneering work of E.W. Graef and developed vee-bottomed runabouts, themselves derived from Chesapeake Bay "deadrise" workboats. In New Jersey Adolph Apel began building wildly fast hulls which were concave aft, giving them a peculiar arched appearance as they ran over the water. In Detroit an alderman's son was experimenting with bow rudders on the theory that placing the rudder near the propeller disturbed the flow of water around both. His name: Johann Ludwig Hacker. On Long Island a Webb Institute mathematics professor, George Crouch, supplemented his scholarly income by designing concave "wave-capturing" vee-bottom hulls. They captured more than waves; they captured trophies at Eastern meets. Vestigial sponsons grew on the forward waterline, first to cure the plunging tendencies of early hydroplanes, then to lift the forward sections. Old hulls sprouted metal plates on their transoms to remedy squatting as bigger and bigger engines pushed them to higher speeds.

The 30' Den was an early attempt at a planing boat. Flat-bottomed for two-thirds her length, various versions broke or sunk. Designer Charles Herreshoff, after many claims of astonishing speeds, finally turned Den into a locally successful class racer.

It was a three-ring circus of invention with strident claims and counter-claims. Members of the once-sedate design community jousted in the press, sometimes openly accusing their peers of gross error and the propagation of false information. Behaving as though the citadel of Naval Science was being attacked by heathens from barns and boathouses, the educated reserved their most excoriating attacks for the practical experimenter, trying to smother the mechanics and woodworkers with erudite theory and arcane equations. One paper was titled "Weary of Practice."

Above the furor had been *Dixie II*. Though sold by E.J. Schroeder in 1910 to a wealthy young New Yorker named Frederick K. Burnham, *Dixie II* with her new hull had continued to win effortlessly, taking prestigious trophies at the major meets. The 1908, 1909 and 1910 Gold Cups had been won, and in a variety of other venues *Dixie II* had emerged victorious. She was now popularly credited with a string of 100 victories — including that symbol of national superiority, the Harmsworth Trophy.

There had been no Harmsworth race in 1909, the British having failed to mount a challenge. But in September of 1910 they crossed the ocean to Huntington, Long Island, bringing three boats, *Maple Leaf III*, *Pioneer* and *Zigorella*. Though all were fast, the pre-race favorite was McKay Edgar's

Clinton Crane's concern with the seakeeping qualities of fast boats was based on practical experience. On the Hudson a combination of modest waves and her own spray nearly swamp Papoose *in this photo.*

William Henry Fauber as he appeared in 1920. Fauber's hulls with their sawtooth-like steps completely destroyed nineteenth-century concepts of streamlined forms as mandatory for speed.

Maple Leaf III. She was rumored to be capable of 45 miles an hour, nearly 25% faster than *Dixie II*. Carrying a 12-cylinder engine, *Maple Leaf* was just a half-inch shy of 40' long. She was planked in 1/4" cedar on the topsides and 1/4" mahogany on the bottom with framing of 5/16" by 7/16" on 4" centers. During a practice run *Maple Leaf* "received a few of Long Island Sound's caresses which proved too vigorous for her delicate constitution." *Maple Leaf III* had broken her back. *Pioneer*, the latest effort by the Duke of Westminster, carried an immense Wolseley-Siddeley 12-cylinder engine displacing 3,715 cubic inches and turning out 400 horsepower. A yellow canvas covered the engine, and with her white paint she presented a deceptively conventional appearance.

The other American starter was called *Nameless*. The work of a talented young designer, William Atkin, who would steer her that day, she was notable largely for the unreliability of her quadruple 8-cylinder engine installation. When the ball dropped that sunny day, all five boats roared across the line. Passing *Dixie II* as if she were anchored, *Pioneer* took the lead, traveling "three feet for every two of *Dixie*." America was certain to lose the trophy if *Pioneer* continued to turn 40-mile-per-hour laps. Within a mile of completing the first lap, *Pioneer* stopped, dead in the water. There she lay for 17 minutes, *Dixie* passing her. *Pioneer* restarted and took off after the distant *Dixie*. The British boat gained; but when *Dixie* completed her second lap and had but 10 miles left to run, *Pioneer* had 17 to complete. It was too great a distance, and *Dixie* crossed the line first with *Pioneer* about 13 minutes behind.

A series of events disabled *Pioneer*. Cooling water intakes plugged by seaweed, the Wolseley engine overheated. While attempting to adjust the carburetion the engineer allowed gas to leak on the hot cylinders, starting a fire. The fire burned the ignition wires, causing the engine to miss when restarted, thereby slowing *Pioneer*. The Harmsworth Trophy stayed in America that year, but there was a certain hollowness to the win. Victory had gone not to the faster boat, but to the luckier.

Fauber's first multiple-step design of 1908 is shown here. There are seven steps and the convex section is clearly visible. Each step was vented by air tubes above the waterline. Fauber experimented at length with different angles of attack on the steps and developed very sophisticated hull forms.

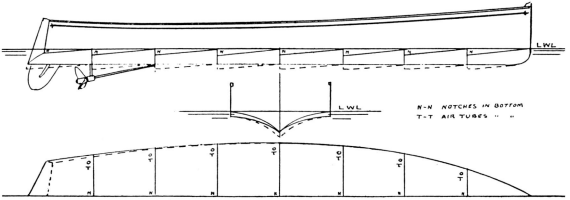

Ironically, *Pioneer* was licensed and built under the patents of William Henry Fauber, a Chicago engineer who had grown wealthy in the bicycle business. Emigrating to France, Fauber developed hulls with multiple steps and obtained his first U.S. patents about 1908. In an early report, *The Motor Boat* of London commented, ''It will be seen that the machine is much more seaworthy in type than the regular box hydroplane, being, as the owner claims, a true boat as far as the upper part is concerned.'' Fauber's 20' prototype was reported capable of 31 miles per hour with a 30-horsepower engine, and 37 miles per hour was guaranteed with 60 horsepower. In America there was not much interest in Fauber's early work. *Pioneer* changed that, and some form of ''gliding boat'' now appeared necessary to win major races. It was not long before Fred Burnham visited Clinton Crane to talk about a new boat. A syndicate was formed with August Heckscher, a ''real estate and steel operator, and a banker'' and another banker, H.H. Melville. Both men had fielded unsuccessful boats the year before.

The syndicate's target was 45 miles per hour — guaranteed. There were, of course, some questions about how to achieve the goal. Clinton Crane admitted that he had not designed a hydroplane before or even ridden in one. ''Few realize, I think, the great advantage possessed by American designers in being allowed to use the Government testing tank in Washington,'' wrote Crane. Four models were tested for the *Dixie IV* development. The 6' 6'' models weighed about 35 pounds, and a series of comparisons were performed. With the help of a photograph of her bottom, a model of *Pioneer* was built and tested. It was then modified, cutting off three of the six steps. Results showed that the three-step boat had less resistance than the six-step type. Also tested was a concave-bottom hull of the form built by Adolph Apel and used by Crane on the unsuccessful *Restless II*. The tank tests showed that a single step about amidships offered the highest potential for speed.

George Crouch's series of Peter Pan race-boats were consistently innovative. On this hull sponsons are attached aft to increase the planing area.

The engine problem was solved by arranging for Henry M. Crane to build a second V-8 identical to the engine in *Dixie II*. The first engine was overhauled and installed forward in the hull with the new engine behind. There were occasional hints that the power had been increased from the prior 250, but this was never confirmed. With the earlier *Dixies* Crane had learned the value of keeping weight well aft to cause the bow to rise and reduce wetted area. It was the movement of the engine aft that had allowed the first *Dixie* to achieve her guaranteed 30 miles per hour, and this time Crane placed the gas tank in the stern and moved all weight as far back as possible. Staten Island Shipbuilding constructed the 39' 6'' by 6'11-1/2'' hull of 1/2'' mahogany on the topsides with a 1''-thick bottom of mahogany and cedar. Fearful of structural failure with a step built into the hull, Crane designed a 3/8'' bronze forward section that was screw-fastened to create a step with a depth of 2-1/2''. Ten months after *Pioneer*, *Dixie IV* was ready. She was called the *IV* in apparent capitulation to the press referring to the second *Dixie II* as *Dixie III*. With Burnham perched on a high seat in the stern so that he could see above the spray, the boat was tested on July 15, 1911. No results of the trial were released, but one observer commented, "She is not a 35 mile boat or a 40 mile boat; she is really fast, much faster than *Pioneer* if I am any judge of speed."

The new *Dixie*'s first race was for the Gold Cup on the St. Lawrence in August of 1911. In the first day's racing she played with the field, winning easily, first with four cylinders and then with one engine shut off for a time. She did not appear on the second day. F.K. Burnham said *IV* had burned a bearing. The race was won on the points system by a peculiar locally built hydroplane called *MIT II*. *MIT* had clamshell-like depressions vented by air tubes in her flat bottom.

Pre-race reports for the Harmsworth showed that a serious attempt would be made to wrest the trophy from the Americans that September at Huntington. E. McKay Edgar's *Maple Leaf III*, the newspapers said, had run 57 miles per hour during tests. This new *Maple Leaf* had been built by John Thornycroft, a man acknowledged to be one of the world's finest ship-builders. Not short of horsepower, *Leaf* carried two W.H. Astell V-12s of 3,464 cubic inches each. The claimed output was 720 horsepower. She would be handled by the engine designer. The formidable *Pioneer* returned with the Duke of Westminster sending the same helmsman as the year before. Rounding out the British team was *Tyreless II*, which carried only 350 horsepower and looked like a cruiser.

Quadruple 6-cylinder, two-cycle Emerson engines drove through two screws on the single-step hydroplane Viva. *Engine problems kept all of her 440 horses from being available at the same time.*

The American team consisted of *Dixie*, *Disturber II*, a Fauber-type hydroplane brought east from Chicago by James Pugh, and *Viva*, a single-step hydroplane with four engines and two screws piloted by *Dixie* veteran S. Bartley Pearce. Under the new rules there would be two races on two consecutive days. The sharp report of the gun found *Dixie* and *Pioneer* across the line within a second; 35,000 people watched as *Dixie* pulled ahead of *Pioneer* while *Maple Leaf* — the pre-race threat — porpoised in a distant third place.

Lap by lap, *Dixie* widened her lead over *Pioneer*. During the second round *Maple Leaf*'s steering gave way, and she was out of the race as unexplained smoke billowed from her engines. At the end of the 30 nautical miles, *Dixie* led by 59 seconds and completed the course at an average 40.4 statute miles per hour. Although none but the crew knew it, *Dixie* had cracked a cylinder in one of her giant Crane-Whitman engines. *Tyreless* had retired, and the balance of the field struggled across the finish line minutes later.

The second day brought a southwest wind, short, choppy seas and a two o'clock starting gun. They streaked across the line, *Pioneer* first, then a repaired *Dixie*, *Viva* and *Disturber*. At the first turn *Dixie* was four seconds in the lead with *Pioneer* running better than the day before. On that first lap *Disturber* hit a heavy packing crate, cutting a huge hole in her port side. As

The profile and plan of Dixie IV. *The boat was started on the forward engine which would take her to about 30 miles per hour. A clutch was engaged and the second engine started by the rotation of its propeller.*

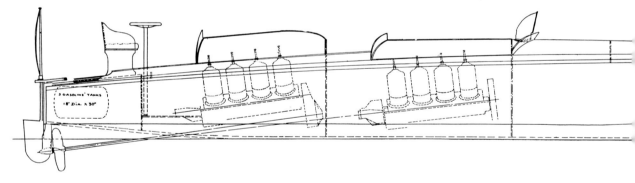

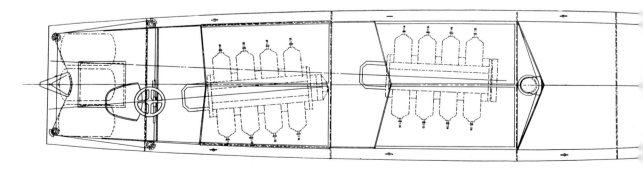

92

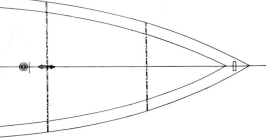

the water poured in, Jim Pugh made for shore; *Disturber* sank to the bottom with a hiss and a gurgle, the exhaust stacks marking her position. On the second lap *Pioneer* was closing on *Dixie* when her overheated engines seized. She was out.

With *Viva* far behind, Fred Burnham slowed *Dixie IV* and cruised to an easy victory with cheers, applause, whistles, horn blasts and the mutilated sound of a cornet accompanying the finish. The Harmsworth remained in the United States in 1911 and more than one citizen of Britain wondered if the trophy was about to become a motorized America's Cup. The phrase ''Dixie Dynasty'' entered the lexicon of sportswriting, and it was not long before *Dixie IV* appeared for public mile trials. The watches showed

The short-lived Crane hydroplane Dixie IV. *At the wheel is F.K. Burnham, and there is a mechanic for each engine. Burnham sometimes raced the boat with a crew of four on board.*

she had run 45.22 miles per hour, barely edging past the mark set by C.R. Flint's *Arrow* in 1902. *Dixie IV* was now the fastest boat to have ever moved on the waters of the planet.

Perhaps it was a harbinger. On September 9, *Dixie IV* ''flopped on her side'' at 45 miles per hour on Long Island Sound. Thrown from the boat was a Crane-Whitman engineer who had accidentally shut off the ignition of *Dixie's* forward engine. Hanging onto the wheel, Burnham was able to bring the boat under control and circle back a half-mile to pick up the struggling man. The ultimate catastrophe still lay six days in the future. At a meet in Buffalo, New York, on Saturday, September 16, 1911, *Dixie IV* was rounding a mark, once again in the lead, when she ''took a sheer'' and headed toward the crowded shoreline. With the boat out of control Fred Burnham shouted

Dixie at full speed off Huntington, Long Island. Her official record was 45.22 miles per hour, which made Dixie the fastest boat in the world in 1911.

for the crew to jump. Two men made their way over the side; two more could not clamber out in time. Burnham himself was knocked from his pulpit-like seat as the boat crashed into the rip-rap. *Dixie* bounded up the rocks, her cutwater slicing off a boy's leg and crushing another boy beneath the hull. A woman was also seriously hurt, but none among the crew was injured.

Some reports said that one of *Dixie*'s engines had been "shut down" to help her turn sharply. The death of young Harold Bell a few days later brought a charge of "criminal negligence and cowardice" against F.K. Burnham. In a later trial the verdict was "accidental death," but neither Fred Burnham nor the fourth *Dixie* raced again. Legend has it that the $46,287 *Dixie IV* was stripped of her engines and left to moulder at the Consolidated yard. The "Dixie Dynasty" had fallen.

Viewed from the stern, the tremendous spray thrown off makes clear why her helmsman sat high. This also helped Burnham to see over the bow as the boat came on plane.

8

MEANWHILE,
OUT IN MICHIGAN

"I have a mile course, chained and land marked and this boat can run at a rate of 24 miles an hour. These miles, I can assure you, are not gasolene miles or india rubber miles, but actual miles. I believe this boat to be one of the greatest pleasure and speed boats in the world today," wrote C.C. Smith. He was describing his new speed launch, *The Morgan*. It was the first national notice of Smith & Company of Algonac, Wisconsin; but if any magazine reader had written to find out more, his letter would have been returned. There was no Algonac, Wisconsin, as reported by *Motorboat*. Algonac was a small village on the St. Clair River in Michigan, and its geography played a crucial role in what transpired there.

The St. Clair River which separates the United States from Canada is the means of communication between Lake Huron and Lake Erie to the south. From this narrow, protected waterway all the Great Lakes are accessible. Behind the river in the 1800s lay thousands of acres of oak forest. "It is doubtful if any county bordering on any one of the Great Lakes was as much interested in the making and operating of wooden boats," wrote a local historian. Beginning about 1820, hundreds of vessels were built at Marine City, Port Huron, St. Clair, Algonac and other river villages. These were not small boats but schooners of up to 1,200 tons and steamers of as much as 6,100 tons. Marine City — 1880 population 1,673 — had five shipyards where more than 200 ships had gone down the ways by the turn of the century. It was there, in Cottrellville Township, that Christopher Columbus Smith was born on a farm May 20, 1861. At age 19 in 1880 he was working with his father as a blacksmith. After marriage in 1884, Smith moved a few miles south to Algonac, and in 1885 he advertised his services as a "Decoy Duck Manufacturer — Also Builder of Duck Boats, Paddles, Etc. — Dogs Broken to Hunt." Henry M. Smith, C.C. Smith's older brother, was gunsmithing at the time, so the two provided a complete range of sporting services within the family. By 1891 the brothers had joined forces as boatbuilders, and in 1895 they were operating a boat livery at Algonac and probably building the rowboats they rented.

Baldy Ryan and J. Stuart Blackton at the Harmsworth Trophy races in 1912. Ryan is on crutches due to injuries he received when a Reliance he was driving flipped and sank.

97

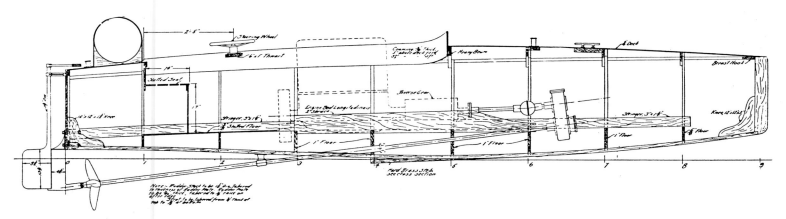

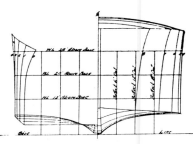

The state of the art in hydroplane design during the winter of 1912. This 19' 4'' by 4' 9'' George Crouch design was intended to be powered by an engine of up to 120 horsepower to achieve 40 miles per hour. Progress in hull design was so rapid that just a few months later Crouch claimed the design was obsolete.

Old records indicate that it was in 1896 when C.C. Smith and his brother first became involved with motorboats. On his seventy-fifth birthday, Smith recalled that he had bought for $125 from its disappointed owner an engine which would not start. The brothers were also unable to make the engine run and contacted the manufacturer, said by another source to be Sintz of Grand Rapids. Disturbed by the proposed service charges, Chris and Henry Smith finally got the engine running, then put it in a boat which was sold to a Port Huron man. With the profits from that transaction they built a four-horsepower 25-footer and sold it to a Detroit milk dealer. This opportunistic approach to boatbuilding must have worked well enough, for by 1900 the C.C. Smith family was able to afford a 17-year-old girl servant, according to census records. In that census Smith listed his occupation as boatbuilder, but by 1901, and perhaps before, he was also postmaster of the Village of Algonac.

The pivotal event in Chris Smith's career occurred when he was 49 years old. It was 1910 when he met John J. Ryan, a Cincinnati theater owner, racehorse keeper and gambler who summered in Algonac. Local legend has it that the Ryan residence was the scene of high-stakes gambling, a frequent pastime at early twentieth-century "watering places." As the legend goes, Baldy Ryan wanted a fast boat, and C.C. Smith & Company, conveniently located, had a local reputation and 10 employees. Ryan's interest was probably more than recreational since large wagers were sometimes placed on the outcome of speed contests. Ryan ordered a boat which could beat another local Smith & Company boat, *Dart*. Powered by a Pope-Toledo auto engine, the monoplane *Dart* was allegedly capable of 26 miles per hour. Back East *Dixie II* had already exceeded 35 miles per hour, so Ryan's request for a guaranteed 30 was locally realistic.

"The man would wager thousands on the turn of a card or the chances of a horse to hit the wire first," wrote J. Lee Barrett. "He'd walk up the slumbering streets of Algonac rolling diamonds in his short, fat hands, looking for excitement." John J. Ryan and Christopher C. Smith became business partners in 1911, forming the Smith-Ryan Boat and Engine Company of Algonac, Michigan. Henry Smith opened a grocery store.

Then was born a series of boats called the *Reliances* which, when they did not swamp, sink, burn or break, won local races. Hull followed hull in quick succession, and by July of 1911 Ryan was campaigning *Reliance III*, a 28' single-step boat with a Van Blerck six-cylinder T-head of 80 horsepower. Joe Van Blerck, a master machinist, had worked at Ford's before setting up his own Detroit engine shop about 1910. Allied with naval architect John L. Hacker, who was acting as business manager, Van Blerck revised standards for power output and reliability, building light, strong engines based on the metals technology he had learned while doing development work on Ford's Model T with Childe Harold Wills. Within a year the power of Van Blerck's engines rocketed from 80 to 275 horsepower, and boat speeds responded more or less accordingly.

In July of 1911 *Baby Reliance III* won a 20-mile race at Ohio's Put-in-Bay with a speed of 29.27 miles per hour. The fastest boat at the meet, it was "irremediably damaged by fire, which was suspected to be the work of incendiaries." A year later the 20' *Baby Reliance III* ran a mile at St. Louis in 1:07 or 53.73 miles per hour. In one year speeds increased more than 80% while engine power more than tripled. Eastern racers sneered at "Mississippi miles" and openly deprecated the performance of the "western" boats.

The snickering stopped in the fall of 1911. Lee Counselman, Vice President and General Manager of the Chalmers Motor Car Company (successor to E.R. Thomas's Buffalo company) sent *Kitty Hawk II* east. On September 16 at Atlantic City *Hawk*, a 26' Hacker-designed, Van Blerck-powered, single-step hydroplane, soundly beat *Sand Burr II*. A highly regarded and widely campaigned boat, the 20' *Sand Burr II* was designed by Adolph Apel and powered by a six-cylinder, two-cycle Emerson. She had beaten the best on the Hudson and the Mississippi and was undefeated until she met *Kitty Hawk II*. John Hacker had built *Kitty Hawk II* in his brother's sign-painting shop on Crane Avenue in Detroit. Something was happening out west.

At Detroit in August *Kitty Hawk II* definitively defeated Ryan's *Reliance IV*, averaging 34.56 miles per hour versus the Smith-Ryan boat's 31.17 for the 5.75-mile second heat. In the first heat *Kitty Hawk II* was also ahead by

Baby Reliance II underway. These round-bilged single-step boats were very unstable and difficult to drive. Depending on conditions, the helmsman sometimes stood up as seen here; at other times he operated the boat sitting down.

One of the famous Kitty Hawks at speed. John L. Hacker built the Hawks in his brother's sign-painting shop in Detroit after one of his boats was sabotaged at the shop of a local builder. This Hawk of 1913 is powered by an inline 12-cylinder Van Blerck.

almost a minute. This did not prevent Smith-Ryan from advertising their *Reliances* as undefeated and *Reliance IV* as the "world champion." Hyperbolic claims ("The only way a *Reliance* can be beaten in any company is by an accident") and open challenges were the marketing strategies of the day. Ryan publicly challenged *Dixie IV* to a $5,000 match race after the boat had been wrecked at Buffalo and her driver indicted. *Dixie* had already defeated *Reliance IV* at Buffalo, averaging 39.71 miles per hour versus *Reliance'*s 36.1; the result could be expected from pitting 40' and 500 horsepower against 26' and 120 horsepower. There was no response.

Neptune was another Hacker design from the same period. A speed of 49 miles per hour was claimed for this 25' 11'' hydroplane powered by a 150-horsepower Sterling turning at 1,550 rpm.

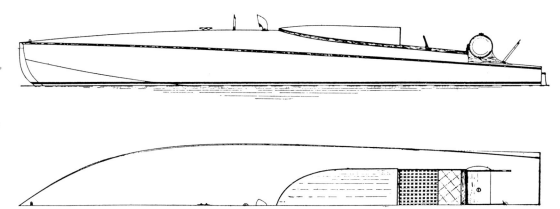

Smith-Ryan *Reliance* types were offered for sale and exhibited at boat shows. A boat with a guaranteed speed of 37 miles per hour was priced at $3,250; a 40-mile-per-hour boat was $1,000 more; and a 50-mile-per-hour boat cost $20,000 in early 1912. *Baby Reliance* plans cost $25. One man who purchased Smith-Ryan boats was J. Stuart Blackton. Born in England in 1875, Blackton worked as a painter of marine scenes and then secured a job as a newspaper illustrator. Sent on assignment to the laboratory of Thomas Edison at West Orange, Blackton encountered Edison's "cinematographic machinery." Taken with the prospects for motion pictures, Blackton and partner A.E. Smith founded Vitagraph Pictures in 1898 and made millions within a few years. Long Island estates, steam yachts (including *Arrow*), games of chance and fast motorboats were all a part of the Blackton lifestyle.

Blackton had been racing two boats called *Vita* and *Viva* without notable success. During the summer of 1912 he bought two Smith-Ryan *Baby Reliance* hydroplanes. H. Cole Estep explained the provenance to his *Power Boating* magazine readers: "Blackton bought two boats . . . . *Baby Reliance* and *Baby Reliance II*. The former is the original 20-footer that was built last winter, the same one that sunk at Detroit and that appeared at Davenport with an eight-cylinder Sterling Engine. *Baby Reliance II* was the same hull that performed at Davenport with a 12-cylinder Van Blerck motor under the name *Baby Reliance III* . . . . A new *Baby Reliance III*, 26 feet long, has been built and entered in the International race. This boat is powered with the same Van Blerck that was installed in the 20-foot *Baby Reliance III* at Davenport." Amidst this game of musical motors and hulls, the "babies" were doing well. After losing $1,500 to Lee Counselman's *Kitty Hawk II* in a close match race at Detroit when *Baby II* flipped on a swell with Jay Smith at the wheel, the Smith-Ryan performance improved.

The 20' Adolph Apel-built Sand Burr II *wedged between two other competitors. Widely campaigned, the boat was undefeated until meeting* Kitty Hawk II. *Blackton's quadruple-engine* Viva *is on the port side of* Sand Burr.

At the Mississippi Valley Power Boat Association's 1912 Independence Day meet at Davenport, the babies swept the field, running in all classes up to 40'. Baldy Ryan himself drove and toyed with his competitors, turning in 27-mile-per-hour heat speeds. It was enough to win against the slow field. Grumbling was heard that the *Reliances* were ''a frost.'' The next day Ryan let the 20-footer run a little harder, and a new 20' class record was established of 35.85 miles per hour. After winning yet another race, Ryan, with Jay Smith at the engine, put on a mile exhibition run. Going with the 3-mile-per-hour current, the Van Blerck-powered *Baby Reliance III* ran the mile before a crowd of thousands at 53.73 miles per hour. The course had been laid out by government engineers, and the run was timed by the Admiral and Commodore of the M.V.P.B.A. Wrote one correspondent, ''Will any gentlemen from the east attempt to impeach such testimony?''

The *Reliances* went east for the Harmsworth Trophy contest on Long Island in late August. Trials to select the American team were in complete disarray, and on the morning of the race the final selection had not been made. J. Stuart Blackton was told that he could not drive *Baby Reliance II* since he was not an American citizen. The fact that he had driven in the race the year before did not change the committee's decision. Bernard Smith was hastily designated as the driver. When the selection process was complete,

Baby Reliance II with Chris Smith's son Bernard at the helm during the Harmsworth Trophy race. The peculiar sheer and round bilges show clearly. The engine turned a V-drive with a 1.25 step-up located forward.

the Babies *II* and *III* were chosen, as was *Ankle Deep*, a new boat designed by Clinton Crane and owned by a Polish count married to the daughter of a wealthy New York lawyer. Count Casimir Mankowski had capsized the boat at the Gold Cup races a few weeks before, and only the presence of an airtight compartment kept *Ankle Deep* off the bottom of the St. Lawrence. *Deep* was a 32' single-step hydroplane carrying a pair of 150-horsepower, 1,283-cubic-inch Sterling engines set well aft and behind the driver, who operated the throttles with foot pedals. A small cockpit behind the engines accommodated the mechanic.

The British challengers of 1912 were *Maple Leaf IV*, fielded by the persistent McKay Edgar, and *Mona*, a 26' Thornycroft hull designed to plane amidships and carrying 150 horsepower. The IV was a Fauber-designed and Saunders-built five-step hydroplane of 39'11'' length and 8' beam. She carried a pair of V-8 Austin engines of 350 horsepower each, and her pilot was the famed aviator Thomas Octave Murdoch Sopwith, who perched high above the hull in a seat like that of *Dixie IV*.

The Easterners were getting their first glimpse of Algonac-style raceboats. Describing *Baby II*, C.G. Davis wrote: "She was full-sided, full-bilged with a rather hard bilge rounding into a bottom that was absolutely flat across and fore and aft also. Just the slightest dimple at the waterline, a very little unfairness of line, showed where the step began aft of her motor. And her step is a very decided one, being about six inches deep, with air fed into it through two big copper ventilators curved up inside the boat above the waterline." He went on to describe a painted canvas deck, an auto steering wheel controlling iron rudders via ropes, and a gas tank all the way aft. The construction was "exceedingly light, single planked about 3/8 inch thick

Count Casimir Mankowski warms up the twin Sterlings of the Crane hydroplane Ankle Deep. *Just a few weeks before, Mankowski capsized the boat while learning how to drive it during the Gold Cup races.*

clinch-nailed to flat timbers, but is greatly stiffened with an arched sort of clamp — a wide flat board, which answered the same purpose as a hog frame on a steamer to prevent the boats bending out of shape . . ." Charles Davis probably did not know that the shore of the St. Clair River was home to many a shipbuilder familiar with "hog frames" and that among the 15 Smith-Ryan employees were at least two such men.

"It looked like a rotten race, about the worst I ever saw," was the blunt assessment of one reporter. *Leaf* was 21 minutes late in starting, a slipping transmission preventing her from getting underway. The problem was solved by a resourceful mechanic who dumped a pocket full of nails into the defective unit, locking it up. Off roared *Maple Leaf IV*. Out on the course, *Baby II* had passed *Mona* and *Ankle Deep*, which went over the line ahead of her. When the little 20-footer completed the first round at a rate of 44.54 miles per hour, cheers, bells, horns and whistles filled the air from the fleet of 600 spectator boats. *Deep* had slowed severely, and *Baby III* went down, engine dead and the boat drifting. *Baby Reliance II* was first across the line, 48 minutes, 39 seconds after the starting gun. *Mona* was next, 12 minutes behind the leader. Ultimately all the boats finished, with *Ankle Deep* taking nearly two and a half hours to complete the course.

In the pits a dog, a boy and miscellaneous spectators survey Ankle Deep. *Clinton Crane believed that the hard chines of* Deep *were the key characteristic of a hydroplane, not the amidships step.*

After a day's postponement for a Nor'easter, the next race was held in the still-rough waters off Huntington. These were conditions which favored the "seaworthy" *Maple Leaf* and *Ankle Deep*. They took the lead, but the failure of a torpedo boat to be on station for the first turn confused both drivers, and *Baby II* caught up with the leaders. It was not long before both *Ankle Deep* and *Baby III* developed carburetor trouble, black smoke pouring from their exhausts. *Leaf* pulled farther ahead in the chop, coming in first but at an average speed of only 30.9 miles per hour. Three minutes behind was *Mona*, followed by *Ankle Deep*, and *Baby III*. *Baby II* was more than seven minutes behind the leader and had managed barely 24 miles per hour. The competition was now tied, one race for the British, one for the Americans.

Wednesday, September 3, 1912, was the day on which the fate of the trophy was decided. It was cool and damp so the engines could develop maximum power while the surface of the Sound was "oily-smooth." It was a day made for the *Reliances*. After a ragged start, *Ankle Deep* and *Baby II* opened a growing gap between them and third-place *Maple Leaf*. Both ran strongly, completing the first lap at 45 miles per hour. Slowing slightly on the second lap, *Baby II* watched *Deep* pull ahead, but *Maple Leaf* was almost a minute behind the leader. On the third lap *Reliance II*'s clutch failed, the result of a faulty overhaul. On that same lap *Mona* went out. Now there were three. *Ankle Deep*'s lead widened to 1:10 over *Maple Leaf* and 3:20 over last-place *Baby III*. On the fourth and final lap *Ankle Deep* had made the final turn and was running hard for the finish when a propeller shaft snapped. *Maple Leaf* drove "majestically" by to win at 43.125 miles per hour. After four years of

The future meets the past. Well behind Maple Leaf IV, Baby Reliance II *and* Ankle Deep *fight for second place. The relative size of the two boats is very clear. The large, high-freeboard Crane boats would soon be superseded by 20-and 26-footers with the largest possible engines.*

The Fauber patent multi-step hydroplane Maple Leaf IV *aboard her lighter,* Commissioner. *The sawtooth-like steps in the bottom and the helmsman's high seat in the stern can both be seen.*

American *Dixie* victories, the Harmsworth Trophy went back to England. Non-plussed by the official time sheets, Smith-Ryan advertised that their boats won two out of three Harmsworth races.

Based on their great success in racing, attempts were made to sell hydroplanes as fast runabouts. Irwin Chase at Elco developed a novel two-step boat with planes made of roofing-like corrugated metal. Taking a page from racing history, a contest with a steam yacht was arranged. This pitted the 60-horsepower, 16' Elco *Bug* owned by J.S. Blackton's partner, Alfred E. Smith, against the 185' *Helenita*, owned by Commodore Frank J. Gould of the American Yacht Club. The stakes were $5,000, winner take all, and the course of 77.1 statute miles was from Huntington, Long Island, to New London, Connecticut, the reverse of the *Vamoose-Norwood* contretemps two decades before. The first race was aborted when *Bug* broke her drive chain within sight of the starting line.

Commodore Gould insisted on a rematch after repairs were made to *Bug*. Four days later the race took place. At the helm of *Bug* was A.E. Smith with Elco's Irwin Chase in charge of the motor. *Helenita* was stripped for action, boiler fires optimized, and manned by her professional crew. Wearing inflatable life preservers, Smith and Chase roared across the line with the gun at exactly 2:00 P.M. At 4:53 P.M. *Bug* pulled up to the New York Yacht Club station at New London, a comfortable

Minutes ahead of the only other boat still running, McKay Edgar's Maple Leaf IV *cruises to victory in the 1912 Harmsworth Trophy races. Leaf took the trophy back to England, where it remained for many years.*

53 minutes ahead of *Helenita*. She promptly turned about and returned to the Sound to escort the steamer in. Massive publicity followed, but sales of Elco hydroplanes were modest. The company offered a line of 16′, 20′, and 26′ "Elcoplanes" for several years and then dropped the boats. The price of $3,500 for a 16′ boat undoubtedly limited the market since the average American labored six years to earn that amount.

No less a firm than Tams, Lemoine & Crane attempted to commercialize the single-step hydroplane, bringing forth a 20′ runabout version called the *Dixie, Jr.* About a dozen were sold with a guaranteed speed of 35 miles per hour and a price of $4,500. The engine was a 60-horsepower Sterling six. W.K. Vanderbilt bought one as a yacht tender, then sold it a few months later. Difficult boats to handle, the *Juniors* were frequently modified by their owners. With extensive changes to the forward section, a *Junior* called *PDQ II* won the Gold Cup in 1912 with a best lap of 36.8 miles per hour. Beaten in that contest — by a small margin — was the Smith-Ryan *Baby Reliance.*

To some the victory of a "stock" boat was laden with social import. John Robinson, editor of *Power Boating*, wrote that the victory of *PDQ II* proved . . . "that the comparatively poor man, who utilizes up-to-date development of engineering skill . . . can put the cleaner on the prodigiously wealthy sportsman. While not socialists, we take a socialist view of the power boat racing situation and when a small moderately powered outfit which an ordinary citizen can afford to own, wins an important series the result is worth cheering." J.G. Robinson was articulating a problem. Racing was in numerical decline. From a peak of 900 races in the summer of 1909, the number had fallen to about half that. Even more significant was that the pleasureboat industry was not growing and was mired at about $3.9 million in revenues, a third below its peak of $6.1 million before the Panic of 1907. Meanwhile, the automobile business had shot to $331 million, over 80 times larger. The vitality of the industry was at risk, and Robinson probably felt that affordable racing would attract new buyers. But it was not to happen anytime soon.

Elco made real efforts to transform the hydroplane from a race boat to a runabout. This huge 35-foot Fauber type carried fittings for an immense canvas top and a windshield in a futile attempt to civilize the boats.

These Charles G. Davis drawings show the sterns of the Elcoplane and Dixie Jr. types. The corrugations on the bottom of the Elcoplane are visible as is the integrated rudder and strut of the Dixie Jr.

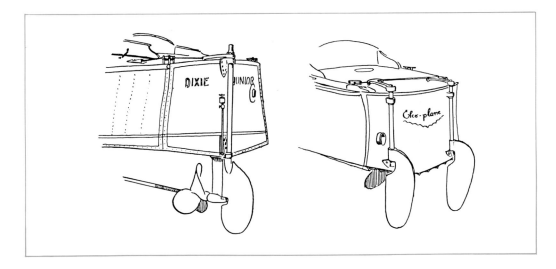

The profile and plan of the Dixie Jr. by Tams, Lemoine and Crane. One of these "stock" boats with 60 horsepower defeated a Baby Reliance for the Gold Cup.

With the industry in stasis, well-known designers were leaving the field. It was about this time that Clinton Crane used his family connections to secure the leadership of the St. Joseph Lead Company, a firm of which he was already a director. After a stockholder lawsuit against Crane, other directors and the executives was settled, Crane became president of the company. Other well-known designers also defected. W. Starling Burgess took up the design of flying machines, and Henry Gielow focused his activity on luxury motor yachts. At Elco Henry Sutphen and Irwin Chase identified cruising boats as the target of opportunity.

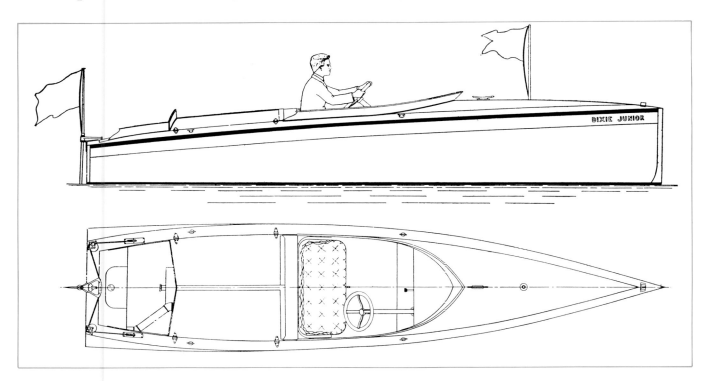

John L. Hacker moved from Detroit to Albany and opened a boat company with L.L. Tripp, who had been Van Blerck's Eastern sales agent. The Hacker Boat Company concentrated on the larger market for fast runabouts. Joe Van Blerck sold an interest in his engine company to a man from Monroe, Michigan, and the company moved there. Before long Van Blerck's connection to the firm that bore his name was severed. The Smith-Ryan Boat & Engine Company dissolved with Baldy Ryan's bankruptcy. Ryan capital and aggressive promotion had moved C.C. Smith from the obscure life of a riverman to a modest prominence. It was Ryan who would now live in obscurity until his death in 1930.

While true planing forms dominated racing, the ordinary launch was still likely to have its bow firmly down in the water, throwing off a wave like the race boats of a decade earlier.

9

WITH LIBERTIES
FOR ALL

The young Bosnian student named Prinzip leaped from the crowd. Three reports from a Browning later, the heir to the throne of the Hapsburgs and his wife were mortally wounded; two hours later Archduke Francis Ferdinand and the Duchess of Hohenberg were both dead. It was Sunday, June 28, 1914, and within two months there were 14 declarations of war among the nations of Europe. It was a war that would envelop 1.7 billion persons, 93% of the world's population. Before it was over, 56.4 million men would take up arms. Of these, 17 million were wounded, and another 7.5 million died in battle. An estimated one million civilians were massacred, and at least another four million died of disease and starvation. More than two dozen governments fell, and the total cost of The Great War was later reckoned at $336 billion.

"Unless a miracle happens there will be no race for the British International Trophy this year," editorialized *Motor Boat* in August 1914. Jim Pugh had taken his *Disturber* across for the race, only to have his boat seized by the British. Ultimately they returned everything but fuel and oil to an America which had declared herself neutral.

On the day Russia began her mobilization — July 29, 1914 — a race was held at Lake George in New York State. It was the fourteenth running of the Gold Cup. Eleven boats entered, nine started and two finished the three-race series. "Some of the owners of the gems of the boatbuilders' art looked at the waves and shivered," was one correspondent's description of the water conditions created by a strong north wind. Cup defender Count Mankowski consented to a postponement despite the fact that his *Ankle Deep* was the boat best suited for rough water. "I'd like everyone to have a chance," was the Count's response.

When the first race was held the next day under calm conditions, *Ankle Deep* placed fifth. In first place was J. Stuart Blackton's *Baby Reliance V.* Following her was another Blackton boat, *Baby Speed Demon II. Buffalo*

Count Mankowski contemplates defeat during the Gold Cup races at Lake George. As the defender, Mankowski agreed to a postponement due to rough water; in the second race Ankle Deep hit a log and was disabled. A few weeks after this picture was taken, Deep was lost to fire.

Enquirer, another Smith-built 20-footer, was third while *PDQ V*, owned by the 1912 Gold Cup winner, A. Graham Miles, was also ahead of the Count. *Ankle Deep*'s 44-mile-per-hour laps were eight miles per hour off the pace of the fastest.

The second day's racing saw more attrition when *Baby Reliance* and *PDQ* failed. *Baby Speed Demon*, with a New York World sportswriter, Bob Edgren, at the helm, and Jack Beebe attending the engine, set a new course record at 50.5 miles per hour. The rest of the field was well behind. With an overnight drop-out the final race started with four boats, but only two finished. On the fifth and final lap the Count's *Ankle Deep* hit "the only log floating in Lake George" and was disabled. *Baby Speed Demon* crossed the line a full four minutes ahead of the second (and last) place *Buffalo Enquirer* with her novice driver.

To emphasize that *Baby II*'s performance was no fluke, the next day she was taken out on mile trials. The average for four runs was 51.8 miles per hour, a new record. The 20' by 7' hydroplane was a new design that differed greatly from the earlier *Reliance* series. Gone were the round bilges, and in their place were hard chines. The step was shallower and placed farther aft while the after section of the bottom was absolutely flat. She carried a bow rudder of the type pioneered by John Hacker on his *Gretchen* hydro. The powerplant was a 200-horsepower, eight-cylinder Sterling that had been extensively modified by Jack Beebe.

Baby Speed Demon II was the new hydroplane type from the C.C. Smith shops in 1914. With hard chines, a forward rudder and much more beam, she was a major advance over the Reliance boats. Demon II captured the mile trophy with a four-run mean speed of 51.8 miles per hour.

While built at the C.C. Smith Boat & Engine Company, it is likely that her design and construction was the work of two brothers, Jack and Martin Beebe. Born in Sackets Harbor, New York, and reared in a family that had built ships since the War of 1812, the brothers left the eastern Lake Ontario village and migrated to Michigan around the turn of the century. They settled in Marine City, probably finding work in the shipyards there. That they were already skilled boatbuilders is likely, since it was not long before they were populating the St. Clair River with St. Lawrence River skiffs. By 1906 they had formed Beebe Brothers and Salisbury to build and repair boats in Marine City. By 1910 at least one of the brothers was in Algonac in another small boatshop, Beebe & Lisee. The other principal was Napoleon Lisee, who went on to build the record-crushing and unremittingly dominant *Miss Americas* for Gar Wood. Not long after Chris Smith and Baldy Ryan formed their joint venture, the Beebes joined forces with Smith and his family. Jack Beebe's specialty was engines; brother Martin's was boatbuilding. Either could do the other's job better than most men. Though neither man completed the primary grades, each was gifted with an uncanny comprehension of the physics of aquatic speed.

Miss Detroit enroute to winning the Gold Cup. At 25' 6'' by 5' 6'', she was an attempt by Jack Beebe to improve the sea-keeping characteristics of the earlier boats.

As the French reeled on their native soil under German attacks, the sixth annual Buffalo regatta was held. It was another set of wins for *Baby Speed Demon II*. On the first day she took a 25-mile event in which *Ankle Deep* was destroyed by fire. On the second day it was a 30-mile race for the Commodore's Trophy in which Edgren and Beebe emerged triumphant over Blackton driving *Baby Reliance V*. In the third race *Baby Speed* was in the lead when the hand pump that pressurized the fuel system failed. Edgren kept driving at full speed, hoping to go as far as possible but certain his engine would die of fuel starvation. Glancing to his left, he saw Jack Beebe whittling something with a knife as they leaped along at 50 miles an hour. Beebe had whittled a washer for the air pump, disassembled the failed unit, and reassembled it. *Baby Speed Demon* had fuel pressure once again, and she went on to win the race at 50.24 miles per hour for 35 miles.

Commodore J. Stuart Blackton did not order a new boat for the 1915 season. His Vitagraph company had exported many films to Europe before the war, and with that revenue gone Blackton apparently felt some need to economize. The Smith shops were turning out the occasional runabout and pleasure hydroplane as well as a few minor race boats such as *Neptune II*. There was, however, one significant new boat from the Smith shops that year: *Miss Detroit*.

''Jack Beebe's latest creation has a world of speed, and after chasing him around thirty nautical miles at Manhasset Bay Saturday afternoon in the cup winner of last year, I'm in a position to know that the new contender for the Demon's honors is as swift, clean running, able a speed boat as ever went after a championship trophy.'' The words were those of Bob Edgren writing in the *New York World* after his defeat by *Miss Detroit* in the Gold Cup races. At 25' 6'' overall and with a beam of 5' 6'', she was larger and proportionately narrower than the earlier boats. A rounded and angled stern reminiscent of the torpedo boats of a decade earlier had the aerodynamic purpose of controlling turbulence. By lessening the angle of the forward plane, the tendency to leap was greatly reduced. This was a departure from the conventional wisdom which held that a leaping boat was faster as long as the propeller did not leave the water. *Miss Detroit*'s engine was the almost mandatory eight-cylinder Sterling with a factory rating of 250 horsepower.

Detroit's construction had been commissioned by the Miss Detroit Powerboat Association, whose officers consisted of some of the city's most prominent citizens. Among them were Hugh Chalmers of the Chalmers Motor Company, William Metzger of automaker E.M.F., C.H. Wills of the Ford Motor Company, publisher William Scripps and Horace E. Dodge, Sr. of Dodge Brothers. A fund drive commenced, and 260 pledges later there was sufficient cash to pay for the new racer. Despite the millionaires heading the Association, C.C. Smith was still due a balance of $1,800 on *Miss Detroit* a year later.

The Gold Cup — now the most prestigious speedboat trophy in the nation since the cessation of Harmsworth competition — was held again at Manhasset Bay in August 1915. A boat called *Tiddledy Wink* that claimed 82 miles an hour by virtue of her flying hull was entered. She was designed and

John "Freckles" Milot and Jack Beebe stand in front of Miss Detroit while an unidentified boy peers around the bow. This was the team that took the Gold Cup west for the first time.

built by A.E. Luders. Count Mankowski entered his *Ankle Deep Too*. The *Too* was a radical design by Fred Chase of Tams, Lemoine and Crane; essentially she was a double-ended hull intended to plane on the center section. She had sunk twice during tests. Blackton's *Demon* and *Reliance* were ever-present threats, and a few other boats, mostly unproven, rounded out the field. An entry list of 17 racers was whittled to seven for the actual start of the first race. Five started the second race, and three began the third. "It was a debacle deluxe for speed work in the east," said one reporter. "Speed boat racing is just like marriage," quipped J. Stuart Blackton, "one damn thing after another." Blackton had lost by almost a minute in the first race and did not start the second.

Miss Detroit's victory was made all the more surprising by the fact that she was driven by Johnny Milot, a Detroit real-estate salesman, who had not driven any boat in competition before. Five minutes before the start of the race the designated driver, William Metzger, could not be found. Milot, who had driven the boat in testing but was there as a mechanic's helper, was hastily drafted and placed in the cockpit with Jack Beebe. Without knee pads, goggles or helmet, Milot was severely bruised by the hard ride and dazed by inhaling the engine exhaust. Holding Milot in the boat, Beebe steered and operated the engine. So confused was the situation that *Detroit*, *Demon* and *Presto* kept racing and completed two additional laps of the five-mile course before officials were able to flag them in.

"I didn't know the race was over. Nobody told me when it would be. I guess they didn't have time to," said John Milot. Astonished reporters would later ask "Freckles" Milot if he had ever driven in a race before. Milot

Described as identical to the short-lived Baby Marold, Whip-Po'-Will, Jr. *was built by the Beebe brothers for A.P.B.A. president A.L. Judson. Campaigned for several years, she sank in England, but not before becoming the first boat to reach 70 miles per hour. She was powered by a Duesenberg-Bugatti aero engine when this photo was taken.*

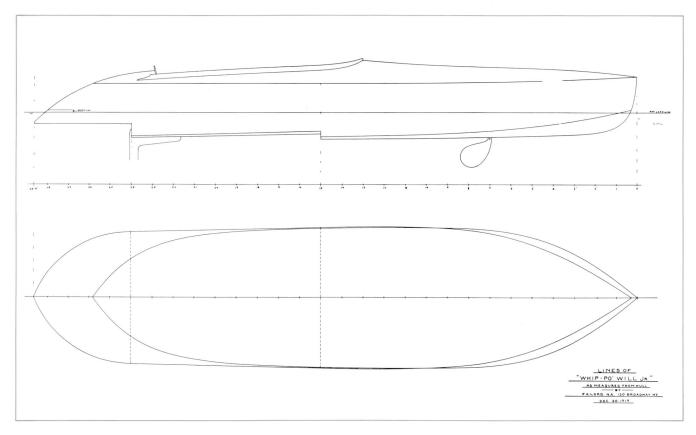

LINES OF
"WHIP-PO' WILL JR"
AS MEASURED FROM HULL
BY
F.K.LORD N.A. 130 BROADWAY N.Y.
DEC 30 1919

responded that he had not. "Have you ever driven a car?" asked another. "Nope," was Milot's reply. Then, after a hesitation: "I've driven a Ford." The nautical demolition derby continued for two more days; when it was over, America had a folk hero in "Freckles" Milot, and Detroit had the Gold Cup.

The Beebe brothers left the C.C. Smith Boat and Engine Company in 1916. Some whispered that it was the end for the Wizard of Algonac and that without the Beebe brothers Smith could not continue. The prophecy proved false, and the Smiths, Nap Lisee and nine other men continued to build fast boats.

The major Beebe project of 1916 was the construction of *Baby Marold* for Childe Harold Wills. Wills, a self-trained engineer, had done extensive work on vanadium steel, and his knowledge of metallurgy played a critical role in the engineering of the Model T Ford. So valuable was C.H. Wills to Henry Ford that there was a special arrangement in which Ford gave Wills a percentage of his profits. This unprecedented understanding created vast wealth for C.H. Wills, and in 1916 he decided to go boat racing.

Martin and Jack Beebe designed *Baby Marold*, and Martin built her in the second-floor shop of the McLouth Shipyards in Marine City. Jack Beebe installed a huge modified Van Blerck V-12 engine rated at 500 horsepower. John Milot was to drive and Jack Beebe was to handle the Van Blerck. Bigger than *Miss Detroit* at 28' by 7', *Baby Marold* was very, very fast.

Naval architect F.K. Lord drew these study plans of Whip *in 1919, probably as part of a project to develop a new boat for Judson. The Beebes lofted their hulls directly from half-models and did not use drawings.*

117

It was a field of six that competed for the Gold Cup in 1916. Chris Smith's shop had built another "syndicate" boat, this time *Miss Minneapolis*. At 20' by 6' 6" she was the smallest of the field. Early in the first race it was *Minneapolis* versus *Marold* with the rest of the field behind. During the first lap, the Van Blerck began to miss, but still the Wills boat was able to maintain a pace adequate to finish third. The trouble was diagnosed as fusion of the spark plug electrodes caused by the high engine compression. There were 48 spark plugs in the 12 cylinders. The fusion caused pre-ignition, which fired back into the inlet tract and blew out valving in the carburetor. C. Harold Wills placed an emergency order for spark plugs, telling a crewman to charter a train if necessary. It did not prove necessary.

Miss Minneapolis under way. She was the first to exceed the magical "mile-a-minute" under officially sanctioned conditions, averaging 61.083 miles per hour for six one-mile runs.

On the second day with fresh plugs *Baby Marold* turned a blistering first lap of 6:14 for 55.3 miles per hour. *Miss Minneapolis* managed 50 miles per hour on the same lap. Then it happened. A fuel line broke, pouring gas into the bilge. The explosion threw Johnny Milot overboard. The unflappable Jack Beebe closed the fuel supply, steered the flaming but still-moving *Baby Marold* off the course, and then went overboard. Firemen were unable to put out the fire, so using pike poles, they drove holes in the boat to sink her. Finally, by towing the sinking boat to deeper water they extinguished the blaze. The hull was a total loss. If *Marold*'s life was fast and short, it was also deadly. The next day Edward Lindow was salvaging the remains of *Marold* in the Wills boathouse. When he disconnected the battery, a spark ignited the remaining gasolene. Lindow was knocked overboard by the explosion. The firefighters did not notice Ed Lindow's absence. Unable to swim, he drowned a few feet from the burning wreck he had helped to build.

Miss Minneapolis, with Chris Smith's sons Bernard at the wheel and Jay on the engine, won the first day's race by 14 seconds. On the second day they squeezed ahead of *Miss Detroit* by a scant four seconds. The third day they lost to *Detroit* by one second. On points, "*Miss Minnie*" took the trophy north. In the traditional mile trials held after the Cup races *Miss Minneapolis* ran up and down the measured mile six times, averaging 61.083 miles per hour. Predicted — and sometimes claimed — for the last five years, the "mile-a-minute boat" had finally arrived.

"The Mile a Minute Boat," reads the sign above Miss Minn *at the New York show. C.C. Smith took the trouble to build up the sides of her cradle so that the details of her bottom construction could not be seen easily, but interested parties were frequently found on their backs under the boat during the show.*

In April 1917 the United States became a belligerent. If the mobilization was late, it was also massive. Spending on the war averaged $1 million per hour for the duration, and the $22 billion expended equaled all government costs from 1791 to 1914. Programs for armament, ships and aircraft were hastily assembled. Sub-chasers were ordered by the score to keep the shores of America free of the "Hun Pirates." Designs for patrol and picket boats were quickly considered, then sent out for bid. Motor manufacturers such as Standard and Sterling received orders for hundreds of engines. But the development which most influenced the future of marine speed came from aeronautics. For a time it was known as the United States of America Standard Aircraft Engine, and according to legend it was designed in six days in a room at Washington's Willard Hotel. Admiral David W. Taylor thought a shorter, snappier name was needed and suggested the "Liberty Engine." So it became, and the government took the unusual step of registering Liberty as a trademark, apparently oblivious to the fact that a small Detroit company had manufactured engines under the Liberty name for many years.

The key figure in the Liberty's development was Jesse Gurney Vincent, chief engineer of the Packard Motor Company. Born on an Arkansas farm in 1880, he worked in a blacksmith shop as a child. By age 17 he was employed as a salesman in St. Louis. Later he labored in Joe Boyer's machine shop, working on the

An eight-cylinder competition Sterling being completely rebuilt between heats at the Gold Cup. These motors were soon replaced by aero engines weighing about one-fourth as much for each horsepower generated.

prototypes of an adding machine which became the basis for Burroughs Corporation. When Boyer and the Burroughs firm moved to Detroit, Vincent went along. Now with the title Superintendent of Inventions and with the benefit of correspondence courses in engineering, Vincent left Burroughs to take an engineering job with Hudson. After a short stay he joined Packard as Chief Engineer.

It was Packard's work on aircraft and racing-car engines that formed the nucleus for Liberty development. In a matter of a few days, Vincent and E.J. Hall of the Hall-Scott Motor Company, together with two draftsmen, synthesized the best aircraft-engine practice from Europe and the United States and developed a preliminary design. After quick approval from the Aircraft Production Board, the complex process of taking the basic design to production began. Within seven months Liberty engines were rolling off the lines, part of a $240 million Congressional appropriation for 45,250 aircraft engines.

The Liberty was one of the great industrial achievements of World War I, and 20,458 engines were built by Packard, Ford, Buick, Cadillac, Lincoln and Nordyke-Marmon. The vast Liberty effort was not without its critics. Among them was the sculptor of Mount Rushmore, Gutzon Borglum. Using his friendship with President Woodrow Wilson, Borglum was authorized to inspect aircraft production. Borglum attacked the Liberty, issuing critical press releases alleging serious design flaws. An immense furor ensued; it was quenched only when Borglum's own plans to produce aircraft were exposed.

What the well-found yacht carried in 1917. Companies such as Elco offered deck guns as options at the New York Motor Boat Show, and cruisers were sold with the claim that they could be converted to naval service.

In the investigations following Borglum's charges, Jesse Vincent was accused of conflict of interest. It was alleged that he had made a profit of $55.00 on the Liberty through Packard stock he owned. The fact that he had also foregone his $50,000 annual salary while in service to the government did not seem to impress the investigators. Ultimately a Presidential pardon relieved Vincent, but the government was left with a much larger dilemma: what to do with 11,810 Liberty aircraft engines now that the Great War was won. The problem was not quickly solved, and in 1924 the Air Service calculated that the supply of Liberties would last until 1950.

There were, however, a few men in Michigan who had ideas about how the engines could be used. One of them was Howard Grant, a former inspector in the Liberty engine program. With considerable foresight, Grant purchased scrap and surplus from the manufacturers when Liberty production was discontinued. There was enough material to allow Grant to build complete engines, and this was exactly what he did. The C.C. Smith Boat & Engine Company was soon offering Grant-Liberty engines. The latest strategic technology, the product of the best engineering and manufacturing minds of the nation, the engine built to help win ''the war to end all wars,'' was now available to anyone able to pay $4,500.

A major war effort for the nation's boatbuilders was the construction of more than 400 of these 110' submarine chasers. Each was powered by three 5,184-cubic-inch Standard engines developing 220 horse-power at 400 rpm. After the war the boats were sold as surplus for as little as $900. While some were converted to yachts, the SCs became a favorite with rumrunners.

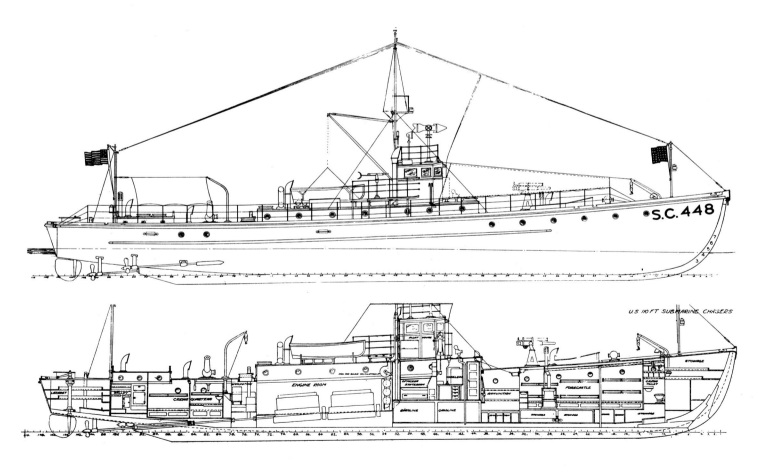

The renowned and controversial Liberty engine as it appeared when completed at the Packard Motor Car Company. The 5'' by 7'' L-12 displaced 1,650 cubic inches and developed 400 horsepower at 1,800 rpm in the first production versions.

Liberties being moved to and from test cells where each was run before shipment. Almost 20,500 engines were produced, and the post-war surplus was soon used for racing, rumrunning and pleasureboating.

While Chris Smith's name was still on the sign, he was no longer in control of the little company. He had sold his business to Garfield Arthur Wood. The Smith family were now employees. G.A. Wood was born in Mapleton, Iowa, near the Missouri River in December 1880, the second-oldest of 12 children. The family moved to Minnesota where Wood's father worked as a harbor pilot, and as an adolescent Wood crewed on lake boats which his father commanded. There were the standard harbingers of success: Wood fixed clocks, sharpened knives and otherwise showed signs of industry and inquisitiveness as a young man. He also briefly attended Chicago's prestigious Armour Institute of Technology. Wood's first racing experience was with a boat called *Leading Lady* that he encountered while watching a boat race. She had been built by a house carpenter from plans by George Crouch published in *Motor Boat.* The engine was a large six-cylinder, 5'' by 5'', 589-cubic-inch, two-cycle Emerson, which was not running well. Wood the spectator used his knowledge of electricity — he was then selling lightning rods for a living — to repair the ignition and then rode as *Lady*'s mechanic.

Finished a few days before the big 1911 Independence Day meet in Davenport, Iowa, *Lady* placed second in one race after cutting a buoy and circling back around it. She failed to finish another. A revised *Leading Lady* appeared in 1912, still under the ownership of W.P. Cleveland of Galena, Illinois. She was soundly thrashed by two of the Smith-Ryan *Baby Reliances* but did place first in a two-boat race on the third day. The season of 1913 brought forth *Little Leading Lady*, a 14' single-step boat "built somewhat on the order of the French bass-fiddle type, her beam narrowing down from a third of her length aft. With her tumblehome this gives a sheerline somewhat the appearance of a dog's hind leg. Her pilot sits out over the transom on a sort of back porch." These boats were Gar Wood's training ground, and it is perhaps as important as anything that at the Mississippi Valley races he was able to see the champions compete. He saw not only the *Reliances*, but *Baby Speed Demon*, "Dynamite" Jim Pugh's *Disturbers* and J.L. Hacker's *Kitty Hawks* at these meets.

If Wood's introduction to racing was inauspicious, a clue to the future was provided at the Gold Cup races in 1916. The *Detroit News* sponsored an express-cruiser race that year, and a totally unknown G.A. Wood entered a boat called *Wood Hydraulic.* By this time Wood had moved to Detroit and was making a fortune with his patent for the hydraulically-operated dump

The excellent power-to-weight ratio of aero engines was considered advantageous in high-speed boats years before the Liberty. J.S. Blackton's Vitagraph Pictures partner, Alfred E. Smith, experimented with twin Curtiss V-8s in Hazel II *for the 1914 season, but he was unsuccessful.*

For many years William Harnden Foster gently satirized marine activities in the pages of Motor Boat. *The amazing new technology of the hydroplane was a frequent Foster subject.*

An early Liberty marine conversion in Miss Toronto, *a Smith design. The port exhaust is bent away from the driver so that hot exhaust gases will not blow in his face. The riding mechanic found a place for himself with the machinery in this 55-mile-per-hour racer.*

The History of the Motor Boat—Part X

By William Harnden Foster

The hydroplane idea reaches the Maine coast.

truck. The "cruiser" was a Van Blerck-powered Hacker monoplane with an improvised cabin attached. Against a field of three 65' displacement cruisers, the result was predictable, and so was the flurry of protests when *Wood Hydraulic* finished well ahead of the field. Garfield Arthur Wood withdrew the boat before the committee could determine its legality.

When Gar Wood appeared at the Detroit Exchange Club with an offer to purchase the well-used *Miss Detroit* for the $1,800 owed on terms of $1,000 cash and a note for $800, he knew both what he was buying and the men who built her. It was not long before he bought an interest in the C.C. Smith Boat and Engine Company. This was only the beginning, and Gar Wood would become as powerful a force for speed on water as the Liberty engine.

10

AMERICA THE WET

*A*lcoholic beverages were big business, very big business. Americans drank an average of 20 gallons per year for each, man, woman and child in the United States in the years before Prohibition. The Department of Commerce estimated that more than $1 billion was invested in breweries, distilleries and wineries; it was more than a quarter of the total investment in the production of all food and beverages. There were accurate data on spirits production, and there was a reason: in the years after the Civil War taxes on alcohol contributed a massive share of the United States government's revenues. In 1900, 35 cents of every tax dollar came from the taxes on alcoholic drinks. By 1915 this had fallen to 30 cents. There was also a reason for this change; a new source of revenue had been tapped. It was called income tax.

Freed of the practical need to permit the consumption of alcoholic beverages, the bureaucrats and politicians were able to listen anew to the moral arguments of the temperance forces. Not a new movement, the idea of outlawing alcohol was almost as old as the nation. Temperance societies were in existence before the War of 1812, and there was also smuggling of rum in that same war. Through the activities of Harriet Beecher Stowe, Carrie Nation and many others, the temperance movement grew for more than a century, and its message made sense to millions. It was argued, for example, that taxes could be cut since poorhouses, asylums and jails would be freed of the victims of alcohol. The proposition was advanced that the grain used to produce alcohol would be more positively turned into bread to feed the poor. The amount was reckoned at 11 million loaves per year.

A critical point was reached during World War I when it was revealed that a brewer's association lobbied not only for beer but for the political aims of Germany. By the time national Prohibition was voted by Congress in the form of the Eighteenth Amendment, 33 states already had dry laws. On January 14, 1919, Nebraska became the thirty-sixth state to ratify the

Captain Bill McCoy is on the right holding a plate. The lady is Gertrude Lithy, an agent for Haig & McTavish's scotch. The ever-gallant McCoy allowed the "Rum Queen" on board to superintend the sale of 1,000 cases of whiskey over the side.

Volstead Act. One year later alcoholic beverages were entirely outlawed, not only in individual villages, towns, cities, counties or states as before, but nationally.

There were, of course, a few exceptions. Alcoholic beverages could be prescribed for medicinal purposes. In the first six months 15,000 doctors applied for the license needed to write such prescriptions. In that same six months more than 100,000 illegal prescriptions were written for alcohol in Chicago alone. The American Medical Association, a supporter of Prohibition before it was enacted, shortly reversed its position and joined the "wet" minority. Industrial use of alcohol was also permitted, and hundreds of new chemical companies were formed to exploit the opportunity. Almost immediately entrepreneurs began manufacturing distillation kits for household use, and the phrase "home brew" entered the language.

A contact boat heads for shore with a load of contraband. Developed from the Jersey shore surf and fishing boats, these matured into fast, seaworthy small boats easily capable of evading Coast Guard vessels.

There were two other basic ways to obtain spirits. The first was to purchase the products of illegal stills that existed not only in rural areas but in major cities with the remunerated complicity of local government. Federal forces seized and destroyed 5,000 stills in 1923 alone. For those with a thirst for quality, there was no alternative but imported drink. Only briefly was there the problem of how to get it. A logistical genius of rumrunning was not long in appearing. His name was Captain Bill McCoy, and his methods were as simple as they were profitable.

Born in New York in 1877, Bill McCoy moved as a boy to Philadelphia with his family. There, on the waterfront, he became fascinated with ships. When his family moved to Florida in 1900, McCoy went along and worked his way up to mate on *Olivet*, a passenger steamer which worked the Key West-Havana route. It was probably at Key West that McCoy first encountered the venerable trades of the smuggler and wrecker, for both had been a source of wealth in the Keys.

Bill McCoy and his brother Ben, however, took up the lawful occupation of boat-building, and McCoy claimed that he had built sailboats for the Vanderbilts, Carnegies and Wanamakers while in Florida. The McCoys' next venture was a motorboat service that worked a route between Jacksonville and Palm Beach, then through the Everglades to Fort Myers. Improved roads and bus service were putting an end to this business when an old acquaintance appeared,

Ready for the "go-through men," an Arethusa *crew member sights down a light machine gun. The ammunition box carries the markings of a New York National Guard Armory.*

driving a big car. Mr. McCoy's nautical skills might have profitable use in transporting liquor, the acquaintance suggested. Before long McCoy sold his boat service and invested the proceeds in a Down-East fishing schooner, *Henry L. Marshall*. The 90-footer cost $16,000 and was refitted at a cost of $4,000. McCoy's first trip — he landed 1,500 cases at Savannah — netted a profit of $15,000, almost paying for the *Marshall* in a single venture. In 1920 bootlegging was a profitable and not particularly difficult business. Neither the government nor organized crime had yet taken a serious interest. Both would.

McCoy pioneered a simple pattern for profit from liquid contraband. Using Nassau as a base, he purchased liquor wholesale, filled out papers saying he was bound for Halifax, then hovered off a Northeast port city and sold his cargo for cash to contact boats which would take it ashore. With the primitive

Stowing cases aboard a seaplane. While the economics of air smuggling were not as favorable as carrying larger loads by boat, this method was favored by some who preferred the reduced risk of capture.

Loading Canadian whiskey aboard Arethusa, *also known as* Tomoka *and* Marie Celeste, *in Bermuda as legal cargo. "Americans would not drink this junk until our American rye and bourbon was exhausted," said McCoy.*

state of the law, the government was unable to prevent this. Federal jurisdiction extended only three miles off the coast, and no law or treaty provision proscribed the sale of cargo on the high seas. To further enhance immunity, McCoy vessels flew the British flag. It was a convenient arrangement to prevent seizure and subtly ironical since McCoy's beverages originated in the United Kingdom. The Bahamian government was more than pleased to accommodate the new trade; they received a tariff of $6 for every case landed on their soil.

Soon others applied the McCoy techniques, so McCoy developed another source of supply: two tiny islands off the coast of Newfoundland, territories of France, called St. Pierre et Miquelon. Not blessed with a tropical climate, but much closer to the major markets, the little village of St. Pierre rapidly grew into a major export facility with a warehouse capacity of 750,000 cases of liquor. Bermuda also became a transhipment point for

spirits, and there appeared off the eastern coast from Montauk to Atlantic City an alcoholic armada called "Rum Row." Up to 150 "blacks," as the Coast Guard called these vessels, stood off the territorial limit. Tramp steamers, coasting and fishing schooners, old military vessels, virtually anything able to float and carry a load, dispensed case lots for cash over their rusty, rotting and unpainted sides to contact boats, which ran the cargo ashore. While the economics varied with supply, demand, enforcement and corruption levels, a wholesale case of fine whiskey cost $12 to $15 at a legal port. Its value might be $25 to $30 over the side and $30 to $40 at the shore three miles away. In New York or Boston the value of the same case was at least double the shore price.

For a time there were only rumors of mysterious ships "lurking offshore"; neither the government nor the smugglers were eager to discuss their activities. But in August of 1921 a reporter made his way to Bill McCoy's

More than 500 blacks were seized by the Coast Guard and converted for government use. One of the prizes was Mary. She represented a typical shore boat of the mid-1920s that was purpose-built for rumrunning.

Arethusa, lying an estimated 20 miles from New Bedford with a cargo of Scotch, gin and champagne. "We transact business here day and night . . ." Bill McCoy was quoted as saying. "Come out any time you want to; the law can't touch us here, and we'll be very glad to see you." With controlled fury and embarrassment, Gordon C. McMasters, the chief deputy for Prohibition field forces in Boston, admitted that he "did not see how anything could be done about it," since his group had no boat and no funds to charter one. Another article stated that $6.25 a bottle was the asking price for Scotch, and champagne was $100 a case. "It is believed the ship is bound for Nassau, Bahamas to replenish its supply of liquor and return for more business outside

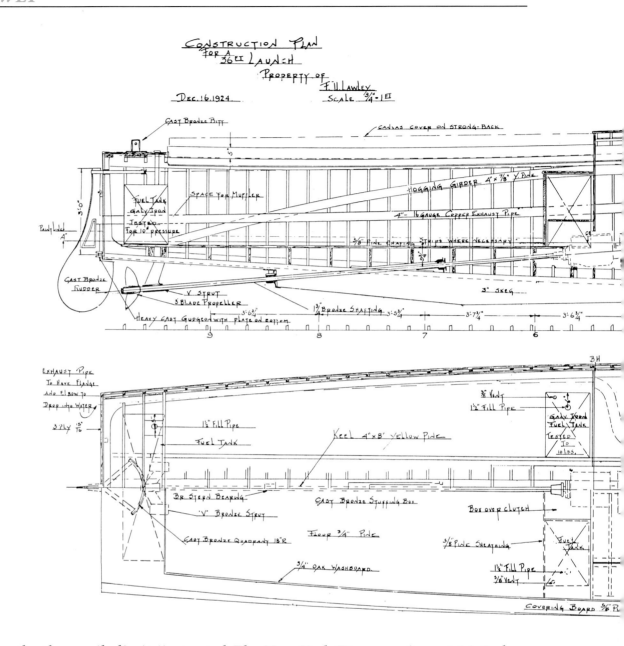

the three-mile limit," reported *The New York Times* on August 14. In less than two weeks *Arethusa* had sold thousands of cases of contraband refreshments.

Like any trade, rumrunning could be improved. Wooden cases were heavy, and they took up valuable space in the hold. Re-packing solved the problem; cases were opened, and their 12 quart bottles were divided into two tightly packed burlap bags of six bottles and some straw. Cargo capacity was doubled and so were profits. McCoy claimed that he was the developer of this packing innovation and another technique which soon proved essential.

The practice of paying cash at shipside meant that the blacks carried huge amounts of cash on board. A 3,000-case cargo might be sold in a week

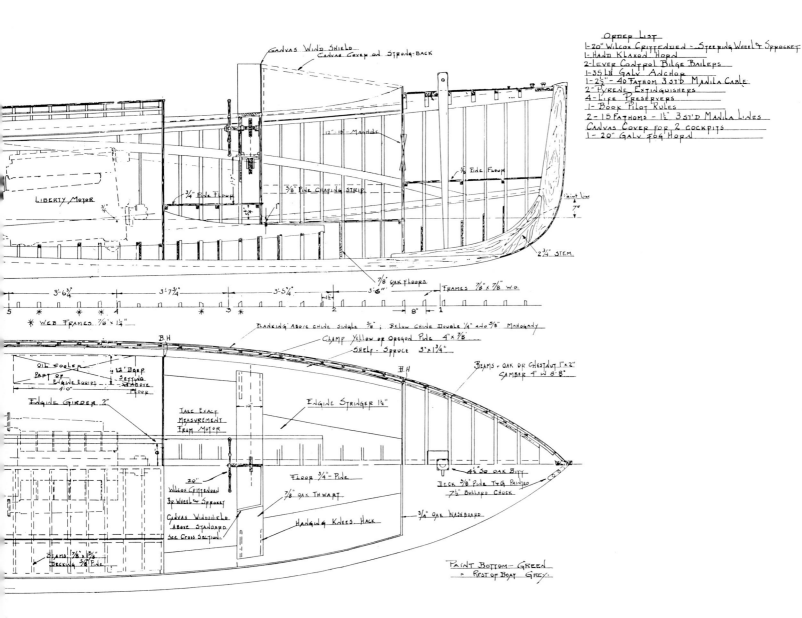

or less, generating a hoard of perhaps $75,000 cash on board. Pirates preyed on the rummies, stealing the money on the high seas. They were called "go-through men," and they would appear about the time that the cargo was gone. Captain McCoy's solution to the problem was the shore-agent system. The cash transaction took place on land, and when the shore boat pulled up for its goods, a crew member presented one half of a dollar bill. If the serial number matched that of a bill on the rum ship, the bearer was entitled to 50 cases. Four bill-parts were presented to obtain the routine 200-case load. Customers also preferred this system since it meant they did not have to carry cash to sea. The "go-through men" could and did still pirate liquor, but this was less convenient.

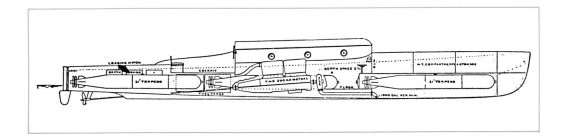

The inboard profile of Sea Hornet II. *The spaces provided for torpedoes were filled with contraband liquor. Watertight compartments, a 2,000-gallon-per-minute pumping system, a 38-mile-per-hour top speed, and a range of 300 miles all contributed to a certain invincibility.*

The inboard profile of Sea Hornet II. *The spaces provided for torpedoes were filled with contraband liquor. Watertight compartments, a 2,000-gallon-per-minute pumping system, a 38-mile-per-hour top speed, and a range of 300 miles all contributed to a certain invincibility.*

The experimental torpedo boat Sea Hornet II *before she joined the wet navy as* Com-An-Go. *The armored hull survived an 800-round fusillade without serious damage when* Com-An-Go *tried to ram a customs cutter off Long Island's Montauk Point.*

All told, Bill McCoy claimed that he sold 175,000 cases during his four years of rumrunning, the value of which would have exceeded $4 million. McCoy seemed unable to resist the lights of publicity and had a penchant for pithy pronouncements: "I sold rum, but I drink water. Congressmen drink rum and vote for water." He claimed, perhaps correctly, that he so embarrassed the government that it had no choice but to "illegally" seize his beloved *Arethusa.* He was sentenced to nine months in jail in March of 1925. "The men who chased and finally caught me were adventurers and sportsmen too," said McCoy. "I have no sore or sour spot in my memory of them, and many of them are to-day my friends." To a public eager for information on a type of smuggling that soon took on aspects of a spectator sport, Captain McCoy was an engaging figure. He sold high-quality goods at fair prices; he openly derided corrupt officials and the "rum mobs" and for years evaded capture while making and spending a fortune. The phrase "real McCoy" came to connote quality and authenticity when used to describe alcoholic contraband.

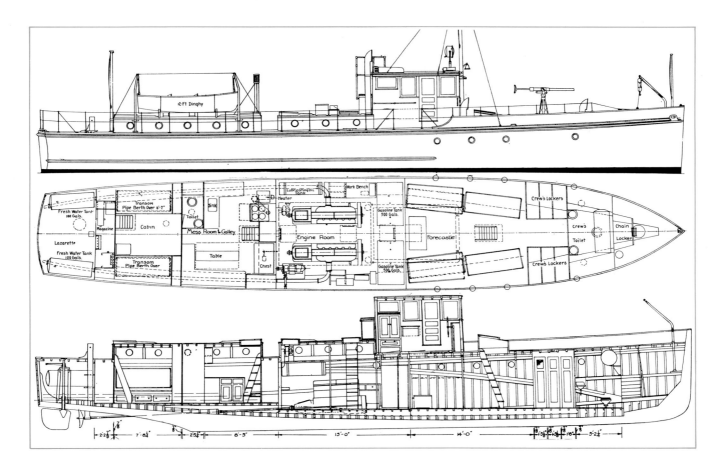

While Bill McCoy may have matched wits and seamanship with government forces, using the sea as an immense and changing playing field where the rules of fair play and ethical conduct were the final arbiters, the game was something entirely different for most of the trade. Industrial alcohol was colored and bottled with counterfeit labels; the rough and sometimes poisonous product of backwoods stills was sold to the unsuspecting; bonded whiskey was diluted; hair tonic was sold as liquor and Colonel Thompson's famous "trench broom" of World War I, the 45-caliber submachine gun, became a tool for negotiations.

It was about money. At first it was fishermen who were lured by it. At $1,000 to $2,000 per night when the average working American made $1,300 per year, there was ample inducement to risk the pirates — always more feared than law enforcement — and bring a load ashore. The federal government was very slow to react; shocked to the point of political paralysis by the lack of respect for law, not until 1923 was the Coast Guard officially ordered to interdict rum traffic. This had been the job of Prohibition agents and local officials. One of the early countermoves by federal forces was the establishment of an expanded zone of territorial waters. The three-mile limit

Fortified by a $14 million appropriation, the Coast Guard responded with the "six-bitter." These 75-footers were powered by a pair of 1,427-cubic-inch, 200-horsepower Sterlings, which could move them at 18 miles per hour. They were used to picket the offshore rumboats.

was broadened to "one hour's steaming," a definition certain to erupt in judicial dispute. A few court cases later, the limit was set at 12 miles.

One response to the widened zone of peril was faster boats. With two nights' proceeds able to pay for a 450-horsepower Gar Wood or Capitol-converted Liberty engine, the greater distance did not long pose a problem for smugglers. Within a few years rum boats with three Liberty engines appeared. They were capable of carrying hundreds of cases at 35 knots. The 12-mile limit translated to 18 minutes from shore, and with such a boat a smuggler could leave at dusk on a winter evening and be back home by 10 P.M., $2,000 richer. The process was repeated, unreckoned thousands of times.

In 1924 a *New York Times* reporter took a trip to rum row and wrote: "The ex-fishermen who have gone into the tricky game have few superiors in the handling of a small boat. Occasionally, one of the smugglers is caught, but for every boat boarded by the government officials, perhaps fifty slip through." There followed a description of a drenching trip to a rum-laden Lunenburg schooner at 30 miles per hour in a sea skiff called *Flipper*. "Cabin boat . . . They is nice and comf-ta-ble alright, but they don't make no time; don't get nowheres," said the skipper as they pounded through the white-caps at Jones Inlet on Long Island. The skipper moved 100 cases that night and made $900, which included $1 per case for storing the liquor for a week.

CG-100, the first of the 75-footers, of which 203 were built. Noted yacht builder John Trumpy was a part of the design team. The vast number of these boats on station ultimately put an end to "Rum Row" by preventing contact with shore boats.

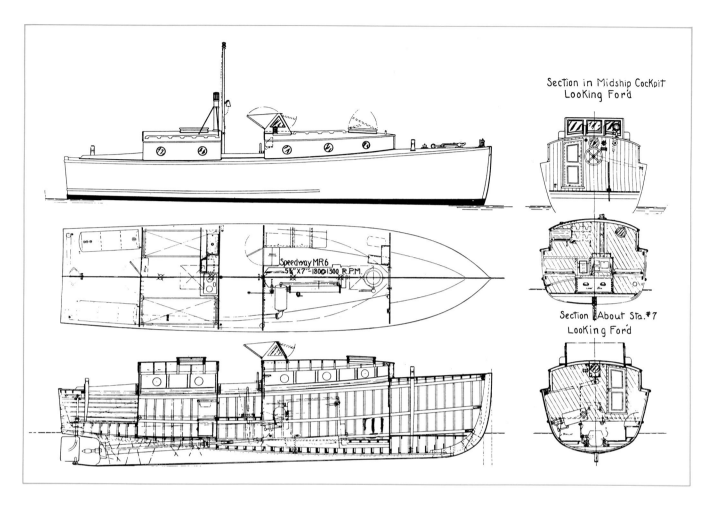

Section in Midship Cockpit
Looking For'd

Speedway MR6
5⅛"X7"–1800 1300 R.P.M.

Section About Sta.#7
Looking For'd

Salty sea skiffs were not the only means of conveyance. One of the most notorious of the Eastern rumrunners was *Cigarette*, a Liberty-powered commuter built for L. Gordon Hammersley, which was enlisted in the wet navy after Hammersley sold her. Claimed capable of 45 miles per hour, the boat was finally seized three months after she rammed the New York City Police boat *Gypsy*. "She would have cut the police boat in two if the blow had been squarely in the middle," but the commander of *Gypsy* ordered the helm hard over, and *Cigarette* hit *Gypsy*'s stern on the starboard side. The crew of the police boat scrambled on board *Cigarette* after the impact and "subdued" her crew. *Cigarette* was quickly returned to duty through the efforts of her lawyers. A few months later she was again captured, this time by the Coast Guard cutter *Argus*. *Argus* seized *Cigarette* and crew at a dock where she had tied up for repairs. No liquor was found, but orders for it were on board as were letters to the crew of an offshore black. Under the new law which prohibited contact with foreign vessels, *Cigarette* was seized and her crew arrested. She became CG-911, but her service record as a part of the "dry" navy was undistinguished.

For inshore interdiction of rum traffic the Coast Guard built more than 100 smaller boats, of which this 36' patrol boat was typical. Able to achieve about 27 miles per hour with a 180-horsepower Speedway engine, it was unevenly matched with the 40 miles per hour which a "fast fisherman" was able to manage.

Wild tales surrounded the movement of contraband. A submarine was delivering spirits at Seattle. A ring had purchased German U-boats and planned to use them to bring beverages to shore. A "booze pipeline" was being built from Canada to the United States. On Lake Champlain ice boats shot across the frozen waters with cargoes of contraband. Radio-controlled torpedoes filled with "hooch" were said to be traversing the Detroit River. It was true that the machinery of war found application in smuggling.

Easily among the most bizarre of the rumrunning vessels was *Com-An-Go*, a 58', 600-horsepower experimental torpedo boat. Called by her designer *Sea Hornet II*, she was a prototype for use in what was apparently a suicide mission in World War I. The plan called for dozens of the one-man *Sea Hornets* to be built and used to torpedo German submarine facilities at Zebrugge.

Com-An-Go had an eventful career of indeterminate length. Abandoned by William B. Shearer, who had promoted the *Sea Hornet* concept, she was stored in a Bayonne yard, from which she was sold for $400 by a federal marshal to satisfy a claim against her. She had cost $40,000 to build. *Sea Hornet II* next came to the attention of authorities as *Com-An-Go* when she tried to ram and sink the customs cutter *Shark* off Long Island's Montauk Point. In the process of defending themselves, the customs men fired 800 machine gun rounds at *Com-An-Go*. These seemed to have no effect on the boat. "I designed her to be completely bullet-proof," said Mr. Shearer in an interview. When found without papers at a Mystic dock, the armor of *Com-An-Go* had more than 50 dents daubed with grey paint, but no serious damage. It

A Greenport Basin & Construction-built version of a Coast Guard "rum chaser" undergoing trials. The huge glass windshield was an obvious hazard in a firefight but was common on many of these boats.

was reported that on the trip back to New York after seizure, *Com-An-Go* made 33 knots. *Com-An-Go* then joined government service as CG-908.

A December 1923 recommendation by President Coolidge that the Coast Guard receive about $14 million in additional vessels and manpower came to fruition by the spring of 1925. The Coast Guard was equipped with a fleet of 75-footers known as ''six-bitters'' and a ''mosquito fleet'' of 36' patrol boats. The latest radio equipment was fitted, and about 3,000 men were added, an increase of 75%. The Coast Guard was now firing on vessels which did not heed their heave-to signal. With the Coast Guard still responsible for its traditional duties of lifesaving and safety at sea and with many inexperienced and low-paid recruits, it was not long before marine mayhem broke out.

A rum chaser fired on Harvard's crew launches when they failed to respond to a signal. On the Great Lakes an auxiliary yawl was rammed and sunk by the Coast Guard. The owner was fined $200. Yachtsmen complained of poor seamanship when boarded. ''I wish they would learn to use fenders,'' said one owner as he surveyed the scarred topsides of his cruiser. At Sandusky, Ohio, on June 28, 1925, CG 2324 fired at a runabout during daylight, seriously wounding the owner. Stray rounds found their way through the Sandusky lighthouse, barely missing the sleeping lightkeeper.

The storm of protest following incidents of this type brought an announcement from the Coast Guard that they would put yachtsmen ''on their honor'' not to smuggle liquor and that they had ''issued orders that vessels which may be *plainly recognized* as yachts or as craft used *solely for pleasure*, be not stopped, boarded or searched . . .'' Yacht prices rose as they were purchased by cash-rich smugglers to take tactical advantage of the new rules.

Not all rumrunners were fast. The rumboat Linwood *was set ablaze by her crew to destroy evidence after evasion failed.*

Lives were lost on both sides as the conflict escalated. Perhaps the most famous incident was that involving *Black Duck*, a Walter McInnis-designed 50' rumrunner capable of 40 knots. *Duck* was spied in Narragansett by CG 290 about 2:00 A.M. on December 29, 1929. Boatswain Alexander C. Cornell was in charge of CG 290. Had it been another war, Cornell would have been revered as an "ace," so outstanding was his record. *Duck* was making fast through the fog for Newport. Sacks were seen piled on her deck, and when she failed to halt when signaled CG 290 opened fire with her deck-mounted machine gun. Three men on board *Black Duck* were killed. The only survivor claimed the Coast Guard did not signal and simply started to "blaze away." A Coast Guard investigation exonerated the crew of CG 290, and a grand jury which was convened failed to indict. Public opinion in some quarters regarded the incident as the equivalent of being shot down for running a red light. A mob in Boston tore down Coast Guard recruiting posters, and two Coast Guardsmen were beaten by another mob. The strengthening wet forces saw a lesson in the episode, and politicians such as Fiorello LaGuardia cited it as evidence that Prohibition could not be enforced.

Illegal alcohol cascaded into the nation, not only from the sea coast but across the Canadian border. Michigan led in this as it did in the development of engines, autos and fast hulls. As early as 1923 reports appeared of an "army" of 25,000 smugglers bringing 100,000 gallons a day across the Detroit River. Once again, geography played a role, and the river, scarcely a mile wide and with a number of small islands, created an ideal crossing point for contraband. "I don't believe a fifty foot wall along the entire Canadian line would make them stop," grumbled a federal agent to a newspaperman.

Five years later Detroit was known as the "Rum Capital of the Nation." In 1927 almost 3.4 million gallons of spirits were legally cleared for export to the States from Windsor, Ontario, alone. It came across with 20 million ferry passengers, a million automobiles and untold thousands of boat trips. A skiff with an outboard would suffice for the 10-minute international journey. One brewery that entertained reporters boasted that 80% of its 60,000 daily pint bottles of beer were destined for America. The $20 million in alcoholic beverages that left Windsor in a single year made a convenient base for calibrating the effectiveness of interdiction efforts. The total value of liquor, boats, vehicles and other property seized was $888,586 or 4.4% of the value of the shipments. The results were not surprising in light of the fact that 30 Prohibition men were detailed to cover 70 miles of waterfront. About 94% of Detroit's policemen said that their only concern with liquor violations was in the area of public drunkenness, for which 23,000 were arrested during 1927.

Meanwhile, the technological sophistication of the rumrunners increased. By 1930 the use of coded radio dispatching was routine. Well-known naval architects such as Walter McInnis, William Hand, William Deed and E. Lockwood Haggas purpose-designed smuggling vessels, sometimes coyly called "express freight" boats or "fast fisherman." The government called six such designers to Washington in 1930 to seek their guidance in improving the capability of the rumchasers. An editorial in a New York paper appeared which slyly began: "The boat racing season is by no means ended with the victory of *Enterprise* over *Shamrock V* . . . It appears we shall see a contin-

Whispering Winds, a Coast Guard prize, was taken after a half-hour chase in which Winds sustained direct hits from machine gun and cannon fire. Burlap-covered whiskey cases had been piled around the deckhouse as improvised armor.

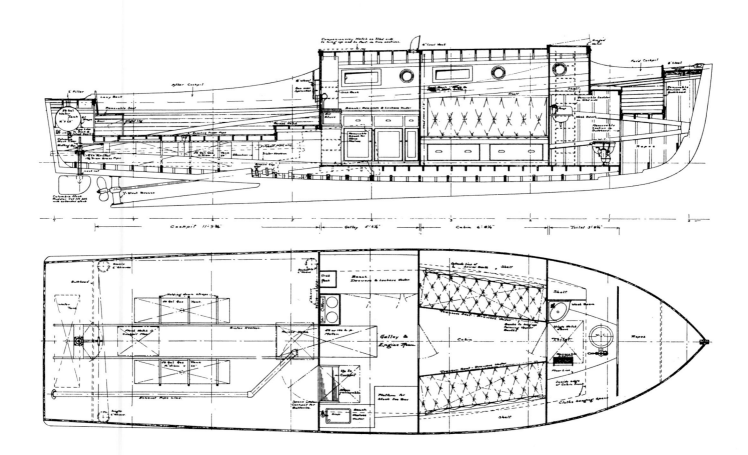

uous marine contest off our coasts." Vessel sophistication escalated, and soon smugglers were using boats with bulkheaded compartments that opened directly to the sea to allow cargo to be jettisoned when in danger of capture. Large blockade runners, 150' long, were built to transport alcohol directly from the Bahamas or Canada when Coast Guard picketing finally dissolved Rum Row. Smoke generators and radios became common on smuggling vessels. Air reconnaissance was used by both sides as were large networks of informants.

Michigan was the first state to ratify the Twenty-first Amendment, which repealed the Eighteenth on April 10, 1933. On December 5, 1933, Prohibition came to an end. Enforcement budgets had already been cut by President Roosevelt, and by the fall of 1933 the price of contraband liquor was dropping rapidly as the bootleggers sought to unload inventory in the face of repeal. There were certain ironies: it had been a call for unity during World War I that triggered Prohibition and another call for unity that ended it. The threat was not the "Savage Hun," but nationwide depression and the hope that making liquor legal would help return America to prosperity. Of course it did not, but beer for a nation to cry in was legal once again.

11

THE NAME BRANDS

A magical word symbolized the economic miracle of the 1920s: *standardization.* It was standardization (some said Fordism) that placed more than 1,750,000 new Model Ts on the nation's roads in 1924. Standardization created an outpouring of new consumer goods such as radios, refrigerators and waffle irons. It was, in essence, a simple idea: concentrate on a single product, make it well, and build in volume. Standardization gave America Colt revolvers, Singer sewing machines, and flivvers. Why not boats?

There was precedent. Three decades earlier, the General Electric Launch Company had created 55 identical boats for the Chicago World's Fair. The hulls were actually built by the Gas Engine and Power Company, which had been selling "stock model" naphtha launches since the 1880s. In 1915 Elco had produced 550 80' British Admiralty Submarine Chasers in 488 working days for service in the North Sea Blockade. In the years just before World War I Elco also introduced a line of stock cruisers that were sold completely equipped to upper-middle-class families, but this experiment was interrupted by the war.

Among the pioneers of production boat-building was Elco. This cruiser was their first standardized model and was produced as early as 1914. Sold completely equipped, it had a top speed of about 12 miles per hour.

A craftsman sanding a small part for a single boat in the famous Purdy shop, perhaps for the huge racing runabout behind him. Such custom building was supplanted by standardized production during the 1920s.

In the main, boatbuilding was a bespoke business, one in which the buyer stated his needs and wants and later received a "custom" boat which more or less reflected the budget and specifications. Many boatbuilders feared that they would lose customers if they became inflexible on the infinity of possible variations. Others argued that the knowledge needed by the buyer to make a "custom" purchase was slowing the growth of motorboating by requiring potential purchasers to make complex technical decisions and that custom boatbuilding created high prices, limiting the number of persons who could participate.

While this modest debate engaged the trade, the industry failed to grow. The value of domestic pleasureboats produced in 1917 was about $3.3 million, roughly the same as it had been 15 years before in 1902. Meanwhile, competitors for the public's increasing discretionary income grew rapidly. The sales of toys, games and sporting goods, for example, grew 425% to almost $200 million during the same period. Auto sales exploded to become a billion-dollar industry, and home appliances grew from a business the same size as boatbuilding in 1902 to one 18 times larger in 1917.

Henry Ford himself had found that building boats was not quite the same as building cars. Contracting with the government to produce 200' "Eagle submarine hunters" at a rate of 156 in the first year, Ford succeeded in building 52 in a year and a half. At the project's peak, 8,000 men labored in a specially built plant on the east bank of the Rouge River. The cost per boat was nearly triple the original price of $275,000, and during the inevitable Senate hearing an Admiral remarked, "Mr. Ford found the job a little more difficult than he anticipated."

Ford also entertained the idea of "mass-producing" boats, consulting with John L. Hacker on plans for a "flivver-boat" with a Model T engine. Ford and Hacker had known each other as young men, both customers of the same Detroit machine shop, both fascinated with gas engines. The plan was to place a boat in each of Ford's 7,000-plus dealerships to sell at a price of $1,000, but this never materialized. Perhaps Ford realized that the market for pleasureboats was 1/250 of that for cars; perhaps it was simply dropped, as were many other projects in fields as diverse as fertilizer and aviation. By abdication, the economic benefits of standardization were left for others to reap in ways less grand.

A pioneer among those who believed in standardization was Edgar M. Gregory. In 1917 the Gregory family opened the Belle Isle Boat Company in Detroit; the address was Motor Boat Lane. No vast enterprise, Belle Isle's financial report filed with the State of Michigan that first year reported cash on hand as $16.07. The "character of the business" was set forth as "the manufacture, sale and repairing of boats, engines, hardware and blocks." In 1918 the cash position improved to $81.85. By the 1920 season Ed Gregory was promoting a "standard" but somewhat ungainly 28' runabout with a choice of four- or six-cylinder Van Blerck engines, a folding canvas top in the fashion of the touring automobiles of the time and a price tag of $6,500 to $7,500, a sum that could also buy a modest home. "E.M. Gregory, the designer and builder of these boats, has made each a complete unit, providing all

Six assembly lines operating at the Dodge works in 1930. The 210,000 square-foot plant was designed to produce 2,000 runabouts a year. Ground-breaking for the plant took place six days after the "Black Thursday" stock-market crash of 1929. Gar Wood and Chris-Craft were also increasing capacity at the Depression's onset.

necessary accessories and equipment so that when filled with oil and fuel the boat is in commission,'' reported *Power Boating*. This was a novel concept, but only the first.

Late in the 1920 season Ed Gregory appeared with a new boat called *Belle Isle Bear Cat*. She was a 28-footer powered by a 200-horsepower, 865-cubic-inch, six-cylinder Hall-Scott. Capable of better than 35 miles per hour, the *Bear Cat* was fast, but more significant was the configuration. The cockpit was split with the engine amidships. The driver steered from the center of the forward cockpit, well in front of the spray and ahead of the engine. It was a radical departure from the long-deck, cockpit-aft traditional runabout and offered greater seating capacity and improved visibility. While Ed Gregory claimed his company both designed and built the boat, the *Bear Cat* was clearly influenced by John L. Hacker's large custom runabouts for the 1920 season that also used the novel cockpit-forward design.

The "indefatigable and omni-present" Ed Gregory roared around the course between Gold Cup races at Detroit, demonstrating the handling qualities of his *Bear Cat* by cutting sharp turns and circles at full speed. Gregory had arranged to have the boat designated the "official" runabout for the races, so his presence on the course was authorized. The boat attracted

The pioneering **Belle Isle Bear Cat.** *At the wheel is actress Peggy Wood. The forward cockpit was both innovative and popular; it increased passenger capacity and kept the driver dry.*

not only attention but orders, and E.M. Gregory announced plans to produce *Bear Cats* in lots of 25 as a standardized 26-footer powered by a four-cylinder, 120-horsepower Hall-Scott. A 200-horsepower Hall-Scott was optional. With prices starting at about $5,000 — almost four years' earnings for the average American worker — it was an ambitious plan for high-quality runabout production. At the New York Motor Boat Show, *Bear Cat* was described as "without exaggeration one of the sensations." *Motor Boat* editor William Washburn Nutting wrote, "If there still remained in the East any of the old prejudice against western boats, this would have certainly been dispelled by such boats as the Belle Isle concern is now producing. *Bear Cat* is an all-mahogany 26-foot concave V-bottom with a hogged unbroken sheer line and beautifully modeled top sides." In size, appearance, configuration and performance, the *Belle Isle Bear Cat* set the standard for runabouts for the next four decades.

Boat sales boomed in 1919 and 1920, reaching almost $15 million, more than four times 1917 levels. Various theories were advanced to explain the new demand; one of the most popular was that people were buying boats to escape the increasingly congested highways. While inexplicably continuing to design for potential competitors, John L. Hacker formed a new company in 1920 to build "pleasure and speed motor boats." The first boat down the ways at the new shop in Mount Clemens, Michigan, was a Liberty-powered 35' runabout for Paul Strasburg, owner of a Detroit taxi dance hall and vice president of The Hacker Boat Company.

A Bear Cat race at the Detroit regatta of 1921. Racing production boats was an ideal way to promote sales, and the similarity of the boats provided close racing. To show that his boats were safe and easy to handle, Ed Gregory also promoted ladies' races with a set of silverware as the prize.

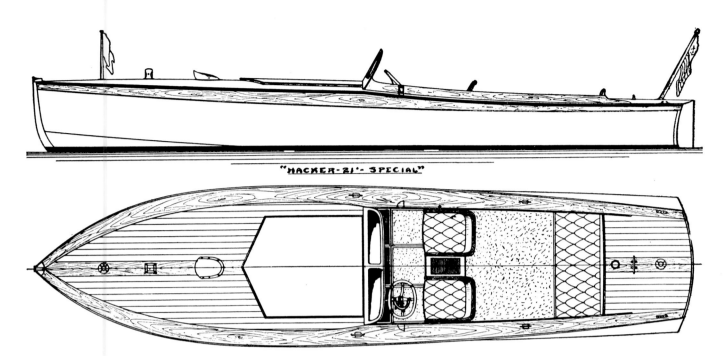

"HACKER-21'- SPECIAL"

It was not long before Hacker's company moved into production boat-building. ''As a culmination of the campaign that has been waged by the boat magazines, standardization and large production of one model of power boat has come,'' reported *Power Boating* in the spring of 1921. ''John L. Hacker, far-famed naval architect of Detroit, has designed a wonderful runabout of a most popular size and is now producing it in large quantities . . .'' While Ed Gregory addressed the high end of the market, J. L. Hacker, perhaps influenced by his experience with Henry Ford, chose the low. Hacker offered a 21' 5'' by 5' 8'' V-bottom runabout powered by a 20-horsepower Kermath marine engine, a boat claimed capable of ''18 to 20 miles an hour.'' Planked in pine with a copper green bottom, white topsides and varnished mahogany trim, the new Hacker had a removable rear seat so that ''the sportsman can sleep in it in comfort.'' The price was a remarkably low $1,975 completely equipped with lights, fire extinguisher, boat hook, lines, anchor, bilge pump, horn and other equipment.

The boat was sold by Central Marine Service Corporation. The impressive-sounding organization consisted of three men, one each in Detroit, Tampa and Baltimore. With a paid-in capital of $2,000, Central had negotiated exclusive rights to sell not only John Hacker's output but that of the C.C. Smith Boat & Engine Company. The Smiths were building a 26' by 6'6'' after-cockpit ''express runabout'' with a four-cylinder, 649-cubic-inch, 100-horsepower Hall-Scott. This double-planked and somewhat tubby runa-bout sold for $3,950 painted white and $4,450 finished bright. A 450-horse-power Liberty called the ''Smith Marine Twin-Six'' was available in a 24' hydroplane capable of 65 miles per hour, and a 35' Liberty-powered 45-mile-per-hour runabout was also offered. To have exclusive sales arrangements with the two most famous names in speedboat building must have seemed something of a coup to the principals of Central Marine Service, but it came to very little.

Almost as rapidly as they rose, boat sales plummeted during the brutal recession of 1921-22. Pleasureboat sales, in synchronism with the national economy, fell 36% in 1921 and 34% further in 1922 to end the year at less than half the 1920 level. Central Marine Service Corporation dissolved. The Hacker and Smith companies struggled along, building what boats they could, when they could, for the few men with both the bravery and wealth needed to disregard economic peril. John L. Hacker's plan to bring boating to the middle class died of economic debilitation, and by the end of 1921 even the Smith family was mostly unemployed. Only Jay W. Smith had work, and he was no longer in the boat business, having moved to Detroit as a production manager with Gar Wood's dump-truck manufacturing company.

C.C. Smith formed a new business in February of 1922 at the depths of the recession. Duly registered with the state of Michigan was Chris Smith & Sons Boat Company. Its resources were the reputation of the ''Wizard of Algonac,'' the energy of a family enterprise, $8,000 in stock, $23,000 in loans and $893.64 in cash. Son Jay W. became Vice President and General Manager; sons Owen N., Bernard T. and Hamilton also played roles in the shop. Daughter Catherine H. managed the office and kept the books.

Smith & Sons did not immediately leap into the volume production of runabouts. Fragmentary records suggest that repair and storage were important sources of the first year's revenue of $53,847.47. Perhaps more important was the association with The Packard Motor Car Company's chief engineer, Colonel Jesse Vincent. Vincent commissioned the construction of two boats, *Packard Chris-Craft* and *Packard Chris-Craft II*. Packard was seriously evaluating boating as a business at this time, apparently viewing it as a potential market for their automotive and aircraft engines and as an additional product for the 800-outlet Packard dealer organization. At the Gold Cup race in September of 1922 *Packard Chris-Craft* with the Colonel at the helm was the decisive winner over a large field. While the victory was Smith's ninth consecutive Gold Cup win as a builder, it was the first under the new *Chris-Craft* name.

Christopher Columbus Smith at the wheel of an early Chris-Craft runabout. By this time active management of the company was in the hands of Smith's sons.

It was also the first race under a new set of rules that transformed the famous Gold Cup from a race for what were essentially unlimited hydroplanes to a new formula for "gentlemen's runabouts." Marine engine manufacturers had seen the small but lucrative and prestigious market for high-powered motors melt under the pressure of inexpensive conversions of surplus aircraft engines such as the Liberty. Following the lead of the racers and the rumrunners, buyers of fast runabouts also chose the marinized aircraft engines. "No sane man who wants an engine for a power boat for practical use will buy an airplane engine unless he is crazy," editorialized one observer, the paradox emphasizing the strength of the conviction.

Responding to fears of commercial annihilation, to Gar Wood's five-consecutive-victory grip on the cup, and to the fact that only two boats ran in the 1921 race, the American Power Boat Association changed the rules in favor of what were called "wholesome" boats. Among other things, this meant no stepped hulls and no large aircraft engines. The ruling came late, and the 1922 Gold Cup boats had engines which were stop-gaps, at best. Colonel Vincent's winner had a V-12 Packard engine from which a bank of six cylinders had been removed in a hull built by Chris Smith & Sons. Gar Wood had an apparently identical hull using a Liberty from which six cylinders had been removed and a new crankshaft fitted to bring the engine into conformance with the new 10-liter engine-displacement limit. Wood finished well back in the field while Vincent won the race at 40.6 miles per hour, 42% off the 1920 speed of 70 miles per hour. For Wood it must have

Packard Chris-Craft, which won the Gold Cup in 1922 and 1923 with Colonel Jesse G. Vincent at the wheel. Modifications to this boat created the highly successful production runabouts of the mid-1920s.

been a particularly bitter defeat; not only had he lost the Gold Cup after a five-year reign, but the boatbuilding Smith family had reasserted its independence. Compounding his difficulties, Wood was storing 50 carloads of recently purchased war-surplus aircraft engines in Detroit.

Vincent's *Packard Chris-Craft* won the Gold Cup again in 1923, this time with a new purpose-built six-cylinder Packard engine called the 1M-621. Based on a Packard design for dirigible power-plants, the ''M''-series engines went on to win 9 out of 13 consecutive Gold Cup races. After the second win the Smith family apparently decided that the future lay with building standardized boats in a new shop just outside Algonac on the Dixon Highway. Former ally Gar Wood was making a similar decision at the Smith family's old Algonac shop, which was renamed Gar Wood, Incorporated.

''On the mezzanine floor will be found a booth where Romance reigns . . . The people have nothing to sell but an idea, which is to popularize the motor boat — to put a boat in every man's possession,'' reported *Motor Boat* in February of 1923. The man with the grand vision was 23-year-old Horace Elgin Dodge, Jr., the son of the late Horace E. Dodge, one-half of the famous Dodge Brothers. After building transmissions for the Olds Motor Works, for many years the Dodge Brothers manufactured the major components such as axles, steering gears and transmissions for Henry Ford's Model T before producing their own vehicle in 1914. It was about this time that John Dodge told newspaper reporters that he and his brother had a net worth of about $50 million. With the popularity of the Dodge automobile, the family fortune grew rapidly, and by the time of the brothers' deaths in 1920 the Dodge plant in Hamtramck employed 18,000 men. Besides Ford, no name had more stature in the automobile business than Dodge.

Colonel Vincent ready to race. The self-educated Vincent co-designed the Liberty, flew aircraft, won two Gold Cups, designed racing and production automobiles and managed Packard engineering for four decades.

For the 1923 season Packard tooled up this special engine for Gold Cup racing. Originally rated at 260 horsepower, the overhead-cam, four-valve six dominated Gold Cup competition for nearly 15 years.

On the right is Horace Elgin Dodge, Jr. suited up for racing in 1924. It was about this time that Dodge decided to enter production boat building. With him is William Horn, who managed Dodge's marine activities for many years.

A lush brochure for the Horace E. Dodge Boat Works, boasting of the ability to build boats of up to 120', was all that was available at the New York Motor Boat Show in 1923; Dodge had no boats to show. The relationship between 120-footers and boats for "every man" was not entirely clear, but within three months Dodge announced stock runabouts of 22', 26' and 32' lengths with speeds of 25, 55 and 45 miles per hour, respectively.

By the end of 1924 Horace Dodge had hired one of the best-known powerboat designers of the time, George F. Crouch, and had made him a vice president of the firm. Born in Davenport, Iowa, in 1880, Crouch attended the University of Wisconsin, where he studied mathematics. In 1901 he graduated from the three-year naval architecture program of Webb Institute and took a job with Tams, Lemoine & Crane. In 1905 he returned to Webb as an assistant professor of mathematics. While his approach to design was disciplined and rigorous, Crouch was no abstract theoretician. Throughout his academic career George Crouch freelanced runabout and racing designs. For many years he conducted a technical question-and-answer feature for *Motor Boat* called "The Forum," in which he patiently but never patronizingly explained the technical arcana of powerboating to the magazine's readership. Crouch's task at the Horace E. Dodge Boat Works was to design new runabouts for production and to work with Dodge on his rapidly growing racing program. The management offices at the Dodge works had revolving doors, and while the door on George Crouch's office revolved more slowly than some, he stayed less than three years before returning to the East and a career as an independent designer.

By 1926 Horace Dodge had poured nearly a million dollars into building production boats and showed a loss of almost two-thirds that amount. The most popular model was the 22-footer, which was powered by a 30-horsepower Dodge car engine and sold for $2,475 through Dodge dealers. It was capable of 20 miles per hour. The same boat was available with a 90-horsepower war-surplus Curtiss V-8 aero engine, which pushed the hull to 35 miles an hour for an additional $500. There was also a Curtiss-powered

Horace Dodge at the wheel of his 22' production runabout. The boats were initially sold with 30-horsepower auto engines through Dodge car dealerships for $2,475.

26-footer priced at $3,475. They were all called Dodge *Watercars*, and despite the promises of a few years earlier, Horace Dodge had not found a way to build boats for "every man." The cheapest cost nearly two years' earnings for the average American — equivalent to more than $40,000 today — and the purchaser of a *Watercar* or other boat paid cash; in the boat business there was no arrangement for "payment out of earnings," a popular euphemism in the 1920s to describe installment sales plans. With the growing prosperity of the decade this was not an immense problem; pleasureboat sales volume jumped 261% between 1922 and 1926, when it reached $22.4 million, while the registered fleet climbed from 159,701 vessels to 208,037 during the same period. Horace Elgin Dodge was learning the lesson that Henry Ford learned during his *Eagle* effort of The Great War: boatbuilding was "a little more difficult than he anticipated." Through the efforts of Dodge, Hacker, Wood and the Smith family, southern Michigan had a new distinction. Not only was Detroit the acknowledged leader in automobile production and the "rum capital" of America, but it was now the epicenter of production boatbuilding.

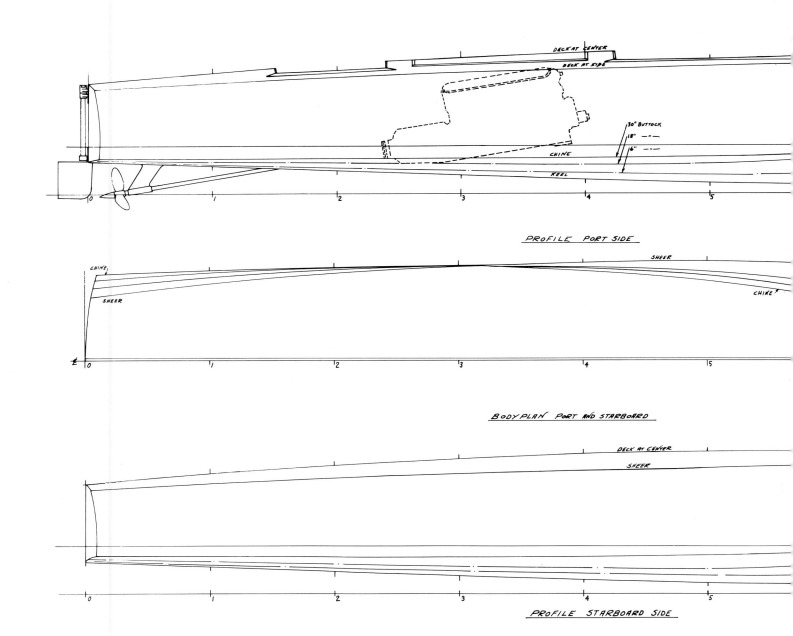

PROFILE PORT SIDE

BODYPLAN PORT AND STARBOARD

PROFILE STARBOARD SIDE

Vast wealth did not seem to guarantee success in the boat business of the 1920s, nor did the existence of pre-established distribution channels such as automobile dealers. It was the Smith family enterprise that showed the way. For the 1924 season they proceeded in typically pragmatic fashion. They took Vincent's 1922-1923 Gold Cup winner, added suitable height to the topsides to transform the profile into something more civilian, and revised the interior layout to accommodate a crew larger than two. The length overall was 25' 10'' and the draft was 22''.

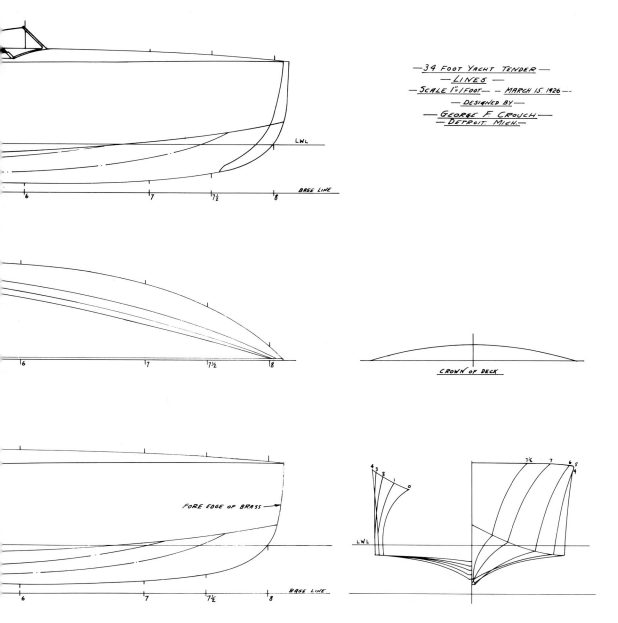

—34 FOOT YACHT TENDER—
—LINES—
—SCALE 1½/FOOT— —MARCH 15 1926—
—DESIGNED BY—
—GEORGE F CROUCH—
—DETROIT. MICH.—

LWL

BASE LINE

CROWN OF DECK

FORE EDGE OF BRASS

LWL

BASE LINE

This custom Crouch design shows the state of the art in fast runabouts in the mid-1920s. The boat was built as a tender for the Dodge family yacht Delphine.

The powerplant was equally expedient. War-surplus Curtiss OX-5 aircraft engines were acquired (reputedly for $50 each), marinized and installed. Rated by Curtiss at 90 horsepower, the Smiths claimed 100 horsepower and said that the boat had a 35-mile-per-hour top speed. Revenues skyrocketed to $165,485.49 in 1924, more than triple 1922 levels. Production for 1924 is unclear but perhaps numbered 50 boats. Sales were strongly regional, and at the Detroit Regatta that September a Chris-Craft Invitational Race was held. In prior years similar events had been held for *Belle Isle Bear Cats*.

Before focusing on the spectacularly popular 26' Chris-Craft runabout in 1924, the Smith family promoted this line of standardized runabouts. The forward cockpit version emulated the Bear Cat, and the Liberty-powered Baby Gar type had a claimed speed of 60 miles per hour. Despite the Smith racing reputation, moderate prices and styling much like Hacker's boats, sales were modest.

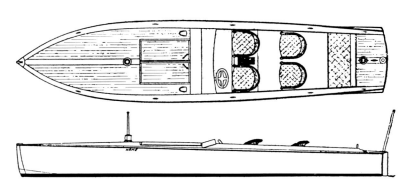

24-ft. runabout, beam 5 ft. 6 in.

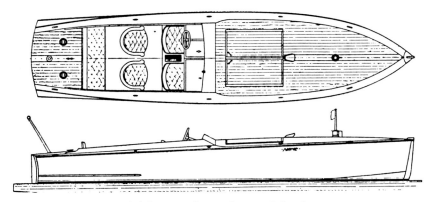

26-ft. runabout, beam 6 ft. 6 in.

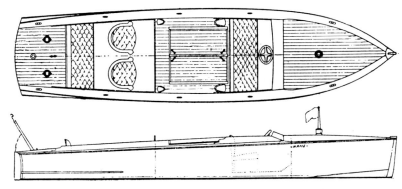

26-ft. runabout with 6 ft. 6 in. beam

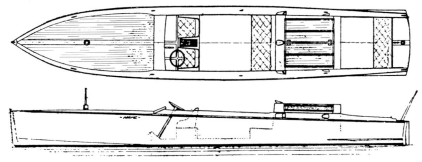

33-ft. runabout of the "Baby Gar" type, beam 6 ft. 3 in.

Twenty-two entries started the 15-mile event; and when it was over a half-hour later, the winner had averaged 29.4 miles an hour. The second-place boat was a slim six seconds astern and the third a mere four seconds further back. Within minutes of the leader 16 more boats roared across the finish line.

The trophy was presented by Chris Smith. He had built his first boat more than 40 years earlier; now Smith and the family had their biggest winner: a standardized runabout. While they certainly could not know and probably did not plan it, within five years the Chris Smith & Sons Boat Company controlled one-sixth of the booming United States market for pleasureboats. Sales more than doubled in 1925, then increased 21% in 1926 as the company started in earnest to build a dealer organization. Prices for the 26-footer, still the only boat in the line, ranged from $2,875 for the Curtiss-powered version to $3,500 for the same boat with a 150-horsepower Kermath six.

In 1926 one magazine reported: ''A year or so ago only one firm could boast of having completed more than 100 standardized power boats in the

Following the lead of Ed Gregory, the Smiths also promoted runabout racing. Speeds were typically in the 30- to 35-mile-per-hour range, but competition could be fierce.

Speed was not the exclusive domain of runabouts and Gold Cup racers. The Gar Jr. was a 900-horsepower Smith-built "cruiser" that could exceed 40 miles per hour. Here she is followed by an airborne newsreel cameraman. These boats pioneered a type called the "commuter" in which the wealthy transported themselves from home to work and back during the 1920s and 1930s.

course of one year. Now we have at least six firms claiming to have bettered that figure." While it may have appeared to be a spectacular achievement, the definition of "standardization" was changing from the earlier concept of a single model built in large volume to multiple models built in small volumes. Chris-Craft was among the leaders in model proliferation, and by 1930 the company offered 23 different models in nine different lengths that included runabouts, sedans, cruisers, commuters and motor yachts, which spanned a price

The boom in boat sales brought forth many innovations. This Albert Hickman-designed Sea Sled was the precursor of modern catamaran-hulled speedboats and also an inspiration for the Boston Whaler. A Sea Sled set a mile record of almost 58 miles per hour in 1921 but never achieved great commercial success. The rooster-tail is the result of another Hickman innovation, the surface propeller, which ran only half-submerged.

range from $1,895 to $35,000. This was a paper fleet, with many of the models existing only as catalog illustrations to be built if orders appeared.

By the close of the decade Smith & Sons could plausibly boast that it was the "largest volume producer of standardized motor boats in the world" with a policy "to build high speed boats which are safe for amateurs to operate, in quantities permitting efficient production at reasonable prices." From its formation in 1922 Chris Smith & Sons Boat Company's growth averaged 80% per year. Even J.P. "Jack" Morgan, son and heir of the great "J.P.," was impressed when he interviewed company president Jay W. Smith as a part of the process which would make Chris-Craft a public company. There had been a stock market crash in the fall of 1929, but orders at the winter boat shows in 1930 were larger than for all of 1929. Horace Dodge was building a vast new plant to manufacture boats and airplanes in Virginia. Gar Wood would soon open a large new facility with two 75-boat production lines in Marysville, Michigan. The Smiths would also expand. Perhaps they all believed the press releases that described speedboat building as "depression-proof." Perhaps they had forgotten the brief but devastating economic events of 1921–1922. Perhaps . . .

Air propellers offered freedom of movement in shallow water, and attempts were made to popularize them. The large number of surplus aircraft engines made the concept attractive to the builders but not to the public. This one was called the Free-Bottom Craft.

157

Garfield Arthur Wood strikes a pose of calm determination at the wheel of Miss America II. The 41-year-old Wood held the world water speed record, captured the Harmsworth Trophy, and won four Gold Cup victories, earning him the title of "The Speed King."

12

A FEW GENTLEMEN GO RACING

I t was 6:52 A.M., Monday, May 27, 1925. Two Liberty-powered *Baby Gars* lay against a float just beneath the New York Central bridge at Albany, their crews on shore. Almost overhead, a train chuffed and rumbled across the bridge. They had been watching trains pass for more than an hour. From the platform of the observation car trailed an orange and white streamer. "Gas!" came the shout, as the crews scrambled for the boats. Starters whined as 24 cylinders hacked and coughed, spitting smoke across the water. Lines cast off, the boats roared down the Hudson at 6:53 A.M. A few miles away at an airfield a telephone rang. "The race has started!" The train was 39 minutes early, well ahead of schedule on a run which began in Chicago the day before. Men ran for the giant twin-engine Sikorsky S-29, its fuselage packed with radio equipment to broadcast the race on WGY, Schenectady, and WJZ, New York. Along the banks of the Hudson crowds gathered to watch Gar Wood race the Twentieth Century Limited.

In a time when the term "media event" had not yet been coined, Gar Wood created one. His announcement on May 15 that he would race the Limited had precedent. In 1921 Wood raced the Atlantic Coast Line's Havana Special from Miami to New York. Delayed by weather and mechanical problems, when he arrived in New York days after the train he declared himself the winner on an elapsed time of 47 hours, 23 minutes for the 1,260-mile trip. The average speed was about 27 miles per hour for Wood's 50', 900-horsepower, twin-Liberty *Gar Jr. II*, which consumed fuel at the rate of 0.7 miles per gallon.

On the 1925 run Wood took steps to increase the publicity yield, giving rides to the Governor's sons on the day before the event, entertaining mayors and other dignitaries from towns along the route and arranging for the radio coverage, a technical feat at least as impressive as the event. The New York Central announced that it was not racing but would simply maintain its schedule from Albany to New York. To emphasize the point, they suspended a crack engineer for arriving two minutes ahead of schedule a few days before Gar Wood's river run.

(opposite)
Wood's Baby Gars *that raced against the Twentieth Century Limited. When the Limited left 39 minutes early, many of the thousands who lined the banks of the Hudson to watch missed the passing of the boats.*

Gar Jr. II on the way to setting a Miami-to-New York record of 47 hours, 23 minutes. From New York, Wood continued on inland waterways to Detroit, setting a record for the passage that remains today.

If the event was redolent of the days of steam when *Vamoose* ''raced'' a train, there was another component: the East-versus-West rivalry that had existed since 1915 when *Miss Detroit* took the Gold Cup to Detroit. As the Wood forces were carefully managing the crescendo of press coverage four days before the event, another boat shot up the Hudson. ''Speedboat Beats 20th Century Time,'' read the headlines in the New York papers. Richard F. Hoyt, partner in the Hayden, Stone & Company brokerage firm and member of the board of directors of Wright Aeronautical Company, had sent his George Crouch-designed *Teaser* up the Hudson 27 minutes faster than the train's scheduled speed. Built at the Nevins yard on City Island, the 39' 10 1/2'' by 7' 6'' *Teaser* was powered with a 600-horsepower Wright Typhoon V-12 engine that sold for $20,000, 15 years' wages for the average American. Wright's chief engineer, R.J. Mead, piloted the boat up the river, averaging 52 miles per hour to Albany and 45 on the trip down, some of it through fog. Foiled by the interloper, Wood issued a $25,000 challenge to Hoyt, saying he would beat *Teaser*'s time on his scheduled run. Hoyt declined, saying that his boat had set a record and it was up to Gar Wood to break it if he could.

So it was when Gar Wood and Orlin Johnson roared off in *Baby Gar IV* that Monday morning. Also on board was *Motor Boating*'s editor, Charles F. Chapman, as official observer, a role he also played on *Teaser*'s run a few

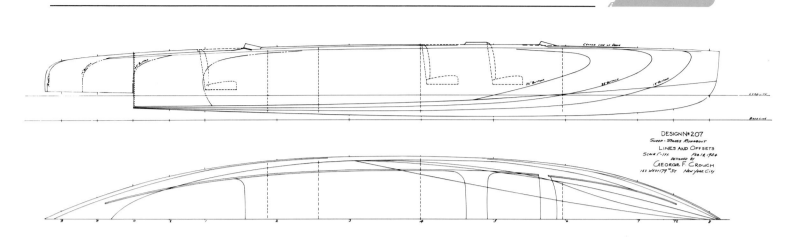

DESIGN Nº 207
Sweep-Stakes Runabout
Lines and Offsets
Scale 1⅛=1ft. Feb 14 1924
Designed By
George F. Crouch
143 West 79ᵗʰ St. New York City

days earlier. In *Baby Gar V* was George Wood, mechanic Joe Kinney, and a reporter. At 50 miles per hour or more, *IV* and *V* roared down the Hudson, sometimes with the train in sight, sometimes not. At 7:13 A.M. — 20 minutes into the run — the first of the airplanes appeared. At one time five planes tracked the boats; three stayed to the finish. Out of the sight of the crowds and 42 minutes from the start, Gar Wood made a decision. Motioning his brother's faster boat alongside, Gar Wood and Charles Chapman jumped from *IV* to *V* while the reporter and George Wood scrambled across to *IV*. The faster *V* boat pulled ahead. Just above Poughkeepsie an hour later *Baby Gar V* came to a halt, her engine dead. Seven minutes behind was *IV*, and when it pulled up another crew change took place. Off went Gar Wood in the only running boat, past Newburgh, West Point, Nyack, Yonkers, 125th Street, finally pulling up to the Columbia Yacht Club docks at 86th Street at 9:50 A.M., the crowd cheering and car horns honking. Slipping out of his oilskins and goggles, Wood presented Orlin Johnson with a crisp $500 bill as a bonus, paused for photographs and moved through the crowds to the Pennsylvania Hotel, where his wife was waiting. She had boarded the Limited in Cleveland and flew the streamer from the last car as a signal for her husband.

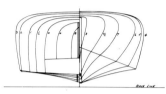

Teaser was basically an enlarged version of Baby Bootlegger. The boat was 39' 10" overall with a 7' 6" beam. She was double-planked with a 3/4" thick bottom. Owner Richard Hoyt used her to commute to his Wall Street office.

The Crouch-designed, Nevins-built Teaser that made a preemptive strike on the New York-to-Albany record. Powered by a 600-horse-power, 1,948 cubic-inch Wright V-12, she ran up the Hudson at about 52 miles per hour.

The first Miss America, *the winner of the Harmsworth in 1920. After the victory the boat set a Gold Cup heat record, which lasted for more than a quarter-century, and a world water speed record of 77.85 miles per hour.*

Baby Gar IV had beaten the Limited by 17 minutes and had averaged about 46.5 miles per hour. At 2 hours, 58 minutes elapsed time downriver, *IV*'s time was slower than *Teaser*'s 2 hours, 40 minutes upriver, but then *Teaser*'s time down was slower than *Baby Gar IV*'s. This ambiguity allowed all concerned to claim records until L. Gordon Hammersley took his *Cigarette, Jr.* up the river two minutes faster than *Teaser* in mid-July but broke down on the return trip. Rail partisans rummaged through piles of old timetables and found that the Empire State Express had regularly made the Albany-New York run faster than any of the boats 30 years before.

If Wood was capable of manufacturing synthetic spectacle on a grand scale, he was also the dominant racer of the decade and beyond. With a firm grip on the Gold Cup, Wood issued a challenge for the Harmsworth Trophy in 1920. The prize had been in England since 1912; a 1913 attempt to recover it by *Ankle Deep* and *Disturber* failed, and during the war years no races were held. Two new boats were built and shipped to England. One was the 38' *Miss Detroit V*, an enlarged offshore version of the typical Smith hydroplane with twin 400-horsepower Liberties. The other was the first *Miss America*, 26' by 7', also with a pair of Liberties. A speed of 80 miles per hour was claimed for *Miss America* in St. Clair River trials.

Arrayed against the Wood boats and the veteran *Whip-Po'-Will, Jr.* of A.L. Judson were two new *Maple Leafs* with similar appearances but different engine installations. *Maple Leaf V* carried four 450-horsepower Sunbeams for a total of 1,800 horsepower. "With that kind of power I could make a grand piano fly," commented one American. A pair of 450-horsepower Rolls Royces powered *Maple Leaf VI*. Both of the Saunders-built *Leafs* had peculiar bottom shapes which were rockered and stepped. Splashing and leaping around the course, "they wasted their energy in useless bucking like the frantic efforts of a pitching cayuse." Rounding out the field was *Sunbeam Despujols*. Built by the automaker of the same name, she was never a factor. Judson's *Whip* burned and sank before the race, leaving only the Wood entries.

"She ran like some fleet, wild thing pursued by a pack of lumbering hounds," wrote W.W. Nutting. *Miss America* finished the first 38.1 mile Harmsworth race more than three minutes and miles ahead of the second-place *Maple Leaf VI* at an average speed of 59.16 miles per hour. With Gar Wood at the wheel and Jay Smith on the engine, *Miss America* finished the last lap almost two minutes slower than her best lap. With a huge lead built up, it was not necessary to push the boat. Sputtering along in last place with fouled spark plugs was brother Phil Wood and Bernard Smith in *Miss Detroit V.*

The second day's contest — August 11, 1920 — saw an orderly procession develop. In the lead was *Miss America*, followed by a refreshed *Miss Detroit V*, *Maple Leafs V* and *VI*, and *Sunbeam*. On the smoother course even higher speeds were timed with a best lap for *America* of 64.96 miles per hour. Almost a mile ahead of the nearest British boat, Gar Wood shot across the finish line and secured the British International Trophy for America. The Wood boats were immediately shipped to America for the Gold Cup at Detroit.

Wood dominated the weak 1920 Gold Cup field of three other entries. Only *Miss America* and *Detroit V* completed the first race. In the third and final heat of the Gold Cup, Gar Wood, apparently sure of victory, displayed the true potential of *Miss America* and made one five-mile lap at 71.43 miles per hour while averaging 70.0 miles per hour for the race. This was 10 miles per hour faster than the next-best finisher, *Miss Toronto II*, and established a record that was to last a quarter of a century. To complete his triple-play of Harmsworth to Gold Cup to Mile Speed Record, Wood took *Miss America* out for timed runs. For three one-mile runs up the Detroit River and three down, the average speed was 77.85 miles per hour, a world water speed record.

Miss America II on her cradle. Quadruple Liberties, propellers aft of the transom and more shapely topsides were the principal changes. II had difficulty planing at first, so her forward plane was widened. The changes are visible here.

Over the winter the Smiths and the Woods occupied themselves with plans for *Miss America II*, this time with four Liberties totaling 1,800 horsepower routed through two gearboxes to twin screws hung abaft the transom. Unlike the crate-shaped earlier boats, *America II* used moderate flare in the topsides and a touch of tumblehome to give her 32' by 8' 4'' dimensions a shape similar to a runabout. Though the power was doubled, *II* was only 3.5% faster than *America I*, managing 80.57 miles per hour for the mile. But, if known, the boat's top speed was a closely guarded secret when she met McKay Edgar's *Maple Leaf VII* for the Harmsworth at Detroit. Apparently the Wood boats had been well-scrutinized by the British the season before, and though *Leaf VII* ran the same 1,800-horsepower quartet of Sunbeams as before, her running lines were an obvious derivation of *Miss Detroit V* with a bluff bow, single step, hard chines and a forward rudder.

It did not matter much as *Maple Leaf VII* tore loose a bottom plank on the second lap of the race and sank before she could reach shore. At the time of the failure *Leaf* was trailing both *Miss Americas*. A procession of three boats — all piloted by Wood brothers — circled the course: Gar was in the lead in *Miss America II*, brother George ran second for a while in *Miss America*, then retired with a leaky hull, allowing brother Phil to finish second and last in the single-engined Smith hydro *Miss Toronto II*. The British returned to England with the Saunders-built *Leaf VII* and did not try to retrieve the trophy for many years. Master boatbuilder John Thornycroft was asked why by a reporter. ''No man in England can afford to build the necessary boat,'' he replied.

The Harmsworth was Gar Wood's final triumph of the Detroit Regatta of 1921. His boats swept the 10-day ''celebration of speed'' wherever entered. He won the Gold Cup again when only *Miss America* and *Miss Chicago* were able to start the race, effortlessly beating his brother George but well off his 1920 pace. He won the Wood-Fisher Trophy for ''displacement'' runabouts with *Baby Gar*, turning a best lap of 46.6 miles per hour. She was a sister to the boat he would run on the Hudson against the Limited. Gar Wood's hegemony earned him the title ''The Speed King,'' a sobriquet bequeathed not only in earnest, but with envy by some and enmity by others.

Rainbow IV under-way during the Gold Cup of 1924. Designed by Crouch but based on the concepts of owner Harry Greening, the double-ended Rainbow planed amidships with her thin stern supported by a surface propeller created by Albert Hickman.

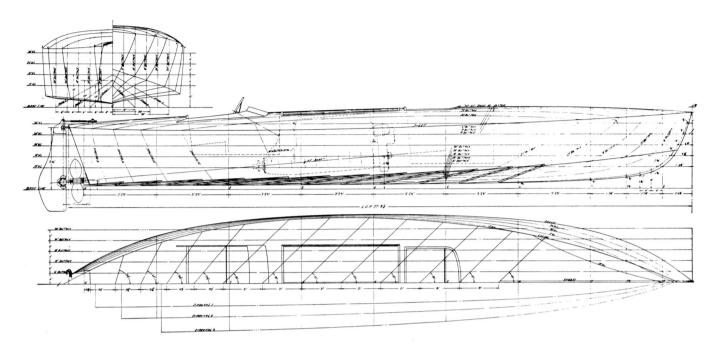

Wood's high-speed hammerlock inspired the Gold Cup rule changes of 1922, but despite the motivation the results were spectacular. In the first two years of racing — won by Jesse Vincent's *Packard Chris-Craft* — practical runabouts were actually, if naively, entered in the race. The Gold Cup class soon became a favorite for the mechanically inclined among the wealthy industrial elite. While the risk to personal welfare was low due to modest speeds, the financial demands escalated rapidly as self-made men invested earnings and egos in sophisticated machines built to rigorous rules.

By 1924 the Gold Cup class had stabilized sufficiently to allow close racing. One man had a better than average chance for the cup that year; designer George F. Crouch had three boats in the field, and two of them won the Gold Cup in a single race. The first winner was *Rainbow IV*, a radical planing double-ender with a surface propeller. While winning the race on points, *Rainbow* was disqualified when the design of the bottom was protested. The bottom was planked in lapstrake across the hull, which created a series of small steps less than an inch high. Although the design was cleared with the sanctioning body before it was built, the ruling was reversed upon protest.

The decision gave the race to the second-place *Baby Bootlegger*, a strangely beautiful and heavily aerodynamic Crouch design owned by auto racer/aviator/industrialist Caleb Bragg. Reflecting Bragg's executive position in the company, *Bootlegger* was powered with a Wright-built Hispano-Suiza V-8 aircraft engine. The hoped-for ban against aero engines was effective for only two seasons as competitors sought any possible advantage. For the first time in nine years the Gold Cup returned to the East.

The lines of Rainbow IV. *The idea behind her unusual shape was to combine the low-speed seakeeping of a surfboat with the high-speed performance of a hydroplane. The small transverse steps that disqualified her after a protest can be seen.*

Caleb Bragg's Baby Bootlegger *was awarded the Gold Cup after* Rainbow *was disqualified in 1924. This Crouch design was among the earliest to show an aerodynamic influence. Her unusually clean lines appeared strange to observers in the 1920s.* Bootlegger *won the Cup again in 1925 and was a contender for many years thereafter.*

Bootlegger won again in 1925, this time cleanly, with two of the three races run at an average speed of about 48 miles per hour. George Crouch designed five of the nine boats entered in the 1925 contest, three of them for Horace Dodge. Of nine boats starting, three finished the 90-mile series; reliability was continuing to be a problem despite the reduced speeds. Even Colonel Vincent was sidelined by failure of his own Packard Special Gold Cup engine that had ceased to produce its rated 260 horsepower. Signs of technological torpor were beginning to appear; one clue could be found in the stock runabout class where Baby Gars were producing speeds of 46 miles per hour, within 2 miles per hour of the fastest Gold Cup boats.

The pattern would repeat throughout the balance of the 1920s: relatively large entry lists, disappointingly few finishers and slowly rising speeds. By the last race of the decade speeds would be where they were in 1916, about 50 miles per hour. Split from the immense spectacle of the Detroit Regatta and raced at yacht clubs with no provisions for spectators, the Gold Cup was losing its popular appeal. To breathe new life into the Cup, the American Power Boat Association once again allowed stepped hulls but hewed to the 10-liter engine displacement limit. The Depression further dampened activity, and in the early 1930s what had once been called the "greatest motor boat race in the world" was the object of openly hostile criticism. "The Gold Cup race is no more indicative of the ultimate in speed boats than a dollar watch is a blood brother to the chronometer. The Gold Cup affair, for the last few years, has become the annual old home week for a select coterie of sportsmen who date back to the days when women swam in bloomers and skirts," wrote the *Motor Boating* correspondent in 1934 after *El Lagarto*'s second win at Lake George. The best heat speed had grazed 61 miles per hour. *El Lagarto* won again in 1935, and in 1936 when *Impshi* took the cup after first racing in

1924, criticism grew strident: ''Two flops in two years! Twice our supposedly greatest motor boat race has produced one ancient and lonely boat at the finish, sauntering along to protect her from falling apart,'' wrote George Sutton, a veteran correspondent for *Yachting*.

In a broader perspective, racing was reflecting the state of the national economy. The average weekly earnings of manufacturing workers had fallen from $24.76 in 1929 to a low of $16.65 in 1933, a drop of 33 per cent among those who had work. As much as one-fourth of the workforce was unemployed. Thousands of banks failed, wiping out the savings of millions of people. More than 4,000 were closed in 1933 alone. That same year pleasureboat sales of $4.8 million were recorded, less than one-fifth the 1929 sales of $26.2 million. Automobile sales collapsed 68 per cent from their

The Hispano-Suiza V-8 of Baby Bootlegger *in aeronautical form. The bare engine weighed only 450 pounds but developed 220 horsepower when built under license by Wright Aeronautical of Paterson, New Jersey.*

peak in the 1920s while spending on all consumer items including food, fuel, clothing and other necessities was halved. Prosperous boat companies such as Dee-Wite and Dart, formed to satiate the demand of the 1920s, evaporated. John L. Hacker lost control of his firm in 1934. The booming Chris-Craft business skidded to a halt, reduced from hundreds of workers to little more than the family firm again. Chris-Craft was saved from annihilation in 1930 by $250,000 cash received from a planned public stock offering that failed. Horace Dodge's company closed in 1935. Production builders tried for a while to build smaller and cheaper boats, but the tactic had only limited appeal; an inexpensive inboard boat was still about twice the price of a Ford or Chevrolet, and cars were not selling.

But there was one man whose resolve to compete was not altered by the crumbling economy. He was Gar Wood. The renewed Wood epoch began in the golden days of the late 1920s when the British once again challenged for

As racing declined during the Depression, El Lagarto accumulated an immense number of wins, including three Gold Cup victories. A Hacker hull from the early 1920s, she was astutely developed and modified by racing veteran George Reis.

167

While the average worker made 44 cents per hour in the early 1930s, there were a few men with money who were not afraid to spend it. Dick Locke commissioned Hacker to create Lockpat II *for the daily 40-mile commute from his home to Detroit. The 40-footer was powered by a 650-horsepower Packard V-12 and could reach 50 miles per hour.*

the Harmsworth Trophy. Save for an abortive attempt to wrest the trophy from Gar Wood and America by the French in 1926, there was no competition until 1928. The challenger that year was Marion B. (Betty) Carstairs, who was born in England in 1900. Carstairs' grandfather was J.A. Bostwick of the Standard Oil Company, who had also invested in the naphtha launch. Inheriting immense wealth from her American grandfather, she commissioned the building of a raceboat in 1925 and began competing in England. Challenging for the trophy in 1928, Miss Carstairs brought across a Saunders-built boat, *Estelle II.*

The real drama occurred before the race when Gar Wood crashed his new *Miss America VI* during testing. The *VI* was built by Nap Lisee and powered by two 2,500-cubic-inch 12-cylinder Packard aero engines developing a combined 2,200 horsepower. At full throttle the *Sixth* nosed in and dived for the bottom, totally destroying itself only 17 days before the race. Within a matter of hours the Packards were salvaged and sent to the factory for overhaul. From his bed Gar Wood ordered the building of a new hull. He had not been seriously injured. Mechanic Orlin Johnson had a broken jaw, severe lacerations and other injuries. On race day Johnson, his jaw in a cast, his ribs taped and head bandaged, was taken from the hospital and lifted into the boat to man the throttles. It was all over in a matter of minutes. *Estelle II* capsized on a swell during the first lap.

Carstairs returned again in 1929, this time with *Estelle IV*. The 35' by 9' 6'' *IV* carried three Napier Lion engines of 1,000 horsepower each, and a speed of 105 miles per hour was claimed for the boat in English tests. The day before the race one of *Estelle*'s propeller shafts broke during testing on the Detroit River; and during the actual race on Saturday, September 1, 1929, *Estelle* hit a log and was disabled. Though there was no chance of winning the trophy, Carstairs repaired her boat and raced Wood in front of a crowd of 500,000 on the Detroit River on September 2. Gar Wood in *Miss America VIII* averaged 75.3 miles per hour for the 30-mile race compared to Carstairs' 64.1 miles per hour.

The year 1930 brought another challenge from Betty Carstairs. The *IV* returned as did a new entry, *Estelle V*, which was built in a yard that Carstairs purchased to build challengers. The *Estelles* faced Gar Wood's *Misses America VII, VIII* and *IX*. When the gun sounded, *Estelle V* was late across the line but by the second lap had passed *America V* and was gaining on the *VIII* and *IX*. She had passed the Wood boats when an oil connection broke, spraying the crew with hot lubricant. A quick repair was made, and off roared *Estelle V*; but within minutes the gas tanks fractured, filling the hull with high-test fuel. The other *Estelle* continued to circle the course far behind the Americas. Betty Carstairs announced that the 1930 race was her last attempt to wrest the Harmsworth from Gar Wood.

Misses America VII and VIII. *After Betty Carstairs' Estelle IV hit a log, the Americas cruised the course to retain the Harmsworth Trophy in 1929.*

Despite the worsening world economic situation, the British tried again in 1931 with *Miss England II*. Originally built for Baltimore-born Major Henry O'Neal de Hane Segrave by Hubert Scott-Paine's British Powerboat Company, *Miss England II* had crashed and killed Major Segrave while he tried to establish a world water speed record. Segrave already held the land speed record of 231.362 miles per hour when the bottom of *Miss England II* failed at more than 90 miles per hour. The boat was repaired and her step covered with stainless steel, then sent to Detroit for the Harmsworth. Driving the 4,000-horsepower, Rolls Royce aero-engined, 38' 6'' by 10' 6'' machine was Kaye Don, a very brave but relatively inexperienced pilot. In trials *Miss England II* had exceeded 110 miles per hour, a world record, with Kaye Don at the helm.

With a fast boat and much better preparation than prior British efforts, Don's practice runs on the Detroit River must have been serious cause for concern among the Wood forces, even with the addition of superchargers to the now-aging Packards that developed 1,400 horsepower under pressure. The concern proved warranted, for Kaye Don and *Miss England* won the first heat for the trophy on September 6, 1931, at 89.9 miles per hour. Over the line ahead of Gar Wood, Kaye Don kept *Miss America IX* and the other Wood boats in his wash for the entire 30 miles. The *Ninth* suffered structural damage, and Wood's crew worked through the night, replacing planks and adding steel braces to the hull. For the first time in a decade, Wood was seriously challenged.

Among the estimated half-million persons who lined the shores of the Detroit River for the Harmsworth Trophy races each year was John L. Hacker, seen here wearing his characteristic Panama hat.

Miss England II as she appeared just before defeating Gar Wood in the first Harmsworth race of 1931 at an average speed of 89.9 miles per hour. A pair of Rolls Royce 2,000-horsepower aero engines on loan from the Air Ministry had already pushed her to a world water speed record of 110.22 miles per hour.

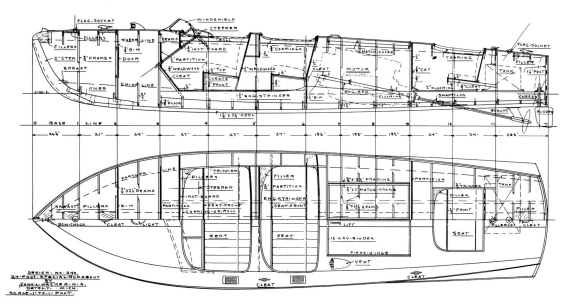

DESIGN·NO·240·
24·FOOT·SPECIAL·RUNABOUT·
BY
JOHN·L·HACKER·N·A·
DETROIT·MICH·
SCALE·1"·TO·1·FOOT·

As race time approached the next day, Wood requested a postponement to allow completion of repairs. Kaye Don refused, saying that the pre-heated oil in his Rolls Royce engines would cool and he would be at a disadvantage. The Wood team scrambled to solder a leaking gas tank full of fuel and reached the course with less than a minute to the gun. At full throttle, Gar Wood roared across the starting line. Kaye Don, seeing *Miss America IX* approaching at high speed, accelerated. The *Ninth* stayed slightly ahead. Wood crossed the line nine seconds before the gun, Kaye Don seven seconds. As they rounded the first turn, *Miss England* went wide, trying to avoid Gar Wood's wash. She skidded, Don corrected and then the boat rolled to port and capsized. *Miss England II* sank to the bottom of the Detroit River. Kaye Don and crew were rescued without injury, and Gar Wood was disqualified for crossing the line ahead of the signal. Wood's *Miss America VIII* circled the course, won the race and preserved the trophy. "Kaye Don fails to win Harmsworth Trophy but his clean racing ethics gain him millions of admirers," wrote *Motor Boating*. Stories circulated in the newspapers, quoting Gar Wood as saying he intentionally led Don over the line early, then swamped him; Gar Wood denied making any such statements. Motion pictures of *Miss England* were reported to show that she was in calm water when she capsized. After a while the furor subsided, and the British returned again in 1932 and 1933, faring little better than they had since 1920. Gar Wood retained the trophy but by 1935 announced he would not compete for it again. Its glow darkened by economic disaster and then war, the Harmsworth Trophy was not contested again until after World War II. Gar Wood watched that race from shore.

Miss America X *at speed. Besides winning the 1932 and 1933 Harmsworth races, Gar Wood set a world water speed record of 124.71 miles per hour on the St. Clair River. The record set by the four-engine, 6,400-horsepower single-step hydroplane stood for five years.*

Racing in general was in a depression-created slump, but by 1937 there were signs of hope for the Gold Cup, if not the British International Trophy. There was a new boat called *Notre Dame*, designed by Clell Perry for Herbert Mendelson, whose wealth came from the General Motors empire. The fall of 1936 also brought forth *Miss Canada II*, a Hacker design built by Herbert Ditchburn in Canada and powered by a sporadically powerful V-12, drawn by the legendary Harry Miller. Rule changes soon aligned the Gold Cup class with the international 12-liter formula, and the 1937 race was the most exciting of the decade.

As if to signal the dawning of the new era, veteran contenders *El Lagarto* and *Impshi* failed early in the first race, leaving eight boats running in a truly international contest with entries from Canada, Italy, France and the United States. *Notre Dame* emerged victorious with the fastest heat speed since

The unusual Notre Dame, *designed and driven by Clell Perry. Her Duesenberg engine was originally built for Horace Dodge but was further developed by a General Motors engineering group at the request of owner Herb Mendelson, who was a large GM stockholder.*

172

1920 of 68.64 miles per hour. With her pumpkin-seed shape, single step, rear rudder and 24-cylinder supercharged Duesenberg engine abaft the driver, *Notre Dame* was both beautiful and fast. She was reported capable of 100 miles per hour on the straight, perhaps due to the attention paid her engine by General Motors' engineering department.

Notre Dame, though impressive, did not point the way to the future. That lay in the direction of an entirely different hull form: the three-point hydroplane. The type was developed by Adolph Apel and his son Arno at their Atlantic City, New Jersey, shop and patented in 1938. Born in Germany and educated in naval architecture there, Apel left the country to avoid military service. Emigrating first to Venezuela, he later arrived in the United States and found work as a boatbuilder with Consolidated, the builders of naphtha launches and many steam yachts.

In 1902 Apel read a newspaper account of a storm at Atlantic City, New Jersey, and moved there expecting to find much repair work. He found instead

that the 800 to 900 boats reported damaged were really 8 to 9 boats. The direction of his life changed by a typographical error, Apel set up shop and began building barges and work boats. Profoundly interested in hull shapes, he began experimenting with different forms. The extremely fast *Sand Burrs* that impressed Clinton Crane, and a boat called *Tech Jr.* for Coleman Dupont, which briefly held a United States water speed record, came from the Apel shop. Apel continued as a small custom builder, turning out very fast runabouts in the 1920s.

The three-point concept was not a new one. It had been proposed by the Reverend Ramus in the 1870s and had actually been built by the Reliance company in a design by George Crouch called *Peter Pan VIII* in 1916. Crouch did not continue to develop the form, and it was almost two decades later that the Apels brought it to practical and spectacular fruition. The shape

A large Apel-designed runabout of 1920. Note that even at this early date there are vestigial sponsons near the waterline that foreshadow later Ventnor developments.

Adolph Apel at the President's Cup Regatta in 1937. Apel and his son Arno filed a patent application for the three-point hydroplane, which was granted in 1938.

they created had two widely separated sponsons forward with the third suspension "point" at the stern. The sponsons let air under the hull, simultaneously creating lift and reducing the wetted surface. First raced in 1935, a 90-cubic-inch, Apel-built three-pointer called *Emancipator* set a one-mile record of 49.3 miles per hour with a 33-horsepower Fay & Bowen engine. Before long Gold-Cup speeds of the 1920s were achieved with engines of one-third Gold-Cup size in the popular 225-cubic-inch racing class.

The Apels had found the road to the future, and orders poured into their Ventnor Boat Works. As a signal of the times, one of the orders came from the Chinese government. The specifications called for a minimum speed of 60 miles per hour from a 20-footer carrying a payload of 650 pounds in the bow with one occupant and a standard Lycoming eight-cylinder engine. The Apels tested the boat, and it ran 66 miles per hour with sand as a substitute for the real payload. This was to be 650 pounds of trinitrotoluene, TNT, and the single occupant was expected to give his life for China in the war against Japan. Twelve of these boats were built and shipped while a thirteenth was powered with a Packard Gold Cup engine and sent racing. She was called *Juno*, and when she flipped in a race, she was given the appellation "suicide boat." Many of the race watchers did not appreciate the irony of the name.

The Apels' patent drawings for the three-point type. From this design flow most of today's hydroplane forms. The Apel design was openly copied, and Adolph Apel once said the patent was only "a license to sue."

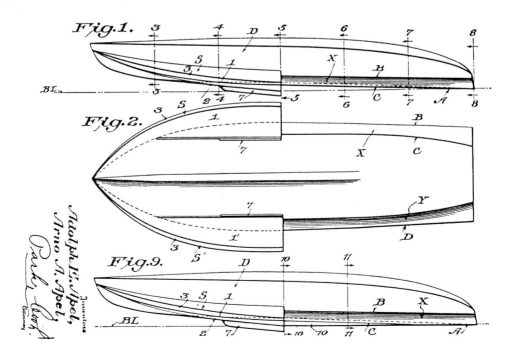

With near-total domination of the smaller racing classes, a Ventnor boat soon won the Gold Cup. The year was 1939, and Zalmon G. Simmons, whose family business was mattresses, assembled a combination of a Ventnor 24' hull and a Miller 16-cylinder engine at a reputed cost of $100,000. True to tradition, competitors *Miss Canada III*, *Why Worry*, *Mercury* and *Notre Dame* experienced mechanical problems, leaving Simmons' *My Sin* with an open field to victory. Despite the unevenness of the competition, Simmons turned a best lap of 70.158 miles per hour, a new record.

The 1940 Gold Cup race was a reprise of earlier disasters. As the field thinned through mechanical failures, only one boat was left running. She was called *Hotsy Totsy III* and was purchased by her owner from the estate of Victor Kliesrath only two days before the race. Like John Milot a quarter-century before, owner Sidney Allen had never driven a raceboat, but with the only boat running at the completion of the three 30-mile heats, he was awarded the trophy. While it did not seem possible, the 1941 competition for the oldest trophy in United States powerboating decayed further when only one boat appeared for the race. That was Simmons' *My Sin*, which after a perfunctory run on the course at Red Bank, New Jersey, was awarded the famous cup. Depression and the widening war in Europe had taken their toll.

13

KEEP 'EM FLOATING

It was the twenty-seventh month of the war in Europe that December. The bombers flew east at 10 angels as the sky lightened in the dawn, a huge red sun climbing over the clouds. On the port flank at 11,000 feet were the torpedo bombers in tight formation; starboard at 9,000 were more torpedo bombers. Flying cover at 14 angels were the fighters, fore and aft. There were 190 planes in all. At 0700 local, Commander Mitsuo Fuchido tuned his RDF to KGMB; its Hawaiian music would take them in.

At 0700 Opana Mobile Radar on the northern tip of Oahu was shutting down as scheduled, but on the 'scope was a strange image, 132 miles out at 0702. The two privates manning the station debated what to do about the blip, then phoned in their report to a central unit. Knowing that a flight of B-17s was due on approximately the same heading, the Lieutenant in charge took no action. At 0755 the first bombs fell on Pearl Harbor; that too was an error. The bomber squadron's flight leader had misread a flare signal and attacked too early. Not that it mattered, for as they broke at 5,000 feet through the scattered clouds that had provided visual cover, they saw below them the battleships *Arizona, California, Nevada, Oklahoma, Tennessee, West Virginia* and a host of lesser craft.

Among them was PT (Patrol Torpedo) 23, moored in its nest with five other PTs awaiting transshipment to the Philippines. Lounging on the forward deck that Sunday morning were PT 23's gunner's mate and a torpedoman. Seeing the unmistakable "meatball" symbol on the wings of a torpedo bomber, they leaped into a gun turret and brought down the plane with fire from the boat's twin .50 caliber machine guns. Later some would claim that it was the first Japanese plane shot down during World War II.

When one of the most effective surprise attacks in military history ended about two hours later and Commander Fuchido winged his way back to the carrier *Akagi*, eight American battleships, three light cruisers, three destroyers and four auxiliaries were sunk or damaged. Dead or missing were 2,403 Americans while another 1,178 were wounded. As in World War I,

This 1943 80' Elco PT was part of an experimental program which tried various paint schemes to confuse and disorient the enemy.

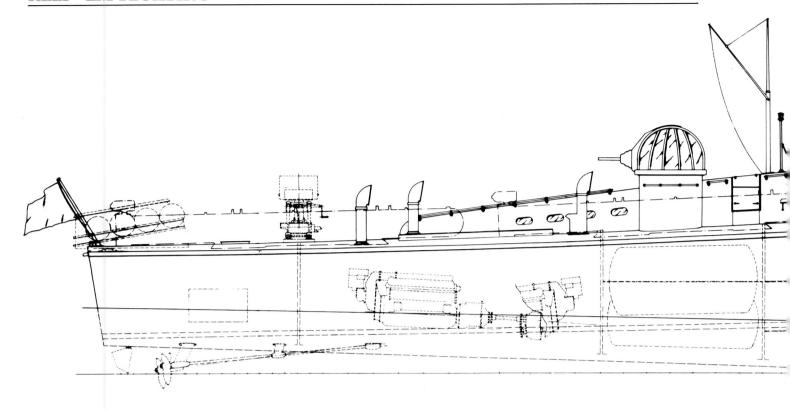

*The first Elco produc-
tion boats were 77'
long. This was the
type which captured
the public ima-
gination with its
Philippines exploits.
They were later
lengthened to 80' to
accommodate im-
proved torpedoes.*

America entered the conflict underprepared. United States armed forces consisted of about 1.5 million men, about two-thirds of them only partially trained. The Army Air Force had but 1,200 planes, including 150 heavy bombers. The Navy had 347 warships, among them 17 battleships — almost half rendered unusable by the attack on Pearl Harbor — and seven aircraft carriers. The Japanese fighting force consisted of 2.4 million men and 3 million reserves. Their air force outnumbered the United States' military aircraft by more than six to one, while the Japanese Navy had 230 combat vessels.

Six months after Pearl Harbor, the Japanese "Greater East Asia Co-Prosperity Sphere" encompassed nearly a third of the earth's surface. Meanwhile, Americans hungered for scraps of good news. There were not many, but among them were the exploits of the Squadron Three PT boats that had reached the Philippines before the declaration of war. Tales of heroism, daring rescues, the sinking of capital ships and bravery in the face of insuperable odds by the PT men were a psychological counterbalance to the darkest of realities: this was a war that America could lose.

The PTs' place in the popular imagination was secured for the duration on March 13, 1942. That was the day when General Douglas MacArthur, his wife and son boarded PT 41 on Corregidor for a harrowing ride and a subsequent escape to Australia. MacArthur and his key staff of about 20 climbed aboard four motor torpedo boats and arrived seasick but safe at Cagayan, Mindanao, several days later. The press seized on these exploits, and it was not long before a book about Squadron Three climbed the best-seller lists. Its title: *They Were Expendable.*

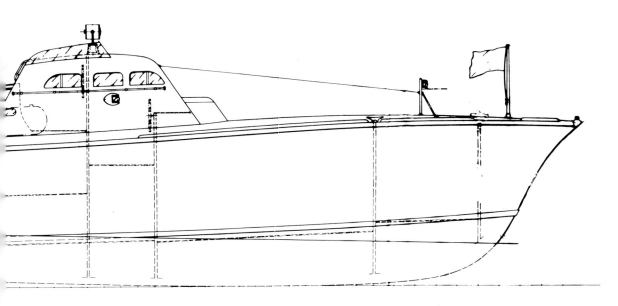

It was no small irony that boats which became famous as symbols of American resourcefulness and bravery were also boats which the Navy did not really want. In the years between the wars little attention was paid to small boats by the Navy. The total activity amounted to little more than the purchase of two of Britain's Thornycroft Coastal Motor Boats, brief experiments with Albert Hickman's Sea Sleds, and a 1920 flirtation with Alexander Graham Bell's radical hydrofoils. The nation that created the torpedo during the Civil War, achieved supreme speed with small steam vessels at the turn of the century and built the fastest raceboats in the world had a Navy concerned — perhaps rightfully — with the projection of blue-water strategic power, not guerrilla warfare with "splinter boats."

Franklin Delano Roosevelt changed all that in 1938. As the geopolitical stew thickened, Congress passed an immense $1 billion naval-expansion measure that included a special provision: "There is hereby authorized to be appropriated . . . $15,000,000 to be disbursed at the discretion of the President of the United States for construction of experimental vessels, none of which shall exceed 300 tons displacement." Roosevelt, a yachtsman and a force behind the submarine-chaser program of World War I that built more than 400 110-footers, was now in charge of a small-boat program for the Navy.

The Packard marine engine of World War II, of which 12,115 were built. This is the rare 1,800-horse-power 5M-2500 W-50 version. First shipped in 1944, it differs in appearance only by the aftercooler mounted above the supercharger. This cooled the air-fuel mix to allow manifold pressures of almost 12 pounds on 100-octane fuel.

179

The Navy's first public act was the announcement of a design contest in July of 1938. To provide motivation beyond the purely patriotic, a $15,000 first prize was announced in each of four categories — a 165' steel subchaser, a 110' wood subchaser, a 70' motor torpedo boat (MTB) capable of operating anywhere it might be lightered and a 54' motor torpedo boat specified as an in-shore coastal defender. The depression-decimated community of naval architects responded to the contest and, after three extensions, the competition was closed with a total of 34 designs received. The ultimate winners were a George Crouch design for the 54' MTB and a Sparkman & Stephens entry for the 70-footer. Contracts were let for the construction of prototypes, and New Orleans-based Higgins Industries began to build two Sparkman & Stephens boats while Fisher Boat Works in Detroit and the Fogal Boat Yard in Miami were awarded contracts for the 54-footers.

In late 1938 — just as the Navy was completing its design competition — the firm that ultimately built the largest number of PTs became involved in the program. This was Elco. They had already won one of the subchaser awards but had not entered a PT-boat design. In a convoluted series of events in which Assistant Secretary of the Navy Charles Edison, the son of Thomas Alva Edison, played a role, the orderly process put in place by the Navy was short-circuited.

Higgins Industries was also a major builder of PTs. With a different, patented hull design, the Higgins boats had many partisans who claimed they rode better than the Elcos. By war's end the measured performance of the two types was roughly equal.

In February of 1939 Henry Sutphen and Irwin Chase of Elco journeyed to England to review torpedo-boat progress there, apparently with a promise from Assistant Secretary Edison that the government would purchase a British boat if they should buy one. Exactly what transpired on the visit is the subject of varying accounts, but it appears that Sutphen and Chase were allowed free access to the British Navy's Motor Torpedo Boats, the future plans of the builders and the general hospitality of the Admiralty.

The boat selected by the men from Elco — along with the rights to manufacture it in the U.S. — was a 70-footer designed by Hubert Scott-Paine. Scott-Paine had devoted his life to speed, first as the manager of Supermarine Aviation Works, then as the owner of a pioneer commercial airline and finally as the founder and guiding light of the British Power Boat Company. Scott-Paine was known in the United States. He had been defeated by Gar Wood in the Harmsworth Trophy races several years before, but he had enjoyed success building crash boats for the Royal Air Force and MTBs for the Admiralty. Involved in the design and testing of these boats was none other than Lawrence of Arabia, T.E. Shaw, who had formed a close friendship with the chief draftsman of British Power. The draftsman and "Lawrence" worked together on a streamlined 80-mile-per-hour MTB, and the legacy of these efforts was seen in the Art Moderne (some said "zoot suit") appearance of what was called PV 70 and soon became U.S. Navy PT 9.

By the middle of the war PTs began evolving into gunboats. Here a cannon is being used against a Japanese shore installation in the South Pacific.

PT 9 arrived in New York as deck cargo on September 4, 1939, the day after Britain and France had declared war on Germany. Less than a month later Charles Edison wrote the President that he wanted to obtain additional boats of the Scott-Paine type with funds that remained in the 1938 Congressional appropriation. Shortly following this request was an ecstatic report from the Navy Trial Board's Inspecting Officer: "As a sea boat, PT 9 has my unqualified approval and I have such confidence in the boat after observing her in rough water that I would not hesitate to take her anywhere under any conditions." It was claimed that the boat would operate at full throttle in eight-foot seas and had a top speed of almost 58 miles per hour. "On the seaward run I do not believe that a destroyer could have maintained the speed which PT 9 held with complete comfort for all aboard," continued the trials report. A scant two and one-half years later a member of MacArthur's evacuation party described the ride as like "being inside a revolving concrete mixer," and an admiral with a half-century of experience at sea called the PT that saved his life ". . . the worst bridge I've ever been on. I wouldn't do duty on one of these goddamned PTs for anything in the world." But that was not the sentiment in Washington — called by some the Arsenal of Bureaucracy — in the closing days of 1939.

When the announcement was made in December that a contract had been signed for Elco to build an additional 23 Scott-Paine-based boats, a political firestorm followed. Leading the protests against the award on the grounds that it was non-competitive, violated the spirit of the design contest and did not represent the best design was Higgins Industries; soon others joined the debate, and the call for a Congressional investigation was heard. Charles Edison was appointed Secretary of the Navy by President Roosevelt, and the Navy indicated to the outraged boatbuilders that the Elco contract was not necessarily the last to be issued for MTBs. The controversy ebbed. Elco's $300,000 investment in the rights to build the Scott-Paine boat paid off with a $5 million contract.

"Late in the Fall of 1938," wrote Packard Vice President of Engineering, Colonel J.G. Vincent, "the Packard Management approved a plan to renew our Government contacts for the purpose of securing some Government business." One Packard project had been a large V-12 aero engine for the Navy that had been built in several versions. The water-cooled, single-overhead-cam, four-valve, twin-plug design was shelved when the Navy standardized on air-cooled radial engines. Originally drawn in the early

Pleasureboat builders such as Chris-Craft produced a wide range of small boats for the Army and Navy. Chris-Craft's primary World War II fleet consisted of a 36' landing craft, a 36' Navy picket boat, a 42' patrol and rescue boat and a 60' Army personnel boat.

1920s, the Packard design was advanced in its use of aluminum alloys; early versions of the 1A-2500 developed 800 horsepower at 2,000 rpm from a displacement of 2,539 cubic inches and weighed about 1,150 pounds dry. The engine set many aviation speed records. Power output rose throughout the 1920s, and in supercharged form Gar Wood claimed about 1,600 horsepower each from the four similar engines in *Miss America X*. In the spring of 1939 Packard received a contract for seven experimental MTB engines.

Virtually the entire United States boat-building industry was mobilized for the war. Consolidated, whose history included the building of naphtha launches, autoboats, steam yachts and torpedo boats, built sub-chasers during World War II.

While the original plan was to use the tooling and parts in inventory from the earlier aero and marine programs, Colonel Vincent felt that the old parts and tools were "not good enough either as to workmanship or metallurgy," and he ordered a redesign, "revising the drawings to current aircraft practice." As in the Liberty program of World War I, Packard once again made investments with no assurance of a return. The result was the 4M-2500 which displaced 2,490 cubic inches and developed 1,200 horsepower at 2,400 with an emergency rating of 1,350 horsepower at 2,500 rpm. It was essentially a new engine on the 60-degree V-12 architecture with revised cylinder heads, crankcase, crank, rods, pistons, centrifugal supercharger and drive, and new accessory locations. Fuel consumption at full throttle was 120 gallons of 100-octane aviation gas per hour. Shortly, the Navy standardized the Packard, and before the cessation of hostilities more than 12,000 engines were built, not only for MTBs but for most of the fast United Nations combatants of World War II. "Thank God for Packard engines," Scott-Paine told a reporter.

If the engine requirements were stabilized, the situation with hulls was not. Operational experience with the prototypes was beset with problems, delays, and disputes over doctrine. Some maintained that PTs should be kept small and low to minimize the target they presented; others argued for larger boats capable of carrying more firepower. Aviation partisans claimed that PTs were superfluous since small planes could carry torpedoes farther and faster. The rejoinder to this argument, in the days before small-craft radar, was that planes were limited in their ability to operate at night. While the doctrinal disputes raged, the operational reports presented a darkening picture.

Rudders on the Higgins boats were being eaten away by electrolytic action, their Vimalert engines consumed spark plugs voraciously, fuel consumption was 12 gallons per mile, galley stoves would not boil water, and the plastic windshields were scratched to opacity by the wipers. Engineering gremlins were everywhere.

The situation was even more serious on the Elco-built boats. By May of 1941 they were experiencing structural failures. In five-foot seas the "frames were moving back and forth so that they worked relative to the clamp a distance of about 1 1/2 inches," said one report. Planking was sprung, frames failed and longitudinals fractured at alarming rates. The pounding ride was injuring crew members, and Navy doctors found blood in their urine. Propellers shed blades, chopping holes in the bottoms of the boats.

While the boats were breaking up in actual use, the public was receiving reports of wonder weapons that would materialize from the mists at 60 knots, launch deadly torpedoes five miles away from an unspecified enemy, and retire as the blasts from the tin fishes tore apart the hulls of capital ships. It was the mission of the torpedo boat of the 1890s brought up to date a half-century later. Actual performance was something less than reported. The maximum recommended speed for torpedo attack was 9 knots and the actual top speed was about 45 knots. The boats were also claimed to take 15-foot seas at 46 miles per hour, and the boating magazines said that it was possible to prepare a breakfast of fried eggs, yolks unbroken and sunny side up, while cruising in a PT at more than 40 miles per hour.

This Army fireboat by Chris-Craft shows the close relationship between pre-war civilian pleasure-boats and their military counter-parts. There was neither time nor funds to develop special military designs in most cases.

The onset of war brought further problems. The stock of torpedoes, most left over from World War I, proved unreliable as a result of age, if not design. One officer testified that about one in four torpedoes would hit a target if fired from a range of less than 1,000 yards. "Inadequate torpedo equipment and control has prevented the PTs from achieving their full military value," stated one officer to the Navy's General Board. But the PTs had already found a tactical niche. In the field the crews converted them to gun boats, particularly in the Pacific. With an ingenuity that would prove characteristic, PT crews scavenged 37-millimeter cannons from downed aircraft, lashed them on the decks and went "barge busting."

The missions involved searching out and destroying Japanese supply and reinforcement traffic. A common type of barge was about 50' long and moved at a speed of 8 to 12 knots. PTs would lie in night ambush or patrol for barge traffic. "Jap barges make very clever use of reefs, islands, shore batteries, mine fields and other conditions that afford them maximum protection from attack," read a contemporary tactics memorandum. The barges were also heavily armed, often with a combination of 37- and 20-millimeter cannons and .50 caliber machine guns plus armor. The basic technique of barge busting involved an approach toward the stern of the barge — its heaviest weaponry was on the bow — with one gun firing at all times. The barge was then riddled with machine gun and cannon rounds until it sank. For particularly difficult barges, a depth charge was dropped alongside the barge during a high-speed pass. The force of the blast was intended to break the barge's back and sink it immediately.

While the PT crews in the Pacific perfected their barge tactics, United States boatbuilders were pouring out an alphabet soup of vessels to aid in the war effort. In addition to the PTs, there were picket boats, mine sweepers, rescue boats, lighters, assault boats, surf boats, sub-chasers and dozens more. All were classified with alphabetical symbols that began with AD, Destroyer Tenders, and ended more than 80 types later with YTT, Torpedo Testing Barges. By 1942 employment at the pleasureboat yards had risen to

Powerboating was curtailed for the duration, and boats such as this Hacker express cruiser were used by the Navy and Coast Guard for patrol duty and personnel transport. Heavy use, operation by inexperienced crews, plus shortages of paint and spare parts, took their toll on the pleasure fleet.

660 per cent of 1940 levels, and a survey by *Yachting* showed that of the 115 pleasureboat builders polled 84% were engaged full-time in war work. The average yard had increased its plant capacity by 175% in the same period.

Meanwhile, pleasureboating — particularly with power — was severely curtailed. Regulations prohibited operation at night, constrained cruising distances, required the sealing of radios, mandated identification cards and rationed gas supplies. An inboard-powered boat was entitled to no more than 500 gallons of fuel per year which was made available in 125-gallon quarterly installments. The practical effect was that few power yachtsmen living in northern climates could legally obtain their 500-gallon allotment. Later this was cut to 144 gallons per year. Racing was suspended for the duration.

By 1944 the United States was spending $250 million per day on the war effort, and at the end of the year nine million Americans were on active military duty. In 1945 this had risen to 12.1 million, or about one in eight of every American over the age of 18. There had emerged a new form of war under an old name: "amphibious warfare." In its new context "amphibious" meant the coordination of air, sea and land forces to seize and subdue enemy-held territory. This often required landing troops on beaches, and for these purposes a wide variety of special boats were developed. These were called Landing Craft (LCs) or Landing Ships (LSs) if over 200' in length. An "LSI" landed infantry while an LCT landed tanks. There were more than 40 specialized types developed by the end of the war, but the basic configuration was a barge-like form with a gas or Diesel engine and a bow that opened to let troops or machines ashore. They were used everywhere, from the Pacific islands to the beaches at Normandy. There they came ashore at 75-yard intervals along 10,000 yards of beach, and for months the landing craft delivered 30,000 troops and 30,000 tons of supplies each day, every day. In 90 days at Normandy almost 2.1 million Allied troops were landed along with 3.5 million tons of supplies. More than 40,000 landing craft were built during the war, principally 30- and 36-footers, along with another 10,000 landing vehicles and 3,300 landing ships; but there were, it seemed, never enough of them.

More than 40,000 landing craft of 40 specialized types were built in less than four years. This group awaits testing at Higgins, a major producer.

On October 1, 1945 — less than a month after the surrender of Japan — the Navy announced its losses in the Second World War: 696 vessels. There remained about 1,500 fighting ships. Only two battleships had been lost, both at Pearl Harbor. Five aircraft carriers, seven heavy cruisers, three light cruisers, 71 destroyers, 11 destroyer escorts and 52 submarines completed the list of lost first-line fighting ships. An additional 545 smaller vessels were lost including minelayers, minesweepers, subchasers, gunboats and PTs. Among the PTs about one in seven was lost, a particularly deadly ratio. Of the losses about 10% were caused by friendly fire, about 37% by the enemy. The balance were destroyed to prevent capture, lost to fire or collision, or eliminated by miscellaneous causes. Much as the nation turned away from the war toward the pleasant reality of peace, the Navy abandoned the PT program. Almost 120 boats were brought to the Philippines and burned at Samar Island. Most of the rest — about 300 boats — were stripped of military equipment and sold, many to foreign governments, some to private parties for conversion to yachts. America finished the war as it began it, largely without motor torpedo boats. At home, the boatbuilders looked forward to a surge in demand. More than 3.3 million men would be returning home from the Navy. Many, it was thought, would want pleasureboats. Racing would soon resume, given new life and higher speeds by wartime technological developments. Boating — and life — would return to normal. Or so it seemed.

Coming ashore from an LC on a tropical beach during a training exercise. These men were preparing for their role in the brutal Pacific "island-hopping" campaign.

14

RECORDS & ROOSTERTAILS

*T*he marquees read "The Sweetest Music This Side of Heaven," and the songs were known note-by-note in America's 33.9 million radio households. Their titles became Americana: *Give Me a Little Kiss, Will Ya Hon?, Boo-Hoo, Little White Lies, You're Driving Me Crazy, Harvest Moon, Moonlight Bay, Easter Parade* and *Auld Lang Syne*. It began in 1927 when Gaetano Albert Lombardo, his brothers and friends ventured from London, Ontario, to Cleveland, seeking work as a dance band in the ballrooms there. Challenged by the complexity of the time's popular songs, they evolved a technique of slowing tempos and simplifying harmonies, then adding a romantic mood by dimming ballroom lights. The mellow brass and saxophone choir became a signature sound. Queried about the minimal role of the drums in his music, Lombardo responded, "I prefer getting the rhythm from the shuffling sound of the dancers' shoes." This proved to be an immensely popular decision in the years before rock and roll, and Guy Lombardo sold 300 million records during his lifetime.

As a boy Guy Lombardo piloted his father's launch on a local river; he watched as his father's friends tinkered with the engines of their motorboats, waiting for spring and the annual tests of speed that determined the fastest local boat. In 1920 Lombardo traveled the short distance to Detroit and watched from shore as Gar Wood set a Gold Cup heat record of 70.0 miles per hour. In one of those peculiar loops of history, the 44-year-old leader of the "highest-grossing band in America" became the first to break Wood's quarter-century-old record.

A scant five months after V-J day the American Power Boat Association announced that the 1946 Gold Cup race would be held at Detroit and that there were new rules. Effectively, the competition was open to any boat with both a propeller and rudder in the water and between 10' and 40' in length. The Gold Cup was once again an unlimited race. There was an avalanche of entries—22 in all; and 17 boats competing in two qualifying heats comprised

Guy Lombardo strikes a pose for the camera at Red Bank, New Jersey, in 1946. The National Sweepstakes race was won by Lombardo that year.

Tempo VI was the two-time pre-war Gold Cup winner My Sin. Lombardo purchased it when the previous owner retired from racing. Here three newsreel cameramen get a moving shot in the pits at Detroit.

the largest starting field in cup history. The 225-cubic-inch hydroplanes that ran nearly as fast as the pre-war Gold Cup boats made up almost half the field; the other half was a mixture of old and new. *Hotsy Totsy*, the 1940 winner, was entered under new ownership. E.A. Wilson's *Miss Canada III*, a Miller-powered pre-war contender, came to Detroit, as did *Miss Golden Gate III*, owned by Californians Dan Foster and Dan Arena. The *III* carried a V-1710 Allison aircraft engine and was considered a "dark horse," even though Arena had driven in three pre-war cup races and countless others. The favorite, it was reported, was Guy Lombardo in *Tempo VI*. After a year of racing in 1942 in a Ventnor 225, Lombardo purchased *My Sin* for $6,001 from Zalmon Simmons, re-named the boat and won the National Sweep-stakes at Red Bank against a modest field.

Through qualifying races the six fastest boats were selected for the Gold Cup heats. Of these, only two were Unlimited boats; the other four were 225-hydroplanes. Among the 225s, Robert Bogie's *Blitz II* was nearly as fast as its Allison-powered competitor, despite having an engine about one-eighth as large. They roared and buzzed across the line that cool and cloudy Labor Day with an audience estimated at 200,000 watching from the banks of the Detroit River. *Golden Gate* was first across the line, followed by two 225s with Lombardo in *Tempo VI* in fourth position. By the end of the first three-mile lap *Tempo* had passed *Gate*, and despite challenges by Dan Arena Lombardo never relinquished the lead. Old lap records were retired as

Lombardo set a new mark of 73.295 miles per hour. Late in the heat Arena's boat slowed with mechanical problems. Lombardo lapped the aero-engined California entry and won the heat at 66.32 miles per hour.

Under the complex points scheme used for the cup, Arena had to beat Lombardo by more than five minutes to win, and this was exactly what he tried to do in the final race. With the revitalized *Miss Golden Gate III*, Arena set lap record after lap record with Lombardo and *Tempo* positioned involuntarily but strategically in second place, the gap between them widening. *Tempo* was a mile and a half behind by the third lap while the remaining 225s snarled along 10 to 15 miles per hour off the pace. Racing veteran and 1932 Gold Cup winner Bill Horn estimated Arena's straightaway speeds as greater than 100 miles per hour, and his best lap reached 77.91 miles per hour. It was a hopeless but glorious run. To win the cup and overcome Lombardo's time advantage, an average speed of 88 miles per hour was needed; and on the eighth lap Arena's Allison lost oil pressure. The boat slumped off plane, and Lombardo motored by to victory and the fulfillment of an adolescent dream: he had won the Gold Cup and beaten Gar Wood's 1920 record. In the process he also set a new 90-mile average for the cup of 68.072 miles per hour.

The sun was rising on a dream world for racers. Thousands of surplus aircraft engines were becoming available at used-car prices. The 1,475-horsepower V-1710 Allisons that powered such legendary fighter planes as the Lockheed P-38 and the Bell Airacobra were the first to be used, but it was not long before the even more powerful Packard Merlin V-1650s — rated at 2,250 horsepower at 3,000 rpm, War Emergency — were available, priced as low as $500, new, complete, cosmolined and crated. This was the engine from the Spitfires, Mosquitos and Mustangs that swept the skies of Europe and established Allied air superiority. As with the Liberties after World War I, the supercharged V-12s were the latest technology, and once again unprecedented power was available to racers.

The Allison aircraft engine soon became the powerplant of choice. The Allison's weight required that it be positioned well back in the hull, and the driver was placed in a race car-like pod aft of the transom in many early post-war boats.

*My Sweetie under-
way during her
immensely success-
ful 1949 season. The
forward step, called
a ''bump-step,'' is
fully clear of the
water. Sweetie set
new records in the
Gold Cup, National
Sweepstakes, Silver
Cup and President's
Cup.*

A world awash in horsepower brought another set of challenges: hulls that could hold the engines without destroying themselves and propulsion systems that could survive the onslaught of power. The 1948 Gold Cup showed the hazards of massive horsepower; this was the first year that the Allisons were widely available. Race day became known as ''Black Saturday.'' A total of 40 boats entered the race and 21 appeared. One entry, *Miss Windsor*, sank on the way to the course.

As events unfolded, new meaning was given to the phrase ''elimination heat.'' After the 1-A and 1-B eliminations, only four boats remained to start the second 30-mile race while 17 left the race due to failures, crashes or black flags. Guy Lombardo in *Tempo VI*, now Allison-powered, swerved to avoid a novice entry and capsized, breaking his arm. *Miss Canada III*, recently Merlin-powered and capable of a reported 119 miles per hour, retired with broken planks on the starboard side. *Such Crust*, a new Ventnor with an Allison driven by Dan Arena, turned the fastest lap of the race at 57.45 miles per hour and then dropped out with a broken back. Even the masterful John L. Hacker was unable to cope with the new conditions. His freshly-built *My Sweetie* led heat 1-A for six laps before a battery came loose and broke through bottom planks. *Sweetie* was beached before she could sink.

In heat three only two boats started. The winner, *Miss Great Lakes*, formerly *Miss Golden Gate III*, limped through the third heat at a speed of 30.66 miles per hour for the victory. The final heat speed could easily have been beaten by *Dixie II* in 1909, while the best lap was about equal to the performance of a Smith hydroplane of 30 years before. There were at least as many opinions about the race as there were observers. Some criticized the

A.P.B.A. for starting the race in rough water; 3' swells were reported on parts of the course. Harry Greening, who lost the cup through protest in 1924, noted that one of his *Rainbows* ran under similar conditions at 64 miles per hour. Bill Horn gave a succinct summary, saying that most "drove with their feet, instead of their heads."

Time provided the solution as designers, builders, mechanics, drivers and owners learned to cope with the surfeit of horsepower and its implications. One year later *Motor Boating* reported, "Never before in the history of motor boat racing have so many outstanding and superior Gold Cup boats run so long and so well." In 1949 15 of 19 Unlimited-class records were broken. Of the new records more than half were set by a single boat, *My Sweetie*. The 30' by 8' Allison-engined *Sweetie* had originally been designed by Hacker for Ed Gregory (the son of E.M. Gregory of *Bear Cat* fame) and Ed Schoenherr, two young Detroit racing enthusiasts. They soon sold her to Horace Dodge. She was built in the shop of Les Staudacher, a Kawkawlin, Michigan, woodworker, who manufactured church pews and built boats as a sideline.

Then in his fifth decade as designer and still innovating, Hacker worked up a two-step hull with a nacelle-enclosed propeller between the steps at the boat's center of gravity. Two small, widely-spaced rudders at the transom provided directional control. T.F.W. Meyer, who designed the propellers for *Sweetie* as well as for *My Sin*, *Miss America X* and many other boats, believed that the shafting eliminated by *Sweetie*'s propulsion arrangement saved about 200 horsepower in friction losses. He also thought that the propeller location aided the boat's turning behavior. Early three-point hydroplanes were notoriously difficult to turn, but *Sweetie* could turn — at least in the hands of driver William "Wild Bill" Cantrell — with "paint-scraping precision." Gar Wood thought that *Sweetie* pointed the way to the future of high-speed boat design. He believed the tendency of three-point hydroplanes to lift and flip over backwards made them very dangerous. Just such an accident killed Kansas City racer and almost perpetual limited-champion Jack "Pops" Cooper in 1948.

The stunningly beautiful Sweetie *being towed out of the pits at Detroit. The success of the Hacker-designed 30-footer, built by Les Staudacher and driven by Bill Cantrell, led many to believe that two-step hulls were superior to three-pointers.*

The three-point boats were operating on the edge of stability at the intersection of volatile hydrodynamic and aerodynamic forces in the domain of what today would be called "surface effects." They were attempting to fly close to the water. Even before World War II, California hydroplane racers discovered the phenomenon of "prop-riding" in the Ventnor three-pointers and in the boats built by Champion in Long Beach, California. On smooth water the stern of the boat would lift, and daylight could be seen under the transom. Some thought the boat was planing on its propeller shaft or propeller; others, that the hull was lifted aerodynamically. It was probably a combination of factors, varying from boat to boat with subtle differences in balance, sponson angle and a host of other variables. But when a boat "prop-rode," it went faster, a result of the reduced wetted area and appendage drag. At 50 to 60 miles per hour the stern lifted, and a surging increase in speed could be felt. In the East, where racing often took place in rougher water, the stern-lifting phenomenon was known but much more difficult to create reliably. Designers and builders stood at a triple-fork in the path to higher speed. Down one path lay the problem of too much lift and a rising hull that flipped over backwards. Down another path — not enough lift — lay the disaster of "submarining" where the bow of the boat caught the water and submerged itself and its occupants at high speed. The third path in the thicket of potentially deadly variables led to dramatically higher speeds. For a while there was a battle of contending design factions — two-pointers like *Sweetie* versus the growing ranks of three-pointers — but this was essentially a skirmish with both sides having access to unprecedented power. Neither type was necessarily faster.

The Ventnor three-pointer Such Crust. *Driven by Dan Arena,* Crust *set an all-time competition lap record of 98.164 miles per hour in 1949 and was the first United States boat to break Gar Wood's 1932 mile record. She ran the mile at 127.063 miles per hour.*

Guy Lombardo demonstrated this in 1948 when he was able to squeeze but 119 miles per hour out of his Allison-engined pre-war Ventnor. With his old Miller-Zumbach engine he had achieved 101 miles per hour with less than one-fourth the power. The answer came on June 26, 1950, as the radio reported that Stan Sayres of Seattle, at the wheel of a boat called *Slo-Mo-Shun IV*, had crushed the 11-year-old world water speed record of Sir

Malcolm Campbell in his Ventnor-derived, Rolls-Royce-engined *Bluebird*. The 141.74 mile-per-hour Campbell mark was bumped 18.58 miles per hour to 160.32 average speed. With Sayres and designer Ted Jones in the cockpit with his foot on the throttle, *Slo-Mo* rocketed through the officially measured mile in 21.98 seconds for a best run of 163.785 miles per hour.

"Stanley S. Sayres . . . seems to be in need of a bit of introduction to the boating world," wrote A.P.B.A racing commissioner Kent Hitchcock, who certified the record attempt. Much as H.J. Leighton went from Syracuse to prominence with a 23-mile-per-hour boat in 1902, *Slo-Mo-Shun IV* materialized before the racing establishment as a 160-mile-per-hour boat, which few away from her Seattle home even knew existed.

But *Slo-Mo* was not new. She had been put overboard eight months earlier; driven on Lake Washington by her designer every morning before he went to work at Boeing as a supervisor, *Slo-Mo* may very well have had more hours at high speed than any Unlimited in America. Rain, snow or rough water did not stop Ted Jones as he gave the boat her daily exercise. A fuel company footed the bill for the thousands of gallons of aviation gas consumed as the boat was developed, tested and developed further. Nor was she designed in a vacuum, despite the distance from Detroit. Stan Sayres bought Pops Cooper's Ventnor and the lessons that boat could teach were absorbed. Reconnaissance at the 1948 Gold Cup and other races gave *Slo-Mo*'s designer and owner an understanding of the character of competitive boats, their strengths and weaknesses. To designer Jones, this was principally a question of weaknesses — metallurgical, structural, hydrodynamic and aerodynamic — as he watched "Black Saturday" unfold.

The legendary Slo-Mo-Shun IV *eases out of the pits. Slo-Mo's tail fin was adjustable to counteract torque-steer at high speeds.*

Jones was apparently more convinced of his ability to build a successful Unlimited "prop-rider" than was Stanley Sayres. The agreement between the two men provided that *Slo-Mo IV* must break Campbell's record or Jones would pay Chrysler dealer Sayres $100 a month until the reported $19,000 expense of the boat was paid off. *IV* was the second boat which Jones designed for Sayres; *Slo-Mo-Shun III* was built at cost and with a guarantee that she would break the national class record. This she did. According to one source, Jones' only compensation for designing *Slo-Mo IV* was the privilege of driving for a record attempt, the Gold Cup and the Harmsworth; and he did drive for the Gold Cup.

*Slo-Mo-Shun V
under construction
in the Jensen Shop.
From left to right,
Ted Jones, Stanley
Sayres and Anchor
Jensen examine a
drawing while crafts-
man Ralph Shamek
poses by the sponson.
The arrow points to
a "non-trip" edge
on the sponson in-
tended to improve
the boat's turning
ability.*

Based on prior experience with what Gar Wood called "paper boats," the consensus in Detroit was that *Slo-Mo-Shun IV* was fast in a straight line, but her reliability was unproven and, like most fast straight-line boats, she would not be able to turn. The consensus was wrong. *Slo-Mo* turned her first Gold Cup lap at 80.119 miles per hour, a new record. It was a short-lived triumph as Bill Cantrell driving *My Sweetie* promptly turned in an 86.200 mile fourth lap in an attempt to catch the vanishing *Slo-Mo*. By the eighth lap of the 10-lap race *Slo-Mo* had lapped all boats but Cantrell's; and in the home stretch of the tenth lap, Jones and riding mechanic Mike Welsch lapped *Sweetie*, setting a new heat record of 80.151 miles per hour.

For the second race of the day Lou Fageol replaced Cantrell as *My Sweetie*'s pilot; Cantrell's injuries from an earlier crash in *Delphine X* did not allow him to continue. The second race looked very different as *Sweetie* held a small lead over *Slo-Mo*, both lapping Guy Lombardo in his recently-lengthened *Tempo VI*. On the back stretch *Sweetie*'s engine coughed, then died. The Allison had lost its oil pressure, and Jones nursed *IV* by the downed *Sweetie*. *Slo-Mo*'s engine mounts had broken, but they were quickly repaired, and for the third heat only Lombardo's *Tempo* was left to compete; the half-dozen other boats that started had all retired. By the second lap *Tempo* was a mile behind and could not win unless *Slo-Mo* broke down. She did not and motored on to an easy victory, averaging about 73.6 miles per hour for the heat. Once again, the Gold Cup went west, this time as far as it was possible to go: Seattle. Driver Jones and mechanic Welsch returned to their homes and jobs. *Slo-Mo-Shun IV* awaited the Harmsworth Trophy races.

Slo-Mo is lowered onto her cradle by Anchor Jensen for the journey to Detroit while a mechanic guides her stern. This 1956 trip was the last for the "Old Lady"; she crashed during qualifications for the 1956 Gold Cup and was completely destroyed.

The Harmsworth of 1950 had but a single ''international'' challenger, E.A. Wilson's *Miss Canada IV*. Failure of a steering wheel bracket, porpoising, and planking damage on *Miss Canada* soon turned the first race into an American contest, one won by *Slo-Mo* at 91.127 miles per hour. Crossing the line first, the boat was never seriously challenged. Interest in the second day's race remained high, the main question being whether a modified *My Sweetie* or the 3-pointer *Such Crust II* could catch what fans were now calling the ''West Coast Wonder Boat.'' They could not, and *Slo-Mo* averaged 100.68 miles per hour for the 40-mile race, the first time a triple-digit speed

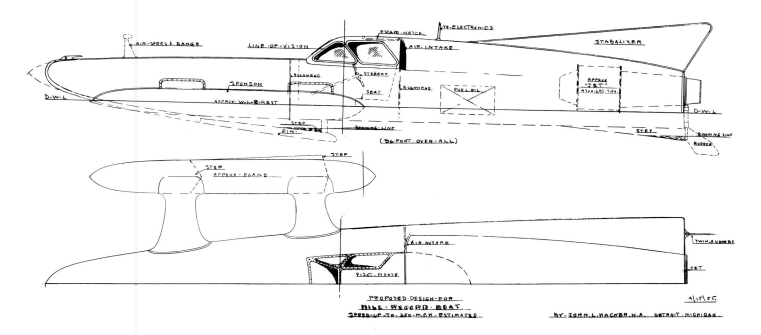

PROPOSED·DESIGN·FOR
MILE·RECORD·BOAT
SPEED·UP·TO·250·M.P.H.·ESTIMATED

BY·JOHN·L·HACKER·N.A. DETROIT·MICHIGAN

There was great interest in jet boats for water speed record attempts after England's Donald Campbell pushed the world record to 202.32 miles per hour in 1955. This proposed design by 78-year-old John Hacker was never built but includes electronic controls among its advanced features.

had been maintained for an entire event. Mechanic Mike Welsch assured reporters that *Slo-Mo* had never been opened up, but it was enough. *Slo-Mo-Shun IV* became the first boat in nearly three decades to hold simultaneously the Gold Cup, the Harmsworth Trophy and the world water speed record.

For the next five years *Slo-Mo* and her sister *Slo-Mo-Shun V* became the boats to beat, establishing a Gold Cup dominance that recalled the days of the *Dixies*, Chris Smith and Gar Wood. The 1951, 1952, 1953 and 1954 Gold Cups were victories for the *Slo-Mo*s, and Seattle became a center for Unlimited racing activity. Searching for a builder to replace Anchor Jensen, Ted Jones struck an alliance with Les Staudacher, and Staudacher learned to build the three-pointers, first with Jones, then on his own. Kawkawlin, Michigan, became the place to visit for those in search of ultimate speed. By 1958, 19 of 29 possible Gold Cup entries — almost two-thirds — were Staudacher-built; of those, seven were designed by Ted Jones. Never before in the history of powerboat racing had a builder and designer achieved such dominance.

The 1955 Gold Cup race broke the hold of the *Slo-Mo*s. That year, while the Jones-Staudacher *Miss Thriftway* won two out of three heats, the boat lost the cup to the 29' 10" Allison-powered *Gale V*. A crowd of a half-million had left Lake Washington thinking the trophy was safe in Seattle for another year, despite the DNF of *Slo-Mo IV* and the crash of *Slo-Mo V* that wrecked the boat and hospitalized driver Lou Fageol. But when the points system used to determine the winner was computed, an extra 400 points were awarded *Gale* for the fastest total time for three heats, giving the trophy back to the Detroit Yacht Club. The already-strained relations between Seattle and Detroit partisans became still more tense.

The tensions erupted in 1956, creating a conflict not seen since the days of Gar Wood, Kaye Don and the Harmsworth Trophy. The charge — brought by a Detroit race official — was that *Miss Thriftway* had hit the number seven turn-buoy. This caused the local race committee to award the trophy to Detroit's *Miss Pepsi*, a twin-engined Hacker step hydroplane. *Thriftway* partisans responded with a kinescope of the race from a Seattle television station, which they claimed showed that their boat had not hit the buoy. A report later surfaced that *Miss Pepsi* had also hit a turn marker. Adding still further complication was a lawsuit by Horace Dodge, asking that the race be declared "no contest" since his entry *My Sweetie Dora* had been bumped from the start by a late qualifier. Meeting followed meeting, and charges and counter-charges were traded while a circuit court judge moved with deliberate speed. Two months later the A.P.B.A. decided that *Miss Thriftway* was the winner. Almost a month later Judge Joseph A. Moynihan dismissed the Dodge suit, deciding that the purpose of the suit had been satisfied when a change in qualifying rules was made. An era had ended, not with the cup in the courts, but with the destruction of *Slo-Mo IV* during qualifications for the race. A few days after he towed the remains of *Slo-Mo* back to Seattle, Stanley St. Clair Sayres suffered a heart attack and died. The boat and one of the men that opened a new chapter in the history of speed on water were both gone.

Racing had changed. Professional drivers and boats named for products were introduced, beginning in the late 1940s. In the 1950s rapid growth of the sport led to the creation of a national championship based on a points scheme. As many as a dozen races were held in a single season. In prior years there had been three major races and sometimes four. In the late 1950s the

The Jones-Staudacher Miss Thriftway *gets a new engine. The boat was ultimately awarded the Gold Cup after a three-month controversy about whether or not she hit a buoy during the race.*

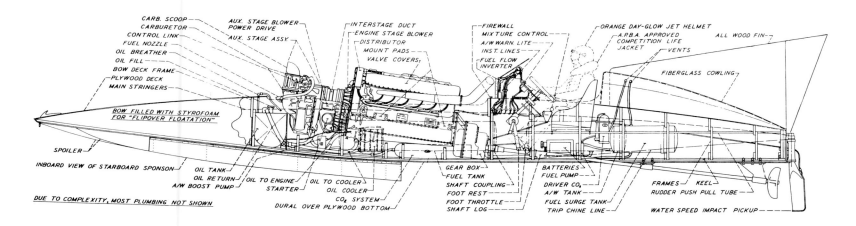

CARB. SCOOP
CARBURETOR
CONTROL LINK
FUEL NOZZLE
OIL BREATHER
OIL FILL
BOW DECK FRAME
PLYWOOD DECK
MAIN STRINGERS

AUX. STAGE BLOWER POWER DRIVE
AUX. STAGE ASS'Y.

INTERSTAGE DUCT
ENGINE STAGE BLOWER
DISTRIBUTOR
MOUNT PADS
VALVE COVERS

FIREWALL
MIXTURE CONTROL
A/W WARN. LITE
INST. LINES
FUEL FLOW INVERTER

ORANGE DAY-GLOW JET HELMET
A.P.B.A. APPROVED COMPETITION LIFE JACKET
VENTS
ALL WOOD FIN

FIBERGLASS COWLING

BOW FILLED WITH STYROFOAM FOR "FLIPOVER FLOATATION"

SPOILER
INBOARD VIEW OF STARBOARD SPONSON
OIL TANK
OIL RETURN
A/W BOOST PUMP
OIL TO ENGINE
STARTER
OIL TO COOLER
OIL COOLER
CO_2 SYSTEM
DURAL OVER PLYWOOD BOTTOM

GEAR BOX
FUEL TANK
SHAFT COUPLING
FOOT REST
FOOT THROTTLE
SHAFT LOG

BATTERIES
FUEL PUMP
DRIVER CO_2
A/W TANK
FUEL SURGE TANK
TRIP CHINE LINE

FRAMES
KEEL
RUDDER PUSH PULL TUBE
WATER SPEED IMPACT PICKUP

DUE TO COMPLEXITY, MOST PLUMBING NOT SHOWN

This drawing shows the configuration and complexity of a late 1950s Unlimited hydroplane as designed and built by Les Staudacher. During his career Staudacher built 56 Unlimited hulls, each varying subtly from the other. Boats of this type remained competitive into the 1980s.

practice of "bidding" for important races was introduced. A winner no longer won an important race for his city and his yacht club. In 1961 further changes were made in the Gold Cup rules. It was no longer an endurance race of 90 miles but was, instead, a race of 15-mile heats, usually totaling 60 miles. Engine changes between heats were also permitted for the first time.

The year 1961 was a watershed in another way. The race for the Harmsworth Trophy was won by Canada with *Miss Supertest III*, driven by Bob Hayward and owned by James Thompson, the same boat that first captured the trophy in 1959 and defended it in 1960. After the 1961 victory, Hayward was killed when *Miss Supertest II* flipped during the Silver Cup race at Detroit. Unable to field a defender, the Canadians suggested that the Harmsworth become a competition for smaller boats. The Harmsworth Trophy, which since 1903 had been a symbol of competition between nations, was shelved.

April of 1962 saw the last great feat of the lineage that began with *Slo-Mo-Shun IV*. At Guntersville, Alabama, Roy Duby, the crew-chief and sometimes driver of *Miss U.S. I*, roared up and down the measured mile at an average speed of 200.44 miles per hour. It was an exercise in frustration and delays. The timing equipment failed, spectator boats crossed the course, and carburetor icing threatened to defeat the attempt; for a while it looked as though *U.S. I* would continue with the bad luck that had marked her career since the boat was built in 1957. Finally everything worked, and Duby shot down the course at 204.55 miles per hour for the mile. A second run was much faster, but the timing equipment failed. It had begun to rain, but Duby steered out on the course again. Partially blinded by the stinging rain, Duby missed the start of the course and corrected sharply at high speed, tripping the starting clocks at 160 miles per hour. Accelerating through the mile, he averaged 196.33 miles per hour for the third and final run. Roy Duby's record of 200.44 miles per hour average stands in the late 1980s as a world one-mile mark for propeller-driven boats.

15

VERY FINNY

*T*o the boatbuilders of the 1940s there was the promise of a golden age after World War II. They had greatly expanded their facilities, often at government expense, and the supply of trained workers was never larger. The industry believed that not only would old boats need to be replaced, but new owners, their pockets filled with wartime savings, would take up boating in vast, unprecedented numbers. New technologies, perfected in the crucible of combat, would bring streamlined, high-performance, light-weight speedboats and cruisers to the multitudes. The millions of men who had served at sea would want boats for personal pleasure. There were even predictions that atomic power would be the prime mover of the future.

But the reality was something else. The first problem was shortages. In 1946 boatbuilding wood was unavailable, engines were scarce, and paint was in short supply, unless it was grey. Materials prices skyrocketed while workers, whose earnings had been frozen since the outbreak of the war, demanded higher wages. These seemed to be transitory problems, and in 1947 pleasureboating boomed with sales exceeding $900 million, a new record. The golden age arrived, but it lasted for only a year. Expenditures on boating skidded downward, dropping each year until they came to rest at $625 million in 1951. The great age of boating waited in the wings as Americans spent for the basics of housing and transportation.

Amidst the frustration of unfulfilled expectations, brave pronouncements that success was on the horizon and the buying, selling and failure of boat companies such as Elco and Gar Wood, a few men were at work on the future, putting to practical use the "scientific miracles" wrought by World War II. It began subtly, almost insignificantly, not with luxury cruisers, flashy runabouts or 150 mile-per-hour raceboats, but with the smallest members of the pleasure fleet: rowboats, dinghies and small one-design sailboats. A revolution in materials was incubating as boating sagged into the 1950s and, like most revolutions, its roots extended far into the past.

This 1947 19' Gar Wood styled by industrial designer Norman Bel Geddes represented the new post-war fashion in runabouts. A top speed of 35 miles per hour was available from a 110-horsepower Chrysler six. Note the "streamlined" stern treatment.

The basic concept was lamination, the fastening together of thin layers of material to form a shape such as a boat hull. In the years just after the Civil War, George Waters obtained patents for laminated boats made of paper and shellac. Phenomenally light, a 28' Waters rowing shell weighed only 22 pounds. The boats were durable; one was rowed from New York to Florida, a voyage that took five months. For almost a decade Waters built paper boats until his Troy, New York, factory was destroyed by fire in 1876. Beginning about 1904, Skaneateles Boats in upstate New York started experimenting with laminating hulls of wood veneer, and in Michigan plywood pioneer Henry Haskell was making molded plywood canoes before World War I.

By the 1920s adventurous designers were specifying plywood bulkheads and other components in their high-performance boats, but World War II gave real impetus to lamination techniques and materials. Concerned about metal shortages, the armed forces invested heavily in alternative fabrication technologies, and soon components of both boats and aircraft were being turned out in molded plywood. The deckhouses of the Elco PTs were made of this material, and it permitted a strong, light assembly to be built in a fraction of the time required for conventional construction.

The basic process required a mold in which thin layers of wood were built up with layers of adhesive between them. The assembly was then subjected to heat in a giant "pressure cooker" called an autoclave. The key was the adhesives, and the war brought forth many new types, including "polyester thermosetting resins." These resins could be combined with paper, cotton, wood, sisal, felt, canvas or other materials to create fuel tanks, radomes, equipment covers and many other items. And, it appeared, some were ideal for boatbuilding. In the years just after the war, literally dozens of new processes were used to build boats.

The Columbian Rope Company developed a method of combining sisal fibers used in ropemaking with plastic resins. It was called *Co-Ro-Lite*, and an eight-foot dinghy hull could be built in less than two and a half hours. In New Jersey, Taylor Winner, a pioneer in lamination, was building dinghies, sailboats and outboards to 14' from a combination of canvas, sisal and Bakelite resin. They were named Plasticrafts.

The potential of alternative materials intrigued many, and, using their wartime manufacturing experience, aircraft manufacturers such as Grumman and Douglas entered the market with aluminum boats. The potential for labor savings was immense. Writing in *Motor Boating*, naval architect William Atkin compared the 3,000 parts needed to build an 18' launch in wood to the 80 needed to make it of metal. There was nothing really new about metal boats. The W.H. Mullins Company of Salem, Ohio, built small pressed-steel boats beginning in the 1890s and sold thousands of them before collapsing in the 1920s; but two decades after the demise of Mullins the idea seemed new once again.

By 1948 the ultimate innovation in boatbuilding materials became commercially available: fiberglass. It was — and is — literally glass. Molten glass is drawn through a die at high temperatures to create thin strands of glass or "glass fibers." Not a new process, cloth was woven from glass fibers by the French in the 1830s, but the method had been unused for a century. With roughly three times the strength of natural fibers, fiberglass proved to be an ideal material to combine via lamination with the new polyester resins. The advantages, compared to wood, seemed spectacular. A boat could be made in one piece by mass-production methods using workers with little skill. A fiberglass boat was inherently watertight, and it soon proved possible to give the hull a non-fading finish, eliminating the need to paint, at least for a while. Such a boat could not rot, required few fastenings and was dimen-

The pre-war trend toward streamlining accelerated after the war, as did the popularity of enclosed boats. John Hacker combined the two in this late 1940s custom "sporta-bout." Hacker's work from this period also presaged the heavy use of shiny trim that would reach a peak in the 1950s for both autoboats and automobiles.

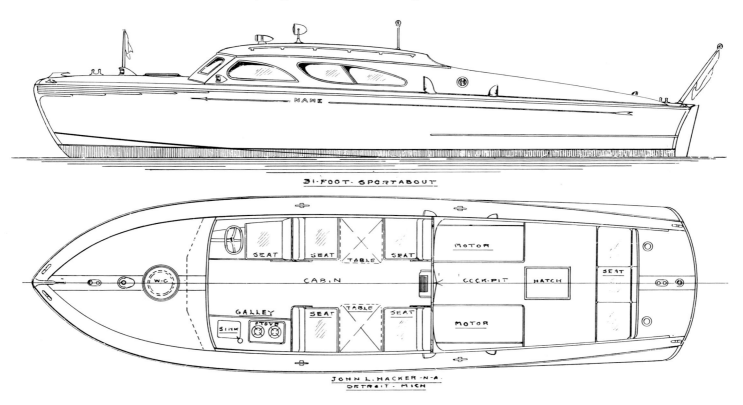

31-FOOT-SPORTABOUT

JOHN L. HACKER · N · A · DETROIT · MICH

203

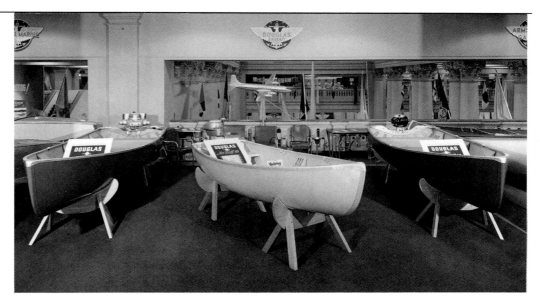

Douglas Aircraft was among the firms which expected a post-war boating boom for which it produced these small outboard boats in a then-novel material, aluminum.

sionally stable since it did not absorb water. It soon became clear that the man-hours needed to build a laminated glass and plastic boat were about one-fourth that of wood construction. The potential to build lighter boats from fiberglass laminates was also present but, as a practical matter, many weighed 20 to 25% more than their aluminum counterparts.

With few exceptions the boat industry did not take to the new material very quickly. Most of the early fiberglass boats were built by ''fabricators'' that made a variety of components in laminated fiberglass. Industrial parts such as tanks, pipes and machinery covers were produced by the same methods as those used to build boats. One exception was Carl Beetle, whose lineage included New Bedford, Massachusetts, whaleboat builders dating back to 1791. For two generations his family had built a 12' one-design sailboat called the Beetle Cat and, through a friend, Carl Beetle heard about General Electric's lamination facilities in Pittsfield, Massachusetts. As a boatbuilder Beetle had always had a penchant for innovation and efficiency.

The trend to alternative materials was in place before World War II. This 1941 cruiser by Revere Copper and Brass was built to show the potential of metal in boatbuilding. It was used briefly as a patrol boat during the war.

He quickly saw the potential of the process and arranged with G.E. to produce his Beetle Cats in fiberglass-reinforced plastic. The resins available at the time required heat and pressure, so special molds were built into which steam could be injected to cure the resin. Taking the technology to its limit, both the hull and deck were molded in one piece, a method more sophisticated than that commonly used today.

To the boat buyers of the 1940s, the sterile, almost appliance-like appearance of the Beetle boats was unattractive, no matter what the maintenance advantages. Buyers stayed away in droves until Carl Beetle made a few concessions to tradition. A wooden deck, coaming and seats were substituted for the original plastic pieces, and the boats began to sell.

Production by General Electric rose to two Beetle Cats and one 10' dinghy hull per day before Beetle began building the hulls in his own plant. This was made possible in the late 1940s by the development of new resins that no longer needed heat and pressure to cure. It was still necessary to paint the boats, but by the early 1950s a special colored resin called "gel-coat" became available. This was used to coat the mold before beginning lamination and created the characteristic smooth, glossy appearance of a fiberglass boat. The technology of today's fiberglass boats was essentially in place, but Carl Beetle did not live to see the results of his pioneering. Disappointed with the lack of acceptance by boat buyers, he sold his company — then producing 10 models, including a 24' powerboat — in 1951 and died in 1953, just as the industry was entering a period of rapid growth.

Carl Beetle was among the pioneers of fiberglass and resin construction. Here he is showing the strength of his boats by shooting at a fiberglass panel. Buyers were unconvinced of the benefits, and seven years passed before the technology introduced by Beetle, Taylor Winner and others became popular.

Beetle was not alone in his innovation; other firms such as Winner, Dyer, Palmer Scott, Western Plastics and Gar Wood, Jr. were working along similar lines with some variations in method. But the new material was simply not accepted in the contracting market. Between 1946 and 1953 — the year Beetle died — industry analysts estimated about 4,000 "plastic" boats were produced. Yet, in 1954 alone that number rocketed to 16,000; in 1955 it leaped 150% to 40,000 and in 1957 grew to an estimated 55,000 boats, consuming 10,000 tons of glass fibers. Total expenditures for boating in 1957 reached $1.9 billion, triple the sum spent in 1951.

Many factors combined to create the boom of the 1950s. Growing discretionary income, government programs that built dams and created recreational waterways in places like Texas and Oklahoma, an interest in "do-it-yourself" activities and a general prosperity brought hundreds of thousands, then millions, into a new recreational activity. The mass market first identified in the 1920s became a reality. The new buyers were not steeped in the traditions of yachting and the sea. They were ordinary people buying a recreational product, often for the first time. The industry responded with fins and rocket-like shapes in open imitation of the styling that so successfully sold automobiles. It was fiberglass which made this possible; it could be molded into forms which were difficult, if not impossible, to create in wood.

Leading the way in this exploration of the potential of the new boatbuilding materials was Milwaukee-based industrial designer Brooks Stevens, who, with outboard maker Evinrude as a client, created "prophetic" one-off boats for the annual boat shows in major cities. The first of these was the Evinrude *Lark* that combined a number of aero and automotive elements including a teardrop windshield, an aircraft-style steering yoke, bucket seats and tail fins that concealed water ski tow-ropes. Stevens' avowed purpose was to shock what he considered a moribund industry into accepting innovation. The *Lark* was judged a success by its sponsors, and a series of increasingly radical designs were produced each year into the 1960s.

The boom market of the 1950s also offered technical innovations in hull forms and propulsion systems. For a while great hope was invested in the hydrofoil as a way of creating high speed from low horsepower. Water-jet drives appeared, giving practical form to Ben Franklin's ideas of 170 years before. Catamarans and multihulls were briefly re-introduced. A few even tried to civilize the hydroplane and turn the hard-riding, hard-turning racing

The first in a series of show boats exploring the new freedom in shapes provided by fiberglass was this 1956 Lark by Brooks Stevens. The fins concealed running lights and a tow rope for water skiing. The boat was put in production by a Michigan company.

The saucer-shaped Fisherman by Stevens probed the parameters of the fantastic in 1957. The electronics panel included a sonar, while a pair of outboards under plastic bubbles for noise control propelled the craft, which was steered by throttle. An ensign appears as the sole concession to nautical tradition.

207

hulls into pleasureboats. Most of these efforts were asterisks to history, but by the late 1950s two innovations appeared that, when combined with fiberglass, formed the powerboat of today.

The potential was dramatically demonstrated on Wednesday, April 13, 1960. In the early morning light, 23 of the fastest boats in Florida rumbled away from the docks of Miami's Dupont Plaza Hotel, destination Nassau, 185 miles of ocean away. Wooden hulls resonated with the roar of 430 cubic-inch hot-rod Lincoln V-8 s, Chrysler hemi's and Cadillac engines as the fleet made its way out of Government Cut to the open sea. It was the fourth running of what race organizer Sherman Crise called "the world's most rugged ocean race." Intended to promote tourism in the Bahamas, the race was first held in 1957 and thereafter became a fixture. In 1960, four days of 20-knot winds brought nine-foot seas to the course, and within a mile of the start the first casualty occurred; a boat called *Miss Palm Springs* retired with structural failure.

In the lead was *Moppie*, a 30' by 11' coral-painted hull powered by a pair of marinized 275-horsepower Lincolns. At the helm was veteran ocean racer Sam Griffith, his face protected from the stinging spray by a skin-diving mask. Also in the cockpit was owner and yacht broker Richard Bertram and, functioning as a writer and reporter, internationally famous sailor, Carleton Mitchell. When the aluminum chairs in the stern collapsed, Bertram and Mitchell were forced to find what purchase they could; for a while Mitchell hugged the port coaming while owner Bertram lay athwartships on the cockpit sole. The compass spinning in impact-induced uselessness, they dead-reckoned their way across the Gulf Stream, cannon-balling from the wave tops. "At times," wrote Mitchell, "the effect was something like diving from a second-story window into a neighboring cellar piled with bricks."

Three hours, 40 minutes into the race *Moppie* had a 25-mile lead on what remained of the fleet. A half-dozen miles from the finish Mitchell checked his watch. It was possible, he thought, to break the race record of eight hours, four minutes. With the wind at 30 knots and nine-to-ten-foot seas running, Griffith pushed open the throttles and brought the V-8s to 4,100 rpm. At 2:53 P.M. lookouts saw a dot on the horizon in a cloud of spray atop the rolling sea. It was *Moppie*.

With that sighting went the old record. The boat had traversed the distance between Miami and Nassau in a record eight hours, averaging about 23 miles per hour. The next finisher was *Aqua Hunter*, a 23-footer skippered by Jim Wynne and carrying his recently introduced "inboard-outboard drives" in a fiberglass hull built by Marscot Plastics. Wynne crossed the line two hours, 25 minutes after *Moppie*. *Moppie* and *Aqua Hunter* were the only two boats to finish the race on Wednesday. The third finisher, an outboard-powered trimaran, arrived with the next day's dawn. When the race officially ended at sunset on Thursday, 13 of the 23 starters had reached Nassau. The rest had broken, sunk, burned or simply given up.

Moppie and *Aqua Hunter* were spectacular demonstrations of the seakeeping ability of an innovative hull form by a 52-year-old Massachusetts designer, C. Raymond Hunt. Not well-known in powerboat circles outside the Northeast, Hunt began designing in 1929 under the supervision of Boston naval architect Frank Paine and marine engineer Norman L. Skene.

High-performance production boats were rare during the boating boom. One of the few available was this Ancarrow Aquilifer. A pair of 300-horsepower Cadillac V-8s pushed the Arno Apel-designed 26-footer to a claimed 60 miles per hour.

For most of his career Hunt's focus was on sail. A superb helmsman and sailing champion, Hunt naturally emphasized rough-water performance as his attention turned to powerboats. This occurred during World War II, when he was detailed by the Coast Guard to the design section of the Navy's Bureau of Ships. After drawing a destroyer that was promising in tank tests, Hunt built a lobster boat along similar lines for his own use. The unusual bell-shaped sections performed well in a seaway, and in 1949 an express cruiser, *Sea Blitz*, was built with what he now called "Huntform" lines. Powered by a war-surplus Packard PT engine of 1,500 horsepower, the 42-footer cruised at 35 miles per hour and had a top speed of 46 miles per hour, an impressive performance for a boat with four berths, a head and a galley.

When the market for outboard boats exploded in the 1950s, Hunt had the opportunity to design — using a novel combination of foam and fiberglass — the 13' and 16' versions of a boat that became known as the Boston Whaler. Initially, these were inspired by Albert Hickman's Sea Sleds, but they were transmuted by Hunt into a novel "cathedral" hull form that led to a host of imitations and continues, with some modification, to this day.

About 1957 Ray Hunt developed the deep-V hull. To that time, the predominant feature of most high-speed boats was a large, flat area aft on which the hulls planed. This might be given a modest "V" of two to six degrees, but it was essentially a flat surface when viewed from the stern. The architecture was traceable through the runabouts of Hacker and Smith all the way back to George Crouch's hulls of 1912. Fast in smooth water, the hulls pounded brutally in a seaway, much as the World War II PTs did. Perfor-

mance in a following sea was poor, and under those conditions they were difficult to steer. Hunt's elegant conceptualization continued the V of the bow all the way to the transom, reducing its angle only moderately. Influenced by designer Lindsay Lord, who had published a book called *Naval Architecture of Planing Hulls*, Hunt kept his V-bottom essentially straight. Lord had written that ''warped planes'' were a source of suction-induced drag.

As a final element Hunt added what were called ''deadrise angle compensators'' to his deep-V planing surfaces. These were longitudinal strips that jutted out from the sides of the V, parallel to the water. Hunt had seen functionally similar strips on seaplane floats. Later these became known as ''lifting strakes'' but served the multiple functions of increasing the strength of the hull, improving lateral stability, reducing spray and adding lift. As the deep-V planed, it rose in the water, and the strakes operated as a chine did on the old runabouts, separating the flow of water from the hull. Requiring more power to drive at low speeds than the old hulls, the deep-V was well-matched to the growing outputs of Detroit V-8s during the automotive ''horsepower race'' of the 1950s. As the deep-V was driven faster, it required less power than the older forms. A new era in rough-water speed was born: an astonishing combination of reduced pounding, better steering and improved high-speed efficiency.

Unlike the hydroplane, the deep-V was a performance advance useful in conventional pleasureboats. Capitalizing on the 1960 victory, Dick Bertram began building cruisers based on the famous *Moppie*. Within a few years,

The 1964 Brave Moppie, *airborne. One of a series of hulls that included* Moppie, Glass Moppie, Blue Moppie, Lucky Moppie, *and* My Moppie, *the Moppie sobriquet first belonged to Richard Bertram's wife.* Brave Moppie *won the World Offshore Championship in 1965.*

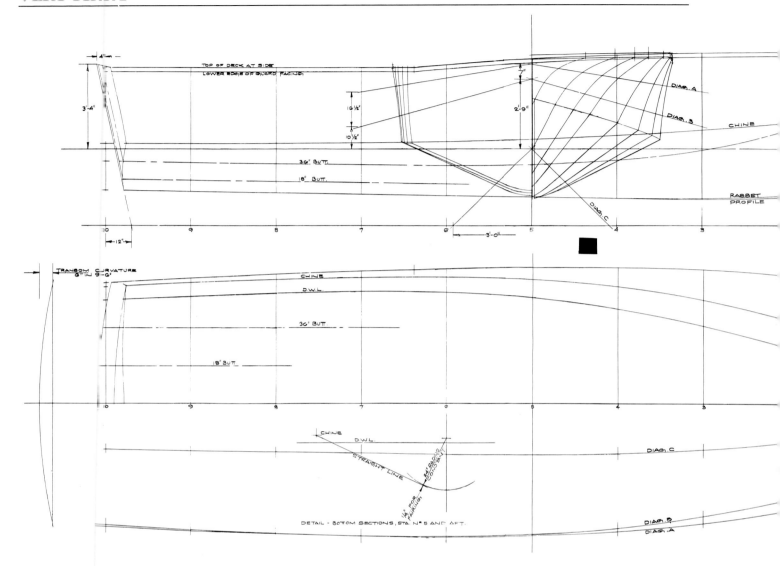

The lines of Brave Moppie, one of the later boats in a successful line of racers. This 36-footer was Diesel-powered and had a beam of 10' 9''. The position of lifting strakes is not shown on this drawing and was the subject of much experimentation.

more than 2,000 fiberglass versions were sold. The second finisher in that historic 1960 Miami-Nassau race carried another innovation that would prove equally significant, Jim Wynne's "inboard-outboard drive." Generically, this was known as a "Z-drive" to describe the path of the power from the engine, down a right-angle turn and out another right-angle turn to the propeller. The purpose was to combine the control of an outboard with the greater power and fuel economy of an inboard. The drive had the additional advantages of an adjustable angle of thrust and the capacity to be swung up for beaching or placing a boat on a trailer.

The attractions of this hybrid had been known for years. In the early 1930s Joe Van Blerck had built such a unit, as had outboard manufacturer Johnson Motors, but it remained for outboard engineer Wynne to create a unit which could be tilted and steered under power. Prior designs did one or the other, but not both. In an elegantly simple solution to the power

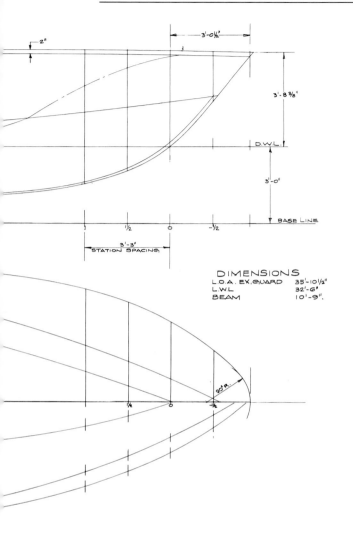

DIMENSIONS
L.O.A. EX. GUARD   35'-10½"
L.W.L   32'-6"
BEAM   10'-9".

transmission problem, Wynne placed a specialized universal joint from a four-wheel-drive truck in the top of the "Z". *Aqua Hunter* carried a pair of these drives, turned by two 80-horsepower, four-cylinder engines from another novelty, a European economy car. So it came to be that the second-place boat in the Miami-Nassau race of 1960 contained all the major features of contemporary pleasureboats: a V-hull, fiberglass construction and inboard-outboard drive. *Aqua Hunter* was the future.

The seminal Aqua Hunter *as she appeared in 1960. Jim Wynne's addition of inboard-outboard drives to a Hunt deep-V hull created the basic configuration of today's high-performance "offshore" racing and pleasureboats.*

SOURCES OF ILLUSTRATIONS

Allen, Everett S. *The Black Ships.* Boston: Little, Brown & Co., 1979.

Barbican, James. *The Confessions of a Rum Runner.* New York: Ives Washburn, 1928.

Barrett, J. Lee. *Speed Boat Kings.* Detroit: Arnold-Powers, Inc., 1939.

Bruce, Robert V. *Alexander Graham Bell and the Quest for Solitude.* Boston: Little, Brown & Co., 1974.

Bulkley, Robert J. *At Close Quarters— PT Boats in the United States Navy.* Washington, D.C.: Naval History Division, 1962.

Bushey, A.C. et al. "Laminated Glass Plastic Construction with Special Reference to Boats." *Society of Naval Architects and Marine Engineers Transactions* 60 (1952): 595–644.

Carter, Samuel. *The Boat Builders of Bristol.* Garden City, N.Y.: Doubleday & Co., 1970.

Clerk, Dugald. *The Gas, Petrol, and Oil Engine.* New York: John Wiley and Sons, 1909.

Cox, D.H. "Gasolene Engines for Marine Propulsion." *Society of Naval Architects and Marine Engineers Transactions* 11 (1903): 33–56.

Crampton, Emeline J. *History of the St. Clair River.* St. Clair, Mich.: St. Clair Publishing Company, 1921.

Crane, Clinton H. "High Speed Gasolene Launches." *Society of Naval Architects and Marine Engineers Transactions* 12 (1904): 321–344.

Crane, Clinton H. "Problems in Connection with High Speed Launches." *Society of Naval Architects and Marine Engineers Transactions* 13 (1905): 365–373.

Dockey, Philip S. *The Liberty Engine, 1918–1942.* Washington: Smithsonian Institution Press, 1968.

Du Cane, Peter. *High Speed Small Craft.* Tuckahoe, N.Y.: John De Graff, Inc., 1953.

Durand, W.F. "Description of the Steam Yacht Ellide and Her Speed Trials." *Marine Engineering* 2 no. 12 (1898): 1–9.

Dyke, A.L. *Dyke's Aircraft Engine Instructor.* Chicago: Goodheart-Willcox Publishing Company, 1928.

Farmer, Weston. *From My Old Boat Shop.* Camden, Maine: International Marine Publishing Co., 1979.

Fostle, D.W. "The Gold Challenge Cup, 1904–1940." *Nautical Quarterly* 28 (Winter 1984): 18–33.

Fostle, D.W. "Vessels of Opportunity —The PTs." *Nautical Quarterly* 26 (Summer 1984): 20–35.

Gardner, William. *The Development of the Sail Yacht, Steam Yacht and Motor Yacht in American Waters.* International Engineering Congress: San Francisco, 1915.

Gillmor, H.G. "Torpedo-Boat Design." *Society of Naval Architects and Marine Engineers Transactions* 5 (1897): 51–79.

Gribbins, Joseph. "Hacker and His Craft." *Nautical Quarterly* 14 (Summer 1981): 2–17.

Gribbins, Joseph. "Ray Hunt — New England Archimedes." *Nautical Quarterly* 25 (Spring 1984): 36–57.

Guthorn, Peter J. *The Seabright Skiff.* Exton, Pa.: Schiffer Publishing Limited, 1982.

History of American Yachts and Yachtsmen. New York: Spirit of the Times Publishing Company, 1901.

Homan, James E. *Self-Propelled Vehicles.* New York: Theo. Audel & Co., 1908.

Hutton, F.R. *The Gas Engine.* New York: John Wiley and Sons, 1908.

Jenks, William L. *St. Clair County Michigan, Its History and its People.* Chicago: Lewis Publishing Company, 1912.

Kimes, Beverly Rae, ed. *Packard, A History of the Motor Car and the Company.* Princeton: Automobile Quarterly Publications. 1978.

Lallier, Ernest V. *An Elementary Manual of the Steam Engine.* New York: D. Van Nostrand Company, 1913.

Lombardo, Guy. *Auld Acquaintance.* Garden City, N.Y.: Doubleday & Co., 1975.

Lord, Lindsay. *Naval Architecture of Planing Hulls.* Cambridge, MD.: Cornell Maritime Press, Inc. 1963.

Morrison, John H. *History of American Steam Navigation.* New York: W.F. Sametz & Co., 1903.

Page, Victor W. *Modern Aviation Engines.* New York: Henley Publishing Company, 1929.

Pitrone, Jean M. & Elwart, Joan P. *The Dodges.* South Bend, Ind.: Icarus Press, 1981.

Prange, Gordon W. *At Dawn We Slept.* New York: Penguin Books, 1981.

Sinclair, Andrew. *Prohibition: The Era of Excess.* New York: Little, Brown & Co., 1962.

Skene, Norman L. *Elements of Yacht Design.* New York: Yachting Publications, 1927.

Stephens, W.P. *American Yachting.* New York: MacMillan & Company, 1904.

Stephens, W.P. *Traditions and Memories of American Yachting.* New York: Hearst Magazines, 1942.

Stokesbury, James L. *A Short History of World War II.* New York: William Morrow & Co., 1980.

Streeter, Robert S. *Internal Combustion Engines.* New York: McGraw-Hill, 1915.

Taylor, C. Fayette. *Aircraft Propulsion, A Review of the Evolution of Aircraft Piston Engines.* Washington, D.C.: Smithsonian Institution Press, 1971.

U.S. Bureau of the Census. *Historical Statistics of the United States.* Washington, D.C.: U.S. Government Printing Office, 1975.

U.S. Bureau of the Census. *Statistical Abstract of the United States.* Washington, D.C.: U.S. Government Printing Office, 1880–1960.

Van De Water, Frederic F. *The Real McCoy.* Garden City, N.Y.: Doubleday, Doran & Co., 1931.

Vincent, Jesse G. *Chronological Development of the Packard Marine Engine.* MS., Detroit: Packard Motor Car Company, [1946].

Vincent, Jesse G. *History of the Liberty Engine.* MS., Detroit: Packard Motor Car Company, [1920].

White, W.L. *They Were Expendable.* New York: Harcourt, Brace & Co., 1942.

Willoughby, Malcolm F. *Rum War at Sea.* Washington, D.C.: United States Government Printing Office, 1964.